THE COMPLETE GUIDE TO
Truck Modelling

The Complete Guide to Truck Modelling
©Canfora Publishing 2023 (first published 2016)
ISBN 978-91-982325-3-0
Project manager: Toni Canfora
Design: Toni Canfora, Marie Göransson
Print: Printbest, Estonia

Canfora Publishing / Grafisk Form&Förlag
Industrivägen 19
171 48 Solna, Stockholm, Sweden
info@canfora.se
www.canfora.se

FOREWORD

For many years truck modellers have desperately awaited the publication of a book dedicated solely to the art of truck modelling. Whilst military modellers have been well catered for with a plethora of titles, their civilian counterparts have had to make do with the odd chapter in general modelling books and magazines, and until the arrival of Truck Model World magazine, a few articles in truck magazines. For many years we have been in the wilderness, so a truck modelling book is long overdue.

I can think of no-one better qualified to write this book than Jan Rosecky; well known amongst truck modellers, Jan has established his credentials both as a modeller and a writer.

As an accomplished modeller he has won trophies and awards at truck model shows throughout Europe, and as a writer he has produced informative articles for modelling magazines such as Truck Model World. Furthermore, Jan has an extensive technical knowledge about trucks, and most importantly, a passion and enthusiasm for modelling.

I know Jan's book will be welcomed by both experienced modellers and newcomers alike. It's what we've been waiting for for a long time. Read, learn and enjoy!

Peter White
Editor, Truck Model World 1991-2014

Thank you

As a truck modelling enthusiast, it's been an honor to see how much the modelling community has embraced "The Complete Guide to Truck Modelling Vol. 1" and "Vol.2" over the years. It's been incredibly rewarding to hear from so many of you who have found both books to be a valuable resource in your own modelling journey.

As I prepared to update this edition, I was pleased with how little needs to be changed after all those years. I went through the entire book with a fine-toothed comb, correcting any errors and incorporating a few updates on recent topics such as the latest kits and accessories. Despite the updates, I still believe that even the original book is as relevant and useful as ever for model truck builders.

While the world around us may have changed significantly since the book's original release in 2016, the fundamentals of truck modelling remain the same. The updated edition of "The Complete Guide to Truck Modelling Vol. 1" provides an essential resource for model truck builders at all levels, from beginners just starting out to seasoned veterans looking to refine their skills.

I'm grateful for the continued support of the truck modelling community, and I look forward to seeing the impressive models you'll create using the techniques and inspiration from these books. Whether you're a seasoned veteran or just starting out, this guide will provide you with the essential knowledge needed to build impressive models.

Happy modelling!

Jan Rosecký

CONTENTS

CHAPTER	PAGE
1. THE WORLD OF SCALE MODEL TRUCKS	6
2. KITS AND ACCESSORIES	14
3. TRUCK DESIGN	20
4. A MEDIUM LEVEL PROJECT	40
5. DETAILING YOUR MODEL	74
6. PASSION FOR SUPER-DETAILING	98
7. LIGHT COMMERCIAL VEHICLES	118
8. ADVANCED RESIN CONVERSIONS	128
9. MODEL GALLERY	138

1 THE WORLD OF S(

When it comes to truck models, first I need to say that it is something that has always been with me. Various creative activities I pursued when I was a kid all led to building my first truck model early in 1998 just days after I turned 13. I still recall my dad bringing the Italeri catalogue home to choose my first kit. That moment has changed my life and truck models have become a passion for me.

1. THE WORLD OF SCALE MODEL TRUCKS

1.1 INTRODUCTION

It may sound an easy start, but it was not, however. I was 13, had no experience with building plastic models, there were no books, no dedicated websites and I did not know anybody with the same hobby. Very soon I found out that the world of scale model trucks has its own features and characteristics that make it very different when you compare it to the others. That difference is actually what made me think of writing a book many years later.

Just the subject of our hobby – trucks – is not in the mainstream. The largest groups among modellers are those who build aircraft and AFVs (armoured fighting vehicles). The rest deal with dioramas, figures, ships, submarines or sci-fi. Last but not least there are three groups (cars, motorbikes and trucks) sometimes labelled 'civilian vehicles' but this is a rather shallow designation. The scale models of trucks have been here for decades but more than a part of the regular modelling scene, truck models have been connected to actual trucking magazines.

The fact that truck modellers belong to a relatively small group is not necessarily negative. It actually can be a lot more interesting to be part of a smaller community where members work together as a family. However, the smaller number of modellers means fewer customers buying products (not just the kits) and this is where many restrictions and problems originate. And these issues are the reason why the world of scale model trucks is so different.

Another fact that make us truck modellers a bit different is the scale we use. 1/24 and 1/25 are rather large and that means the models we build are big and provide much space for the finest details. In fact, these are the biggest scales commonly used with plastic kits. All the details such as bolts, nuts, rivets or even welds are big enough to be seen on a model and therefore worth making. Most of the vehicle components are large enough that they should be present on the model at least in a simplified form. Wiring and electrical harness, air lines and all their fittings; this is a significant part of every vehicle and should be visible on a model too. Certainly, one cannot tell apart a metric and a UNF bolt, but 1/24 scale allows one to go deep into the details if this is the desire.

If you compare the two last paragraphs, you might see the conflict where a relatively small group of modellers wants to build one of the biggest and most detailed kits on the market. It does not work like this of course. However, the biggest scale truck kits are not always the most detailed. The level of simplification on truck kits is relatively high. Why? Because otherwise the kits would be too expensive and nobody would buy them. For an average 1/35 military kit the level of detail is therefore higher than in any 1/24 scale item, just because the tooling costs split into many more kits…resulting in a reasonable price for the customer.

The level of simplification is not a problem at all. First, this is something we are used to and second, this gives the same starting point to everybody. Furthermore, we have many ways to improve the subject. There is quite a wide range of aftermarket parts and accessories available through international e-shops so accessibility is not a problem and scratch building has been very common among truck modellers to ensure extra detail.

SIMPLIFIED KITS

However, there were two moments that influenced the world of scale model trucks when the kit simplification went too far. The first was back in 2001 when Italeri's new concept kits appeared on the market. These had a single-piece chassis with non-steerable front axle, no engine and no tilting cab but were meant to be cheaper. The idea was not bad, but the final models were generally considered too simple for such a big scale and were never really any cheaper. The second happened even earlier, in the mid-1990s, when the Italeri Volvo FH12 was introduced. This kit has created an unfavourable precedent because it was based on updated moulds from an older Volvo F12 kit. A significant percentage of parts from the previous F12 (chassis, engine) was used as a basis on which new exterior components of the new FH12 models were assembled. Commercially, this meant lower costs for a new kit. For the modeller this means an inaccurate kit with no price advantage at all. This has happened with other kits since then and unfortunately, the Volvo FH series is not the only one with the wrong genes. You might say "Who cares?", but the problem is that Italeri is a major plastic kit manufacturer and if such a company behaves inappropriately, there is nobody else to provide optional products. The larger scale only emphasises the problem because the bigger the parts the more obvious the kit

This Scania R500 from well known Belgian Ceusters transport is based on Italeri 3850 kit and decals provided by Flemming Pedersen.

faults are and these can hardly be covered simply with new cab panels. The impact of the market size and kit scale on tooling cost reduction for new kits is obvious here, as well as the impact of the cost reduction on quality.

Due to these facts, building scale truck models became a very challenging activity. No matter what kit you choose, there is always plenty of detail that can be added to your model to make it more realistic. No matter what kit you buy, there are always a few bolts or air lines you can add. It starts with bolts and rivets and some basic wiring and ends up in complex conversions. You can hardly say this about the world of aircraft or AFV models, though, because most of these kits are very accurate when built just out of box and for an average model builder there is no need to go any further than that.

There we are…the world of scale model trucks. In the arena of beautifully detailed truck models where childhood dreams come true but also in the tricky world of faulty kits, where knowledge and information is as valuable as gold. This is the reason why I decided to write this book. A book that should help all truck modellers to find all the information they need. It does not describe any generic tools or activities you can find in almost any modelling book or a magazine. The focus is on trucks and truck model-building in particular. Something that is not easy to find…even in today's world of the internet.

1.2 BASIC TERMS

To avoid confusion, there are some basic terms I would like to define here. First, there are many different types of activities called modelling or model-building. In this book, unless otherwise specified, the terms modelling, modeller and model are related to assembling and finishing scale plastic models, as we are not going to deal with anything like radio controlled or die-cast models.

Truck model or a truck model kit in particular will always mean a model or a kit either in 1/24 or 1/25 scale. There are a few more scales related to truck models (1/35, 1/87, 1/50) but for this book we will focus entirely on 1/24 and 1/25 with just a few scattered remarks about 1/35 scale, which is the main scale for the builders of armoured fighting vehicles, AFVs. The scale of 1/50 relates more to collecting and rebuilding die-cast models and 1/87 scale for collecting and rebuilding plastic models; however, some plastic 1/87 kits are available too.

The 1/24 and 1/25 scales co-exist together in the world of scale model trucks. Some companies (Ertl, AMT, Moebius) provide kits in 1/25 scale, while others prefer 1/24 (Italeri) and some actually use both (Revell).

1. THE WORLD OF SCALE MODEL TRUCKS

The thing is that there really is a difference between the size of a 1/24 and 1/25 scale model. If an average truck is 2,500mm wide, the 1/24 scale model width should be 2,500/24 = 104.2mm wide, while the 1/25 example just 2,500/25 = 100mm wide. The 4mm difference is something you really see on a model and combining 1/24 trucks with 1/25 trailers is something that generally does not look correct. However, the truth is that many modellers mix these scales and use 1/24 Italeri wheels on 1/25 Revell kits for example…and often it does not look so bad. Once I measured a Volvo engine block length in the 1/25 scale Revell kit, along with that in the 1/24 scale Italeri kit and guess what? The 1/25 scale Revell engine was longer! This indicates that sometimes the difference between these two scales is rather formal. I do not want to underrate the difference but for our use there often is no difference in the size of the kit parts at all, but the difference still exists and cannot be denied.

In strong contrast to the Scania on the previous page, this 1/24 Emhar Bedford OSBT tipper was built straight from the box..

> *What we are talking about here is a hobby; therefore, it is something we do because we want to, and we have fun doing it the way it suits us.*

The correct heavy-duty look is provided by wheels and a front drive axle sourced from British after-market company Kit Form Services.
The range of 1/24 kits can be extended by combining them; this Italeri Iveco 190.38 (No. 767) carries a BRO wrecker body from the Scania wrecker (Italeri No. 3838).

1.3 ATTITUDES TO MODELLING

Before we move to building models there is a matter I would like to discuss briefly in a separate chapter. From my perspective this is a very important topic but rather overlooked. However, it can be a source of misunderstanding or even conflict and disappointment.

There is a very basic question that everyone should be able to answer themselves. The question is: "What do I want to do?" or maybe "What is the point of my activity?" Answering these questions should be fairly easy. I want to build a model. Ok, good but there is another question and this can actually be pretty tough. The question is "Why am I building a model? What is the purpose of this model?" You might also ask this differently, such as: "Why do I want that model? What is my motivation?"

Let me help you with this for now because the purpose of this discussion is to show that there are no wrong answers.

"I want to build a truck model because I like trucks. I have never built any model so I actually do not know what the chosen subject should look like or what is the point of doing it. I just want to have fun and relax."

"I am building my model for a competition. I am competitive and I enjoy comparing my skills and my models with other people. I want to build a good model and I want my it to be better than those of my peers. I have already built some and every new model I finish is better than the older one. I enjoy improving my skills."

"I build truck models for my collection. I already have some and I enjoy building new ones. I am not interested in visiting model shows or in competing with anyone. I am just having fun with extending my scale fleet."

"Although I am a beginner I already know a couple of skilled builders and I like their work. I do not have many skills yet but I would like to build as good a model as my friends build or like those that can be seen at big model shows. I want to learn step by step, model by model and once my models will be good enough I would like take part in a competition."

You can see that different people may like different things and there is nothing wrong with it. What we are talking about here is a hobby; therefore, it is something we do because we want to and we have fun doing it the way that suits us. Otherwise it would not be fun anymore and there would be no point in

TRUCK **MODELLING**

doing it because a hobby is something you do for fun, isn't it? It is not a duty.

Now the critical point. Because we are free to build models the way we like them it is very probable that sooner or later we will come across someone who will not like our models, just like we will come across a model that we will not like. What happens? Well, if you have your builds locked in your modelling room this situation is rather unlikely, but if you post pictures on an internet forum or bring a model to a show it may look like you are asking for opinions. You should be ready for potential criticism at that moment because this is part of the creative process. It may be gentle or heartless but you should be prepared for both and be ready to accept that and take it easy. On the other hand, when you are about to express your critical opinion on someone's model you should think twice before you say something, because the fact that you dislike someone's model does not mean anything in fact…because the builder of the model is free to work according to his/her own standards. Criticism should generally be positive, and should be accepted humbly on one side but expressed wisely on the other.

MODEL QUALITY

Throughout the years the term 'model quality' has evolved and we use it to describe kit properties or features that are generally accepted as good and positive. When you say a model is good it is expected to have some qualities. For most modellers these qualities are something that they generally agree on and it does not have to be anything really special; just a **general tidiness, correct geometry and authenticity**. That is something an average modeller is able to reach. The term quality is not necessarily related to the amount or fineness of the detail added by the builder, but to a general ability to assemble the model as per instructions and paint it with no glue or brush strokes visible, for example. Of course there are masters who can do a lot more than that, but an average modeller with average skills is able to build a quality model within the generally accepted standards. However, as the whole hobby develops, average model quality goes up and what is extra today may be just average tomorrow. This is valid especially for painting and weathering styles and techniques.

Correct geometry is a straightforward term. What is parallel on the real vehicle should be parallel on a model, all perpendicular edges should be perpendicular on a model too. This works for the frame geometry as well as for any attached components. Correct geometry of wheels is particularly important and both the toe and camber angles should be set to zero precisely.

Model authenticity in other words means that the models represent the reality well enough. Of course, for different scales there are different requirements. For example, an engine and gearbox of a 1/87 model will be just a schematic component whereas in 1/24 scale, the engine is bigger than a 1/87 truck and therefore has many details so it cannot be generic. You can tell the various engines and other components (axles, suspension) apart in this scale easily. That is why so many model builders complain about 'messy' Italeri kits. In such a big scale the difference between similar components from different vehicles is not negligible and correcting some kit faults is not easy. Besides the physical shapes and sizes of the parts there is another level of authenticity in modelling, and that is the paint job. Not only should the model have correct

General tidiness is mostly related to clean working, with no excess glue and obvious faults in the fit of parts. Weathering is beneficial, but can be overdone and in general is considered as an advanced skill-set.

components but these should also be painted and weathered appropriately. Here, good reference photos cannot be emphasized enough. These show not just the correct vehicle structure, different components' positions, wiring and other details but also the colours and surface structure of different parts that will guide you through the painting and weathering stages. It really does not matter, though, if you build a clean vehicle or a worn-out workhorse.

MODEL TIDINESS

General tidiness means the model is clean and free of any technological defects. The paint surface should be smooth (no orange peel) and free of any dust and dirt. There should be no finger prints on the model's surface and there should be no excess glue visible. The clear parts such as windows and lights should be clean with no scratches or damage. Decals should be placed correctly and the clear decal film should not be apparent on the subject's surface. If model parts consist of two components while the real part is a single piece (such as an air tank, fuel tank or suspension air bag) the join line should be sanded or filled with putty so that it is not visible on the finished part. All the visible technological features related to injection-moulded kit production should be removed from the parts too. These are the **ejector pin marks, witness marks and moulding flash at parting lines and gate marks**. **Ejector pin marks** are circular depressions or elevated surfaces where the ejector pins touch the sprue during the manufacturing process. Sometimes these locations can be located on the sprue itself and not the parts, but often they get in touch with the particular components when pushing them out of the mould. To remove ejector pin marks, fill them with putty or sand them away.

Witness marks appear as a low rib that runs along the mould parting line across the component's surface, and may eventually contain excess plastic that leaks into a narrow

Correct geometry and alignment is a must when assembling the vehicle frame. This 1950s GMC chassis earns its points in authenticity, as well as featuring the classic Page and Page suspension I bought as a limited-run resin detail set.

TRUCK **MODELLING**

gap between the moulds. Removing witness marks and flash is relatively easy as you usually scrape it off with a sharp knife or a scalpel.

A moulding gate is the location at which the molten plastic enters the mould cavity. On a plastic part a gate is the thin area that connects a part to a sprue. If you cut it off, often a visible gate mark is visible on the part surface. Removing moulding gates is automatic as you always cut off the part from the sprue. Use a sharp knife or side-cutter pliers to remove the gate precisely so that no excess plastic remains on the part…but be careful and do not damage the parts themselves.

The requirements above are in fact the first thing you should try and achieve before you move from building out-of-box models to conversions and expensive aftermarket parts. It is up to you to decide whether you will follow these simple rules or not of course. The point is to try and define what is generally accepted as standard or normal, what could be the possible questions you might try to answer yourself, and which path you could take when exploring the world of scale model trucks. It is all about fun and joy. However, different people have fun with different things. One with looking at the finished model, the other when rebuilding the model with Evergreen profiles into something completely different. Just as I wrote before: there are no wrong answers and no wrong paths. Make your choice and have fun.

Note the clean and smooth paint on this GMC Cannonball. Although not discussed extensively in this book, good painting skills are vital for a good model.

1. A typical example of flash at the parting line, which has to be removed.

2. Parts with fine feaures (such as wood) sometimes have ejector pin marks located outside of the component, to prevent any surface damage during neatening work.

3. A partial seam runs around the whole part following the mould parting line. On more curved components, this trait is always quite apparent.

4. Flash on a sprue from one of the old 1970s AMT kits. These always have been a bit rough in some areas, but feature pleasing details in others.

5. Note the deep ejector pin marks on the inner door of Emhar's Bedford. Leaving the door open calls for filling and sanding to remove them.

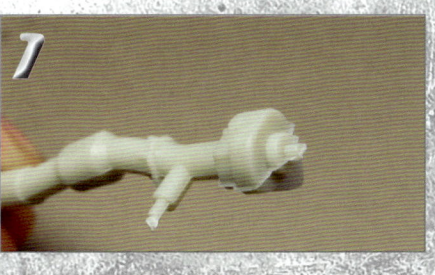

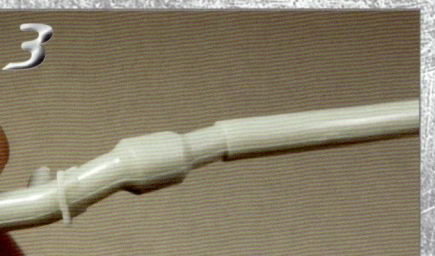

2 PLASTIC KITS AI

Before you start building your first model, there are things that you should know. As this book is intended to make your life in the world of scale model trucks easier, it's appropriate to addresses these matters now.

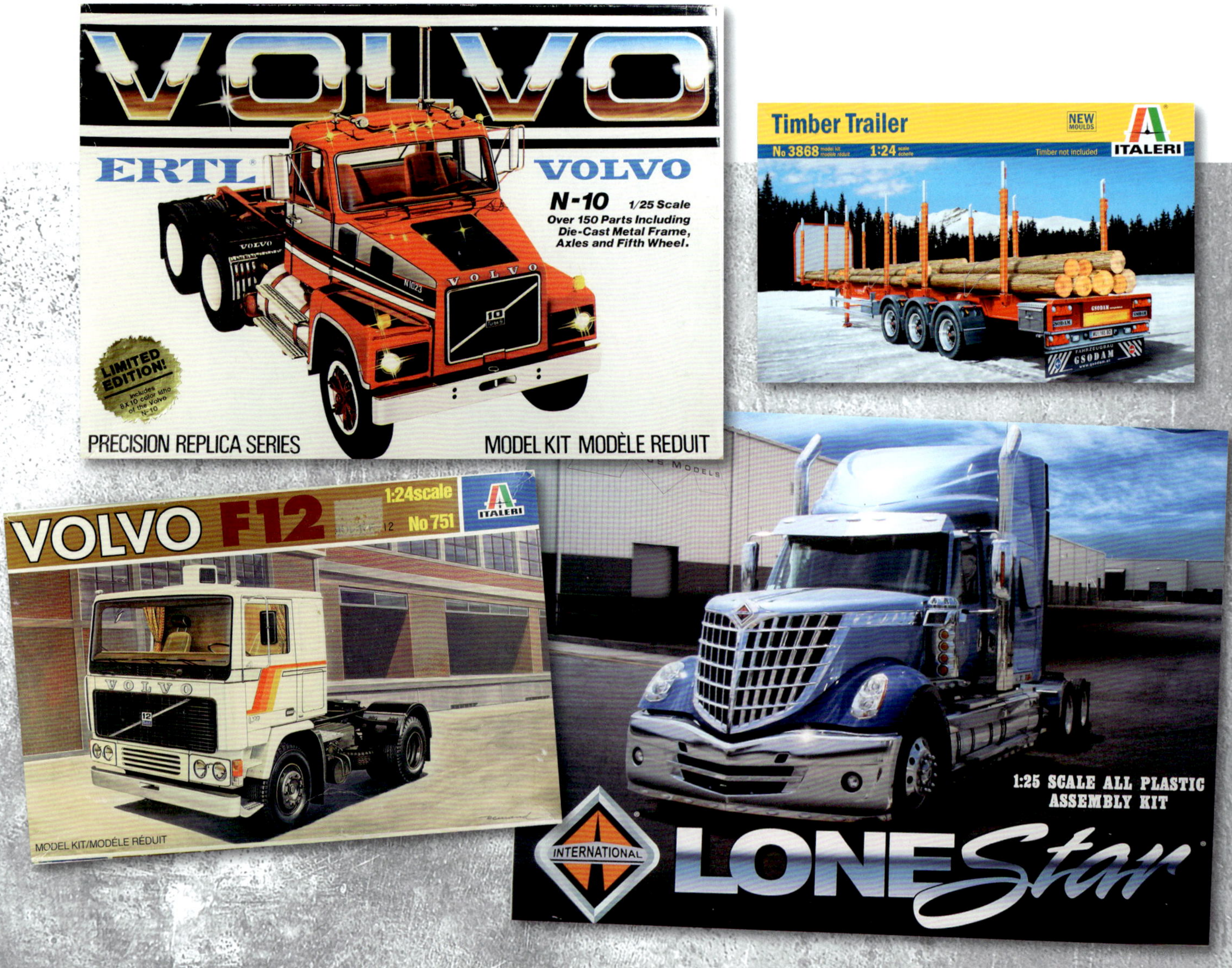

TRUCK MODELLING

2. PLASTIC KITS AND ACCESSORIES

2.1 INTRODUCTION

There are three main topics I'd like to discuss here before we cut in plastic. It is kits, truck design and wiring. Kits because you should know the basics about the products you'll explore. Trucks because you should know something about the real vehicles you'll portray in scale form and wiring because this is probably the very first modification of a standard model you will carry out. It's not necessary to employ this in your first model, but it is always handy to know more and learn about it in advance.

2.2 KITS

Truck kits in 1/24 and 1/25 scales can be tricky. If you compare it to a range of AFVs or aircraft you might think the choice is rather narrow. Still, there are more than 100 kits available on the market that represent various types and makes of trucks, and from different time periods. For most of us it's more than we are able to build in a lifetime so choice is actually not a problem.

What happens in the world of aircraft or AFVs – that every kit producer has the same mainstream kits available in their portfolio, such as Spitfires, F-14 fighters or Abrams and T-34 battle tanks – is not common in the world of model trucks. When a producer makes a kit of a particular vehicle type, nobody will offer a kit of the same subject again because the market is too small. Instead of this, the producers share moulds and sell the same plastic parts in different boxes (Revell in particular). If an inaccurate kit of a particular truck is made, most likely it is definite and there will be no other choice than to buy a poor product and rework its mistakes.

What is also special about truck kits, is that most of the liveries are fictional and are barely based on something realistic. There are exceptions, but the fact that the model represents a fictional vehicle has never been a problem for truck modellers. Another interesting fact is that most truck kits are still available although they are more than 30 years old. However, they sell well because there is no replacement. Therefore most of the companies making truck kits re-issue a couple of old items every year so that most of the truck kits are easy to buy.

2.2.1 KIT MANUFACTURERS

As for the aforementioned, there is just a handful of companies. Italeri is the major player in the 1/24 market and has made truck kits since the early 1980s. They are still designing new kits, or are at least trying to update the old examples. A large amount US truck (and even some construction equipment) kits were produced by American companies such as AMT and Ertl of which most were designed back in the 1970s and early 1980s. Obviously these kits fall behind Italeri with tooling quality due to their age but are still popular, as there is no replacement for the classic 1970s vehicles. Another company

MANUFACTURERS and their scales

Brand	Scale	Comment
Italeri	1/24	All kits designed by Italeri.
Revell	1/24, 1/25	Partially own kits, partially shared products designed by Italeri and Moebius models, boxed by Revell with their own instructions and decals.
Moebius models	1/25	Relatively fresh and new products, modern US trucks and classis US cars.
AMT / Ertl / Matchbox	1/25	Classic golden era of classic US truck kits mostly (although some construction equipment and European kits were made or boxed by them as well) with old tooling of which most of them have been re-issued recently.
Emhar	1/24	A series of four Bedford lorry kits, nice new tooling, welcomed addition on the market.
Heller	1/24	Classic French kits, a couple of trucks and trailers that are continuously re-issued.
Meng	1/24	They made a nice 1/24 heavy duty Ford F-350 pickup, top quality tooling.
Trumpeter	1/25	They made a nice 1/25 American LaFrance fire pumper.
Monogram	1/16, 1/25	A couple of large scale us trucks including trailers and some US trucks as well, old tooling kits being re-issued from time to time.

that deals with truck kits is Revell, with their Revell Germany and Revell USA (Monogram) product streams. While Revell USA and Monogram made a few 1/25 scale truck kits, and some 1/16 and 1/32 plastic kits in the past, many are now actually out of production, Revell Germany is still active and together with selling some re-badged Italeri kits, they also introduce brand new items from time to time. In Europe, Heller is another manufacturer that has rather a narrow array of kits in 1/24 scale and is barely active on the truck market, with just some of their older products being re-issued sporadically. Recently, the new US-based company Moebius appeared on the market, designing a fully detailed 1/25 scale replica of an International Lonestar, followed shortly by an International Prostar and a couple of Great Dane trailer kits...which brought fresh perspective to the model truck market. Some of the Moebius kits were re-branded and sold by Revell Germany with their own decal sets. Some years ago, British company Emhar introduced two 1/24 Bedford O series kits (a tipper and a flatbed truck) in two versions and recently they have provided a pair of new kits using the same chassis, but with new bodies (tanker and recovery).

Except for the aforementioned, there are companies that enter the 1/24 scale market afresh on occasion. Some have provided just a kit or two with no successors. Trumpeter has made a modern American LaFrance fire engine in 1/25 scale, while Mitsuwa has offered few Japanese truck and trailer kits; recently Meng has provided a 1/24 Ford F-350 Super duty pickup which, with its size, is somewhere between a car and truck kit.

2.2.2 QUALITY AND AUTHENTICITY

The tooling quality and amount of detail in the aforementioned kits is equal to their age and cost of mould design and production. There are differences, especially between the old AMT/Ertl/Matchbox kits designed back in the 1970s and later Italeri/Moebius/Revell kits. However, if you compare a 2010 Italeri or Revell kit to a 1990 example the difference in tooling quality improvement is barely visible and almost negligible. A significant step forward in 1/24 truck kit tooling is exemplified by Italeri's Iveco Stralis introduced in spring 2014, but still uses wheels and rims from early 1990s kits so the tooling is not 100% new. Moebius Prostar and Lonestar kits are equal to the latest Italeri products, but even these do not provide any extra detail when compared to the average 1/24 model. If you compare the best 1/24 truck kit to the latest 1/35 military vehicle, the former fall behind significantly. In other words, 1/24 kits are not as detailed and finely moulded as the latest 1/35 AFV scale kits. It does not mean that 1/24 products cannot be more detailed but that would make tooling costs too high and increase the price, number of parts and complexity, which would be rather counter-productive. Therefore, kit quality has been balanced on a certain level and does not change much over time.

While the tooling quality for most kits is generally equal, variation in authenticity is very high. Some kits are very accurate and despite their age they represent the real vehicle very well, while others are highly inaccurate as they simply share some of the moulds with ostensibly similar kits. This creates two basic categories we could label: good (accurate) kits and wrong (inaccurate) kits where the accuracy proportionally depends on the amount of parts from shared moulds. The following lines should provide you with basic information on the most common kits and prevent any unwanted surprises.

As for the good kits, the list is rather long. Generally speaking, all the 1/25 scale offerings are accurate and there has never been any inappropriate mould sharing. The only problematic kit is the Marmon Conventional from Revell. This is based on the same firm's Peterbilt 359 with just the hood changed to provide a Marmon truck look-alike. Except for this one all the Revell, AMT, Ertl, Monogram or Moebius kits are great representations of the real subjects and you do not need to worry much about authenticity.

In 1/24 scale the situation is rather tricky. As for Emhar, the Bedford kits are great and of high quality. The rest of the 1/24 scale world is split between Revell and Italeri. As for Revell kits, there are actually two groups. Those that Revell produced on its own and those coming from Italeri moulds. The original Revell kits are accurate and most are pretty interesting subjects (Mercedes Atego fire engine, Neoplan Cityliner, London bus). Several Revell kits designed in the 1990s, Büssing S8000 and Krupp Titan, are actually some of the best-detailed kits in 1/24 scale. The Italeri production, whether sold directly by Italeri or re-badged by Revell, contain some great kits as well as poor examples. A general rule is that the older the kit the more accurate it is. All the 1980s and early 1990s Italeri kits (and all their re-issued versions) are more than fine. Volvo F12 (Italeri 751, 752, 797, 724), Renault R series trucks (Italeri 759, 761, 771, 787) and Magnum (Italeri 723), 2nd and 3rd generation Scania trucks (kits No. 755, 762, 772, 780, 792, 726), Mercedes NG series (No. 757, 786), SK series (793, 729, 734, 739) and MAN F8 (756), F90 and F2000 trucks (795, 732, 741, 714, 3901), Iveco 190 and TurboStar kits (767, 768, 775, 796) and DAF kits (777, 765, 760) are pleasing items and although there has been some mould sharing it did not have any serious effect. The trailers designed in this period are very good too (766, 758, 754, 737, 725, 774) as well as the Freightliner trucks (779, 783, 785) and the Iveco/DAF/Volvo/Magirus fire ladder (Italeri 784).

1990s COST SAVINGS

Later in the 1990s the situation became worse (and confusing) as there were decent new kits introduced on one side but mould sharing was employed much more than before. Various well-detailed Peterbilt kits were introduced. Both the Peterbilt 377 A/E (Italeri 740) and Peterbilt 378 (Italeri 746) are great and accurate, as well as the Freightliner FLD kit (738) while the remaining US trucks made by Italeri (Mack, Ford and Western Star) are pretty poor as they are built on the Freightliner chassis. Among the European trucks, one of the borderline kits was the DAF 95 (Italeri 788) which is actually a 760 kit chassis with a new cab and a couple of updated details... however, the real vehicles are relatively close to each other. A similar thing happened with the Scania T143M (736), which is a mixture of the old Scania T142H (753) and later 143M Streamline (726). There are some little issues with the engine (no intercooler in the kit) and the most significant problem is that the wheelbase was taken directly from the 143M Streamline and is too short for the conventional truck; but the remaining parts are not so bad. The situation became much worse when the Volvo FH16 kits (Italeri 733 and 735) were introduced. In the early 1990s the Volvo FH was a clean-sheet design of a heavy truck range but Italeri had no respect and used the old 751 kit chassis as a basis for the new Volvo kits. At that time kit No. 751 (Volvo F12) was more than 10 years old, the real F12 design has just turned 15 and its obsolete moulds were used for a kit that should represent a state of the art FH16 model. A disaster in other words, because all the Volvo kits Italeri ever made are based on the very first Volvo designed by Italeri in 1981. There is no possibility to hide the difference in 1/24 scale so all the later Volvo kits have obsolete engine, chassis components and an antique leaf spring suspension. In terms of accuracy this kit is hopeless. Later, Mercedes Actros (715) appeared; its tooling was 100% new and the kit is great. At the same time, the Scania 144

The International Prostar designed by Moebius Models is sold by Revell, but with different decals..

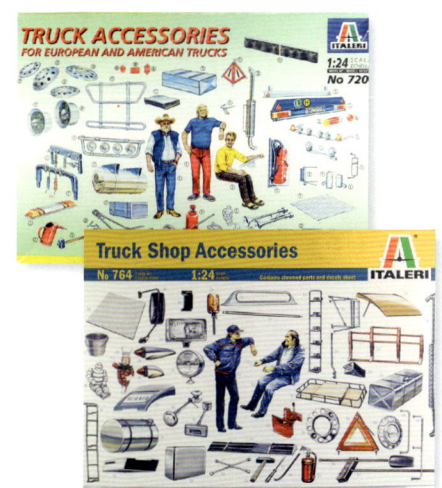

Italeri accessory sets are a great source for truck conversions and customising.

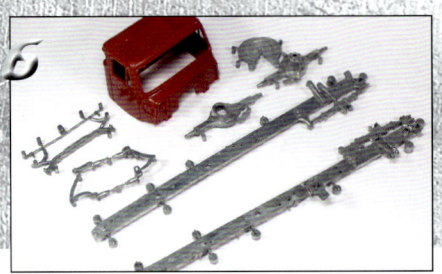

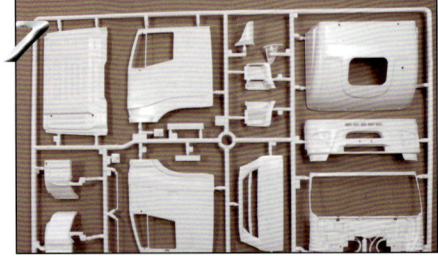
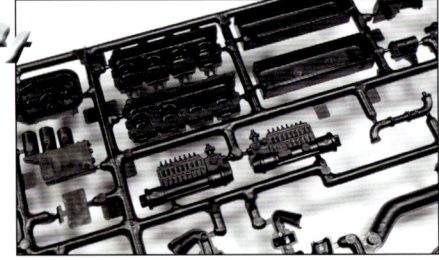

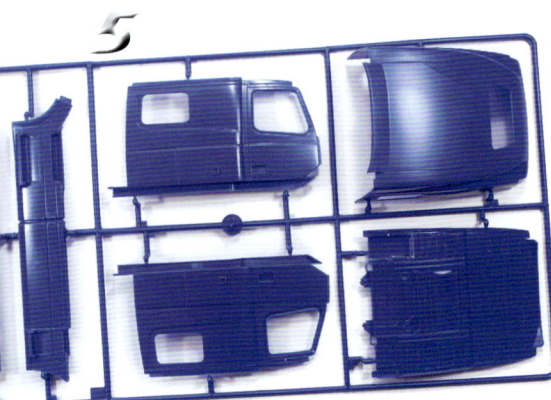

1. Old and new, every kit comes with an instruction sheet that will guide the modeller through assembly and painting.

2. Self-adhesive decals were supplied with the oldest kits, such as this Italeri Volvo F12 and Matchbox Caterpillar dozer.

3. Plastic injection-moulding technology allows the creation of large and complex assemblies to be rendered as one part, as with the floor from the Iveco 190.38 kit.

4. Some kits offer extensive engine detail. This injection pump comes from the Iveco 190.38 kit.

5. A typical cab sprue from an Italeri kit. The cab shell usually consists of separate panels.

6. This rare Ertl Volvo N10 was supplied with diecast metal parts.

7. Painting large US truck cabs can be a challenging task. While the Moebius Prostar and Lonestar cabs are virtually one piece, the Italeri Volvo VN cabs are split into separate panels.

8. 'Daily bread' for most truck modellers are Italeri wheels. This sprue has been a part of most of the company's kits since the mid 1990s.

9. When compared to modern AFV kits (Asuka 1/24 Bantam shown here) most truck kits fall behind in terms of fine details and moulding quality.

kit (Italeri 712, 743) was introduced and was also brand new and very authentic. However, an updated Renault Magnum (716) was based on the previous AE Magnum kit (723) and received an incorrect engine.

Just after the year 2000, two important kit lines appeared on the market. Italeri introduced a regular 13.6m Schmitz curtainsider trailer (3809) that set the foundations for a new series of modern European trailers (later a reefer, a canvas and a dumper from Schmitz were introduced and even an Austrian Gsodam logging trailer based on the same moulds were released)...very welcome and beautifully detailed kits. The others were the new concept kits of which the DAF 95XF was the first, followed by Volvo VN and MAN TGA. These were of a completely new design. In these kits the chassis was a one-piece moulding together with other parts such as the battery box, fuel tank and mudguards. There was no engine though, and the argument was that these kits should be easier to assemble and cheaper, but there was never a significant price advantage and many modellers complained about the simplicity. Although simple, the DAF 95XF, Volvo VN and MAN TGA kits made by Italeri (and sold by Revell), were pretty accurate and easy to build. However, later DAF XF and XF105 models and MAN TGX were again based on the previous kits

2. PLASTIC KITS AND ACCESSORIES

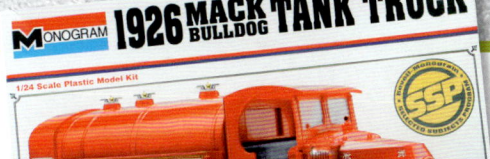

An exotic touch from the past in 1/24 scale comes from Monogram. This kit was re-issued many times and represents the oldest truck available in this scale.

Many AMT kits have been re-issued recently and are still popular among truck modellers, despite their age. The truth is that for classic US trucks, AMT is often the only way to go.

In the early 1990s, the golden era of truck model kits gave birth to some of the best detailed and most authentic products. Revell's Büssing 8000 was just one example.

While the Mack from Monogram kit is old the Bedford O series by Emhar, it is relatively fresh and available with four different bodies and with various liveries.

The latest Italeri kits in the line below: Volvo FH4, S730 Scania Highline and Mercedes Actros MP4.

and the accuracy was poor again due to significant chassis changes on the real vehicles. The same goes for the Mercedes Actros MP2 and MP3 (3824 and 3884), both based on the first generation Actros. One of the most popular subjects in this scale, the Scania R series kits, unfortunately, are again based on the Scania 4 series. But the exterior was updated and even the latest 2009 R series model looks quite good; but most of the cab interior, engine and chassis components remain old and the overall kit accuracy is rather poor.

In 2007 a first sketch of an Iveco Stralis appeared in the Italeri catalogue however it was not until spring 2014 when a new updated Stralis kit was introduced and became one of the best-ever 1/24 truck kits. Later in the same year a facelift Stralis Hi-Way was introduced by Italeri, which is also good and accurate as the chassis and driveline in both Stralis kits represent a standard Euro 5 specification.

Besides the truck and trailer kits, Italeri has also provided some interesting and useful accessories sets in 1/24 scale. The catalogue numbers are 720, 764, 776, 3854 and 3870. These contain a wide array of both the classic and modern truck accessories, and decals, and are highly recommended as a basic source of custom parts and accessories for your models.

RECENT RELEASES

Since the first release of this book in 2016 five major kits were introduced by Italeri and these are a vital contribution to the hobby. The 100% new MP4 Mercedes Benz Actros kits (Italeri 3905 and 3948 and their other decal versions provided by Italeri and boxed by Revell) are a beautiful example of the recent Mercedes heavy duty range and represent nicely detailed kits. The same goes for the Volvo FH4 (Italeri 3940), again a new kit with many nice details, high conversion potential and all new parts. A pair of new trailer kits have also appeared (Italeri 3887 and 3929): a short three axle modern European container trailer (based on the design from the Italian company Tecnokar) either with a box 20ft container (a previously known one) or an all new 20ft tank container. Again, something that modelling community was been asking for since a long time ago. In 2022 the next generation Scania (Italeri 3927) kit was released that has caused some mixed emotions as the kit only has a new cab and external body parts while some 50% of the parts in this kit come from the old Scania 144 (Italeri 712), nearly 25 years old kit. Other new kits that appeared in the Italeri range after 2016 are only a new combinations of old parts with new decals or minor updates. The lates contribution from Revell in the truck category was the 07452 Schlingmann HLF 20 firetruck on MAN TGM chassis that came out in 2015 and all that Revell does since then is re-issues and so is done on the american side except for two interesting contributions: the AMT/Ertl International Transtar CO-4070A that looks like and old kit but is actually 100% new and it really makes a difference when you compare it to the old original issue and the Ford C-900 Refuse truck (AMT1247) that is based on the old Ford cabover kit but an all new refuse body.

3 TRUCK DESIGN

A general knowledge of how trucks are built and how the basic systems work is more than handy when building scale truck models. If you have an idea about what the different components look like on the real vehicle and their purpose, it is easier to work on their scale representation.

TRUCK MODELLING

3. TRUCK DESIGN

3.1 INTRODUCTION

With som basic knowledge, you can easily see the errors, areas where details could be added, and you become familiar with the surface structure and colours of the components for painting purposes. Your knowledge is a great source of useful reference data you have in your brain. This will help you in every phase of the kit's construction.

You might ask: "What do I need to know?" Of course, you do not need to be a skilled mechanic. Trucks comprise many parts and assemblies. Some of them may look and work just like those you have in your car, while others will look completely different and there are some you can't even find there. The fact that you know something helps, but it is not essential. However, there is no doubt that it has a positive effect on detail and model accuracy. This chapter is here to help you with the basic terms and generic information you may need when building a scale truck.

3.1.1 THE FRAME

The basic component of a heavy truck is a ladder frame. It has a basic support function and holds together all the vehicle components. It consists of a pair of frame rails and cross members that are either welded, bolted or riveted. All the parts are steel sheet metal pressings. The frame rail material thickness is roughly about 8 mm. In the US, aluminium was a very popular construction material in the post-war period and except for standard steel frames, some truck producers offered aluminium frame components and even the frame rails. However, while the ladder frame shape and form hasn't changed for decades there are some unique systems such as the central load-carrying tube with independently suspended swinging half-axles (Tatra).

The frames in truck kits generally represent the real thing rather well. Often the assembly is just like on the real trucks (except for the new concept kits of course) and the only think that may be an issue is the wall thickness…especially with some of the older AMT kits. The plastic injection moulding has its limits and the frame is a basic model component, so a certain stiffness is required here and hence the wall thickness may be somewhat out of scale. For easier and more precise assembly the frame rails sometimes have large rectangular holes, indicating where all the chassis components should be fitted. However, the real frame rails never have this type of hole (small circular ones are preferred) as they would act as a stress concentrator and could initiate cracks in the material.

3.1.2 CHASSIS PARTS

The frame is fitted with all the vehicle components. The most basic are the axles and suspension parts as these carry the vehicle's weight and transmit engine torque. There are two basic suspension types used on trucks and heavy commercial vehicles. The classic steel suspension that consists of separate leaf springs, or an airbag suspension where the acting parts are tough rubber cylinders with compressed air at about 0.8 MPa. Both systems have their pros and cons. The steel suspension is more robust and is used for heavy duty and construction vehicles. The airbags came into use during the 1970s and have a very positive effect on driving comfort - and through pressure regulation, the driving height of the vehicle can be controlled which is widely used in practice. On modern vehicles shock absorbers are a common part of the suspension. To improve vehicle stability, anti-roll bars came into use in the 1970s, acting

> The frames in truck kits generally represent the real thing rather well.

A rear view of a Scania tractor chassis nicely reveals how packed it is with components.

©Scania

as a torsion spring to reduce body roll during cornering. Various versions of radius rods and bars are used for wheel torque and braking force transmission from the axle to the vehicle body, and for the axle lateral location. While the leaf springs can be seen on antique wooden carriages, the rest of the previously mentioned components were employed with increasing vehicle speeds and comfort; safety requirements, therefore, cannot be found on each vehicle. Even today their use depends on the vehicle type and use.

A beam axle is an axle type common to all trucks and trailers and has many functions: a drive axle or a dead axle, and both can also be steering axles. A most common truck configuration is a front dead steer axle and one or more rear drive axles. In many applications another rear dead axle is added to a vehicle to increase its payload. Depending on its position to the drive axle it is either called a pusher axle (when located in front of the drive axle) or a tag axle (when located behind). Again, these dead axles can also have a steering function. Furthermore, most of the dead axles also have a lifting function to reduce drag when the vehicle drives without a full load. The lifting mechanism used to be rather complex before the airbag suspension came into use, and some additional mechanisms and parts such as hydraulic pumps and cylinders were required, but modern lifting axles work just on inflating and deflating airbags and are therefore lighter and more simple.

Now we know that there are various axle functions on trucks. To capture the vehicle axle arrangement there is a common formula used that covers all necessary information. The formula AxB provides the total number of vehicle wheels (A) and amount of vehicle driving wheels (B). So, a most common car configuration is 4x2 (and most European trucks are 4x2) while in the US it is 6x4. In the world of trucks, you can find anything from 4x2 to 12x12. Adding another level of the formula to AxBxC (or sometimes AxB/C or AxB/C depending on the particular vehicle configuration) a number of steer axles (C) can be also des-

TRUCK MODELLING

3. TRUCK DESIGN

1. This nice 3D view shows the internals of heavy duty Scania reduction axles. Note the planetary reduction gear in the wheel hub, the frame rail thickness and the crossmember details.

2. A bottom view of a truck shows the front axle with leaf spring and an engine oil sump. The large vessel in the top center is an intake filter bottom.

3. A close-up drive axle view shows a pair of large spring brake chambers. Note the rubber caps which allows access to the inner part of the chamber in case of an emergency brake release.

4. Clearly visible is the size difference between the service (in the front) and spring brake chambers on these double drive axles.

5. A modern fifth wheel mounted on a Blue Stream Scania limited edition. Note there is no base plate and the fifth wheel is mounted directly to the frame rail sides.

TRUCK **MODELLING**

This nice detail of a classic truck driveline shows a straight six cylinder engine, a gearbox and a driveshaft transmitting the torque to the axle. Note the position of the spring brake chambers and the typical Scania shaped wheel hubs.

cribed. This is quite handy because often a pair of the front axles are steerable and, both the pusher and tag axles can provide steering to allow as many wheels as possible following the ideal track, reduce drag and tyre wear significantly and increase manoeuvreability.

3.1.3 ENGINE AND TRANSMISSION

Once the frame is fitted with suspension and axles, both the engine and transmission are next. An upright longitudinal four-stroke direct injection turbocharged diesel engine is the most common. Usually it is fitted in the frame just above the front axle, but there are some anomalies such as a horizontal engine mounted under the cargo body just between the axles (Büssing/MAN), or an inclined engine (MAN/Saviem/Rába or Liaz 100/110 trucks) but these are not common in today's world. Modern heavy duty truck engine displacement is somewhere between 10 and 16 litres and provides roughly 300 – 500 kW (400 – 700hp). The most common arrangement is an inline six-cylinder, however eight-cylinder V engines are still provided by

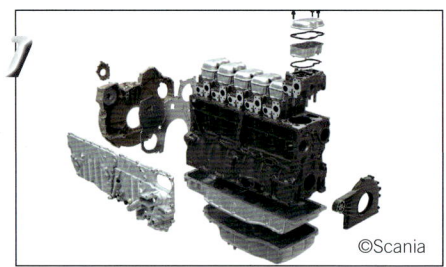
©Scania

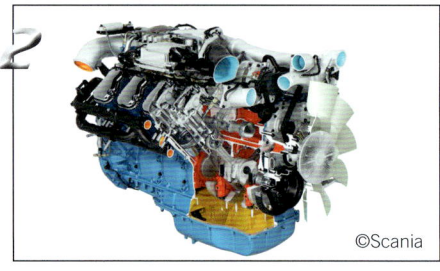
©Scania

1. A modern Scania six cylinder engine block assembly, note that both cast iron and aluminum are used on various components.

2. A section through a 16 litre Scania V8 engine, note the complexity of the whole assembly. Unfortunately, although stated, all the Italeri Scania kits including the latest one have the old (and wrong) 14 litre engine.

some manufacturers (Scania). As the brake mean effective pressure (bmep) has increased significantly in the last 30 years, production of larger engines with more cylinders and large displacement was reduced and these were replaced by smaller and more effective designs. Heavy-duty V10 and V12 truck engines with a displacement of up to 22 litres were common in Europe during the 1970s (MAN and Mercedes). A US speciality was two-stroke engines produced by Detroit Diesel. The most common and popular series 71 was introduced in the late 1930s as an inline six and later also in a V configuration, starting with V6 and going up to 24 cylinders produced until the mid-1990s and replaced by state-of-the-art four-stroke inline six-cylinder Series 60 engines. Although also used, two-stroke engines were never employed widely in European trucks.

With conventional trucks, the engine is covered with a hood and the cab sits on the frame behind the engine, just above the transmission. To access the engine a hood is tilted. On a so-called 'cabover' truck, a cab is fitted above the engine and there is no hood at all. On early cabovers the engine cabs had various door and service hatches to access the engine during maintenance. It was not until the late 1950s when tilting cabs came into mass production, introduced in 1958 by Freightliner, in 1962 by Sisu, Volvo and Foden, in 1967 by MAN, in 1968 by Scania, in 1969 by Mercedes and in 1970 by DAF, allowing much better engine accessibility. However, the tilting cab is rather a complex mechanism but its advantage is a shorter cab length (as the hood is missing) and therefore longer cargo body within a limited overall vehicle length.

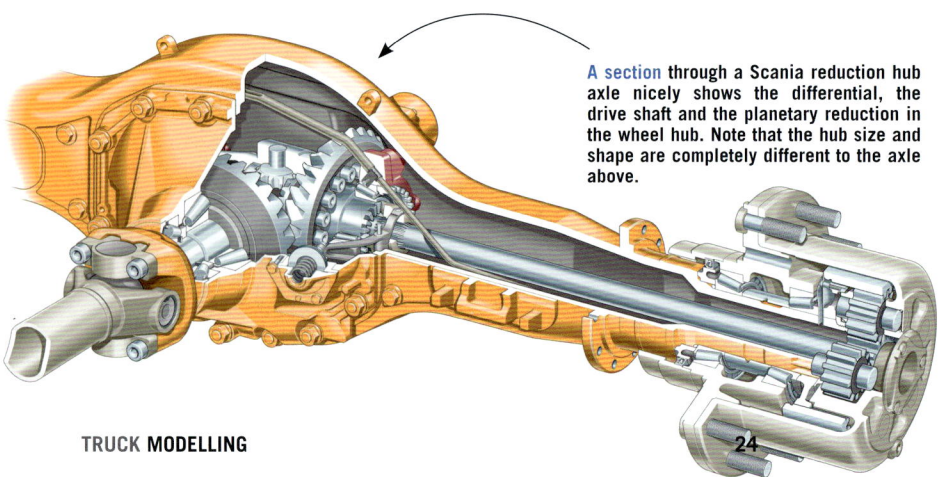

A section through a Scania reduction hub axle nicely shows the differential, the drive shaft and the planetary reduction in the wheel hub. Note that the hub size and shape are completely different to the axle above.

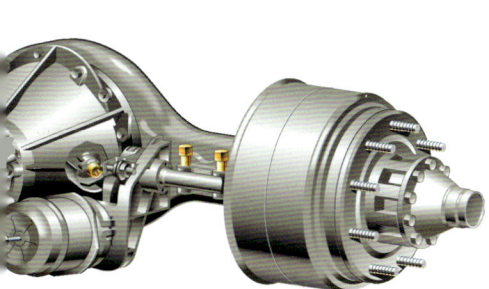

An engine radiator is usually mounted on rubber blocks in the frame just in front of the engine. There are some historical exceptions such as Volvo F88/89 series and Scania 1, 2 and 3 series, which had their radiator fitted to the cab. Because the radiator was tilting together with the cab it was connected to the engine via a flexible rubber hose. Various coolers are usually attached to the main cooler, such as an intercooler, air-to-oil cooler or an A/C heat exchanger. All the coolers are usually made of light corrosion-resistant materials such as aluminium or brass. Close to the engine there is always a large cylindrical vessel mounted either on the frame rail under the passenger seat or on the chassis behind the cab. Usually, it is a thin sheet metal or plastic and contains an air intake filter. A filter outlet is connected with an air intake manifold (or a turbocharger inlet) while the inlet is fed with an intake pipe that sucks in ambient air. Classic American trucks often have chromed air intake filters mounted on either side of the cab or under the hood.

The vehicle transmission is usually one piece with the engine. In today's world a mechanical gearbox within a range of 10 to 16 gears is the most common hardware. It usually consists of the basic and reduction gearbox within one case, but a separate reduction transmission has been very common in the US in the past. Modern European trucks have either synchronised manually controlled or fully automated transmission, while in American trucks, classic non-synchronised simple and robust transmission is still widely used for its durability. However, a clutch servo mechanism has been common in Europe; classic American trucks often remain simple and have no clutch servo at all because with non-synchronized transmission, gear changes are possible even without a clutch engagement. This makes the system very robust but requires some driving skill.

Another part of the driveline is a propeller shaft connecting the transmission and the drive axle. This shaft drives the final gear in the

A detail of an axle with the brake drum and hub removed. The axle shaft on which the hub bearings are fitted is visible.

Note the brake S cam between the pads which pushes them to the drum's inner surface. The reverse motion is done with the spring.

A reduction hub fitted on the axle. Note that the internal planetary gears are not fitted, and the spline on the hub OD for attaching the planetary gear.

The typical shape of brake pads with lining from heavy duty drum brakes.

For adjusting the vehicle riding height a load sensing valve is often used on vehicles. Mostly as a simple mechanical connection between the frame and the axle. Note the thin arms attached to the air valve just above the drive axle.

A detailed view of the front steer axle's brake system showing a spring brake chamber, a slack adjuster, a brake cam and cam rollers. The red parts are the brake shoes with lining.

drive axle and the differential. If the vehicle front axles are driven too, there usually is a transfer case that sends the power to both the front and rear axles.

An interesting thing you will not find in your car is a brake retarder. It is a device used to augment or even replace the function of the primary vehicle friction brakes, especially on a long decline to prevent any brake fade during extended and continuous operation when the friction brake power might drop below what is necessary to stop the vehicle. There are more principles, but the basic two-brake retarder types are hydraulic or electromagnetic. Brake retarders are usually mounted on the transmission output.

3.1.4 BRAKES

Although axles have already been discussed, a very important part was left out and that is the brakes. Brakes are vital for reducing the speed of a driving vehicle, and for secure parking so their function is very important for overall safety. There are two basic brake types that are common on trucks…drum brakes and disc brakes.

Drum brakes are a classic system used worldwide on all types of vehicles. The speed reduction comes from friction between the brake shoe lining and the brake drum internal surface. During acceleration and driving there is a clearance between the lining and the drum surface. During braking the brake shoes are pushed away by a brake cam acting on cam rollers. Resulting force pushes the lining to a drum surface that spins with the wheels and arising friction reduces the wheel rotational speed. In today's world, drum brakes are being replaced by discs because of their effectiveness and better cooling properties; however, for some markets and applications drum brakes are still used because of their better resistance to dirt, lower price and more robust design.

Disc brakes first appeared on heavy vehicles in 1991 when the Renault Magnum was introduced. Its front axle disc brakes were a world premiere. In about 15 years, disc brakes became standard on most European heavy trucks and trailers due to their better performance and cooling, but production costs are higher compared to drum brakes. The friction on disc brakes is caused by pushing the brake pads to either side of a brake disc that spins with the wheel.

The contact between the brake lining and drum or a disc surface is a final result of the system operation, although the whole brake assembly is more complex. From the brake pedal to the brake lining there is a long chain of components and those on trucks are very different from cars. While the brakes on cars and small commercial vehicles are hydraulic, the main acting medium in heavy commercial vehicle brakes is air at the pressure of about 0.8 Mpa. On car brakes, the brake fluid can act directly inside the wheel in the piston, pushing the brake lining to the drum or disc surface. This is not so easy on trucks, because there are much greater forces transmitted over greater distances. With air this can be done much more easily through rather simple components.

As the acting forces are rather high, the air piston that applies the brakes would be too big to fit within a wheel. Instead of this an air-operated piston in a device called a brake chamber is mounted externally on the axle. Each wheel has its own brake chamber so there is always a pair of these per axle. The brake chamber is nothing but a cylinder where compressed air is converted into mechanical force to apply the brakes and stop the vehicle. The air pressure has to be high enough to move the piston within a chamber, and provide a linear motion that is transferred via the slack adjuster and the brake cam to either brake shoe or a brake pad.

There are two basic brake chambers commonly used and combined on trucks: service and spring brake chambers. A service brake chamber contains a flexible rubber disc called a diaphragm and a piston connected to a pushrod. When you press the brake pedal, compressed air fills the brake chamber, causing the diaphragm and piston to move and apply the brakes via the brake linkage. When air pressure is released out of the chamber, the piston returns to its original position by the return spring inside the chamber and the brakes are released again.

In a spring brake chamber there is a large compressed coil spring acting against the piston. The compression force is about 5 kN. This spring force is used as a parking brake when the vehicle is at full stop, and therefore the brake chambers are actually not air applied but air released when air pressure builds up behind the piston, pushing against the spring and releasing the brakes. When you press the brake pedal, compressed air acts against the spring force, moves the piston and applies the brakes. Once the braking power is no longer necessary, you release the pedal and the piston is pushed back by the spring and the brakes are released.

During an emergency situation, if there is a sudden air leak (a blown hose for example), the pressure drop in the spring brake applies the brakes automatically because the spring is what actuates the brakes and not the air. On the other hand, the service brake chambers are air operated and therefore if there is an air pressure loss they simply stop working. This is why both types of brake chamber are combined on modern trucks, but on older vehicles sometimes just service brake chambers were used, on which another mechanical emergency and parking brake was fitted. Due to the coiled spring inside both, the service and spring chamber are easy to tell apart as those on the latter are significantly larger.

If a vehicle brakes down and it has no engine power (and therefore no pressure air source) an external hose from the towing vehicle is used to fill the vehicle air system and release the spring brakes and allow the vehicle to be towed away. If this is not possible, most spring brakes are equipped with a special bolt which, when screwed in, releases the brake without any need for air. Speaking

of towing broken-down vehicles, another act can be considered and that is removing the propeller shaft. This is done because of the fact that when a vehicle is towed, its wheels touch the ground and spin. With the wheels, there is also the differential and final gear spin and these move the drive shaft. The drive shaft spins the gearbox shafts so all the gears inside the transmission move too. However, there is no engine propulsion and the gearbox lubrication is not fully operational. Therefore, to prevent any transmission damage a drive shaft has to be removed.

To complete the story, I should say that on some vehicles an air-over-hydraulic brake system was used, combining both systems together. This was mostly on light- and medium-duty commercial vehicles in the past, but is now uncommon.

3.1.5 PRESSURE AIR CIRCUIT

I have already mentioned that trucks need pressurised air for many functions. It is not just the brakes but also the airbag suspension, clutch and shifting controls, differential lock engagement and even the cab and seat suspension. Obviously this means that a truck engine has to be equipped with a compressor and the truck itself needs a whole system for pressurised air storage and distribution.

The compressor itself, either single or two-cylinder, is always engine-mounted and driven from the engine timing gear. From the compressor the compressed air goes to the air dryer to remove any excess oil or moisture; an air dryer usually has an outlet for tyre inflating. From the air dryer the air travels to various valves and into separate circuits, of which those for the brakes are the most important. If you add some electronic regulation valves and sensors that modern vehicles use, it is not very difficult to realise that all the air-lines and circuits are a significant part of every vehicle, but you can hardly find any evidence in an average truck model kit. Therefore, having an idea about how the vehicle works is very useful for adding all these details to a model when improving its accuracy.

Because of the amount of compressed air necessary on an average truck, and to store back-up air in case of an emergency (a compressor failure for example) trucks are equipped with multiple air tanks installed all around the vehicle. The air tanks are either welded steel or aluminium with various threaded inlet and outlet holes. There is a drain valve on the bottom of each tank, allowing moisture and oil drainage.

3.1.6 ELECTRIC CIRCUIT

The electric circuit of a truck does not differ much from an average car. There is a pair of 12V batteries connected in series with a chassis used as a ground on a modern European truck. A 24V circuit is used on Euro-

The very first component of the air system is always an air dryer used for removing any moisture and oil from the air before it reaches the air tanks. This is the large white cylinder, the attached valve underneath also acts as a pressure regulator.

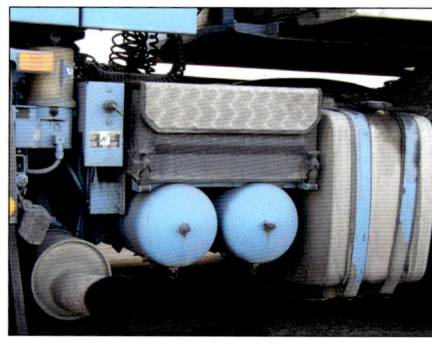

A typical setup of components you can see on a truck. An exhaust with an end silencer, a battery box with its plastic cover under which the air tanks are fitted. On the right side is a diesel tank.

TRUCK MODELLING

pean trucks while 12V is common in the US. The batteries are rather large and heavy and therefore have a dedicated battery box on a chassis. The energy is supplied by an engine-mounted belt-driven alternator. As with the air-lines and pipes, no electrical harness is present in model kits and to make a realistic model, some wiring should be added to connect the alternator, batteries cab, lights and the other electric systems.

3.1.7 TRAILER COILED CABLES AND BRAKE HOSE

To supply air and electrical power to trailers, coiled cables and hoses are used on modern trucks. There usually are two air hoses and two or three electric cables. They have distinctive colours that may vary from country to country. The current European arrangement is: yellow and red for the air lines, green is often used for the ABS cable and a pair of the standard electric cables are in black. In the UK, a three-line brake system for trailers was used in the past, with the third air hose in blue. The modern US trucks use a green electric cable and a red and blue air line. The classic coiled shaped hose and cables appeared in Europe in the 1970s. Before then, straight black rubber hose and cables were used, also being common in the US and they can still be seen there. All these cables are also missing from the kits, but they are an essential detail that should be added to a model.

In Europe the following standards for electrical trailer connections are used: ISO 1185 (7 pin, black socket) as the main classic type. ISO 3731 (7 pin, white socket) used on newer vehicles in addition to ISO 1185 and finally ISO 12098 15 pin connector that combines ISO 1185 and ISO 3731 together. Furthermore there is another 7 pin connector for ABS/EBS connection (ISO 7638-1) on vehicles equipped with these systems.

A nice view of the susie cables typical for the UK where the three line system was used - yellow, red and an additional blue one.

3.1.8 FUEL SYSTEM

The fuel system consists of a fuel tank made of either steel or aluminium and mounted on the chassis. Recently, fuel tanks made of plastic have come into use as well. Long-distance trucks can carry more than a thousand litres of fuel. From the fuel tank the diesel goes to a low-pressure supply pump that feeds the fuel filters and the main high-pressure injection pump. On classic trucks, the high-pressure fuel pump is mounted on the engine side and feeds the separate injectors through high-pressure fuel pipes. Excess fuel from the injectors is collected by an overflow pipe, returning it back to the fuel tank. A common part of an average fuel system is an air bleeding hand pump, usually mounted on the high-pressure fuel pump or near the fuel filters. Modern trucks with advanced high-pressure fuel systems often have many components mounted internally inside the engine, and covered so that the amount of external fuel lines is reduced significantly.

Another device is that of independent heating common in today's vehicles. This is usually mounted somewhere in the interior or underneath the cab. This type of heating is used when the vehicle is parked in cold weather to heat the interior without any need to start the engine.

On the subject of fuel, economy has become one of the most important heavy com-

Batteries: A pair of large 12V batteries on European trucks such as this Iveco EuroStar, are stored in large rectangular boxes that are often grouped with the exhaust system. Note the white air drier cap mounted nearby.

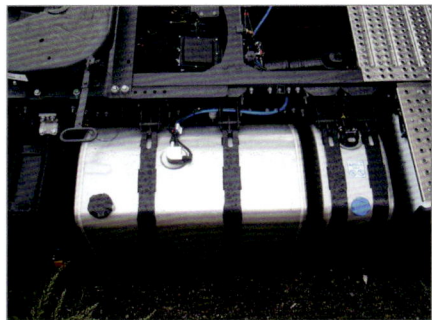

Large aluminum fuel tanks occupy a lot of room along both frame rails. Note the smaller tank with blue cap used for Ad/Blue or DEF (Diesel Exhaust Fluid).

An x-ray view reveals the amount of space occupied by modern exhaust and after-treatment systems. The black plastic tank is used for the Ad-Blue storage.

©Scania

A nice view showing the steering box linked to the front axle via a push rod. Note the single leaf spring suspension and anti roll bar mounted underneath.

mercial vehicle characteristics in the last decade. Good fuel consumption of a modern European truck and trailer combination is just below 30 litres per 100km, although in heavy conditions the diesel consumption can double easily.

3.1.9 STEERING

The steering system, and power steering in particular, represents another hydraulic circuit that can be found on modern trucks. In the 1950s trucks were produced without any power steering so driving them was a tough job. Soon the first air and hydraulic power steering systems appeared. The steering box is mounted on the chassis under the driver and is linked to the front axle by a push rod. An engine-mounted power steering hydraulic pump is driven from the engine timing gear and has a separate oil reservoir mounted on the engine or chassis, usually near the steering box. Vehicles with multiple steering axles have more advanced systems, either with a set of push rods connected to the front axle or with hydraulic cylinders that control the steering function.

3.1.10 EXHAUST AND EMISSION CONTROL SYSTEMS

Fifteen years ago there would not be a chapter such as this at all. Truck exhaust systems were just pipes and silencers back then. No electronics, no chemistry, all simple. Times have changed and more restrictive emission standards were introduced (Euro IV in 2005, V in 2008 and finally VI in late 2013). Those simple exhaust silencers became complex, electronically regulated chemical reactors that consist of hundreds of components and cost thousands of Euros. Their task is rather simple. When the fuel injection and combustion control had reached their limits and it was no longer possible to keep the engine emissions within the allowed range just by affecting the fuel burning, after-treatment methods came into use. These work with raw emissions and change their chemical composition to reduce their negative impact.

The most common terms used recently are EGR, SCR and DPF.

EGR is an engine-mounted system and is

3. TRUCK DESIGN

1. A modern six cylinder Scania engine and transmission assembly coupled to the complete Euro 6 spec exhaust system. Compare the volume and size of the exhaust components to the engine.

2. The view of the exhaust section shows how complex assembly of the exhaust actually is. An advanced system control is required as well which all together make this system an expensive and sensitive component

3. EGR (exhaust gas recirculation) shown in the picture is one of the basic principles of emission reduction used on modern diesel engines.

4. The SCR (selective catalytic reduction) principle is shown in this picture. Note that the Urea (Ad-Blue or DEF) is injected into the exhaust system and not the engine.

©Scania

©Scania

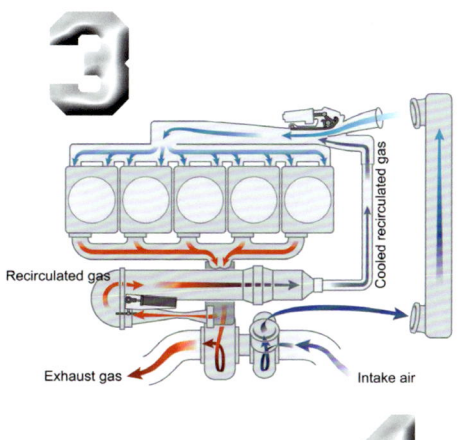

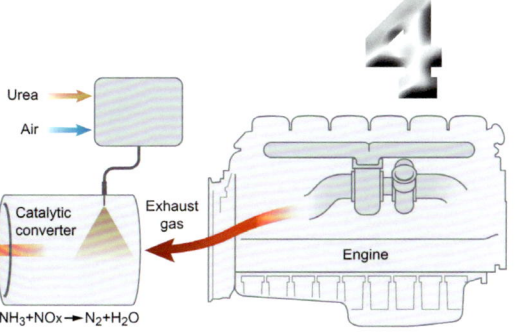

actually not a part of the after-treatment but its function is vital for modern engines. The abbreviation stands for exhaust gas recirculation. This means that a certain percentage of exhaust gasses is mixed with intake air and introduced into the cylinder again (up to 50% in a diesel engine). In the cylinder the exhaust fumes act as an inert gas and reduce the amount of air available for burning the fuel. As a result, fuel burns at lower temperatures. This reduces the amount of nitrogen oxides formed in the exhaust fumes as the higher the temperatures are, the more nitrous oxide forms within the exhaust gasses.

DPF stands for diesel particulate filter. It is a part of an exhaust silencer used to remove any particulate matter from the exhaust fumes. The filter acts as a trap, collecting the particles and where they burn at high temperatures to carbon dioxide, the least harmful form of a carbon we can get from the combustion process in a vehicle engine.

SCR (selective catalytic reduction) is a method to chemically reduce the amount of nitrogen oxides in the exhaust gasses. This is done in a special chamber integrated into an exhaust silencer, where a special liquid called AdBlue is injected and mixed with exhaust gasses. A chemical reaction causes the nitrogen oxides to turn into clear nitrogen and water vapour. The ideal reaction temperature is approximately 400 °C. This puts an immense requirement on the engine and the exhaust system heating. To keep the system heated the exhaust pipes and silencers of the latest vehicles have a temperature insulation, and even combustion chambers appeared within the exhaust manifold 'downstream' of the turbocharger.

AdBlue or DEF (diesel exhaust fluid) is an aqueous urea solution made with 23.5% urea and 67.5% de-ionised water. It is stored in a separate so-called AdBlue tank on a vehicle, often located near the exhaust system. You can easily tell the tank apart from a diesel tank by its blue filling cap.

Depending on the vehicle specification and the emission standards it meets, the truck may be equipped with either an EGR or SCR and DPF or all the previously mentioned systems. There has been a rapid development in this area and these systems have changed rapidly since 2005. From a modelling viewpoint these changes are rather significant because most of the components, the advanced exhaust silencers together with the AdBlue tank, are mounted externally on the chassis and are therefore clearly visible…both on the vehicle and the model. However, as the design has changed rapidly, none of these systems in any form were captured by Italeri in their mould updates and are missing entirely in the kits except for the Iveco Stralis.

3.1.11 TRUCK DESIGN - CONCLUSION

Truck design and architecture is an amazing story, which started more than 100 years ago and contains many interesting chapters. The topic itself would fill a book easily, but for modelling purposes we do not need to go that deep. The aim is to literally help you learn the ropes and become familiar with the basic terms. Once you know how trucks are built, tackling a model will be much easier and many things will come to you automatically.

BEFORE WE START MODELLING, LET'S TAKE A CLOSER LOOK AT
Wiring and plumbing
3.2

3.2.1 GENERAL INFORMATION

Certain wiring and plumbing is usually missing in every kit. However, it represents an inevitable part of every vehicle that is visible well enough, so it cannot be neglected in 1/24 or 1/25 scale. Therefore it deserves a separate chapter. This will show you which materials can be used, where to add lines and which components they should connect. Some basic modelling skills are required of course, however, wiring a model is not so difficult. With practice and the following information, it may soon become an activity you will enjoy. Wiring should be one of the first advanced techniques you should consider after you manage the basic steps. All you need to know is in the lines below and it does not matter how long it will take you to employ it on your own model. It is a fundamental section of this book so you can return to this chapter and study it anytime in the future, if you feel this is too complex at this time.

WHAT IS WIRING?

Wiring technically means all cables, and pipes in the chassis that represent the real vehicle systems. It is not just the electrical harness but also all the air, diesel and hydraulic lines visible on a real vehicle.

WHERE IS THE WIRING LOCATED?

Well, that is the problem. The answer is: everywhere in the chassis, all around the engine, underneath the cab, around the axles and air tanks. Of course the wiring is more complex on modern vehicles whereas older trucks had just basic air piping and few electrical cables. In any case, if you look at the real subject there is no doubt that wiring should be present on a model in at least a basic form.

WHAT DO I NEED?

Wiring the model does not require any special tools. The material you will need is not expensive and sometimes even free of charge. The most worrying part of the process is the basic technical knowledge of the real vehicles. It is good to know some basics prior to your first wiring attempt, but often modellers do not know much at all. Still, wiring is something that can be created on your model. You do not need to know the precise path of every pipe or cable, or its purpose. If you have good reference photos you can just follow them as a guide. There are so many wires and pipes on an average truck that no-one will track each single pipe on your model to revel an error. Therefore, replicating the reality may even be a waste of time as just an approximate representation is good enough in most cases.

The basics of vehicle architecture were described in the previous chapter. If you need any reference material, electrical harness or air system schemes from instruction manuals for various vehicles can be very useful. Of course, when building a particular vehicle the more reference photos you have the better.

TRUCK **MODELLING**

3. TRUCK DESIGN

1. These pictures will guide you through the basic materials suitable for wiring. One of the first items on the list is the black fishing nylon. It is super fine and does not need any painting.

2. Resin air valves are important aftermarket item when it comes to chassis plumbing.

3. Wiring is not just about cables and pipes. Various sizes of fittings are helpful for detailing your model as well.

4. For larger diameter hoses and pipes various cables good to have at hand. These are the ones used for the susie cables as well.

5. Various copper wires are a must for a classic truck wiring where most of the air lines are in steel pipes.

6. Super detailing of the wiring can be done with the CTM etched cable ties. These are also handy for making cable bundles as shown in this picture.

7. Just as with the materials, all the tools you need are rather basic. In addition, some Evergreen and Plastruct profiles may be handy for creating your own air valves and fittings.

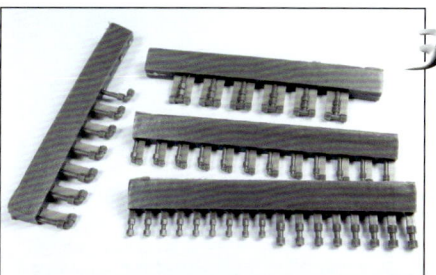
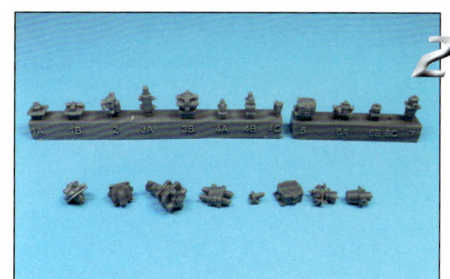
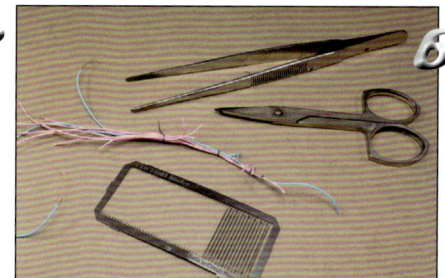

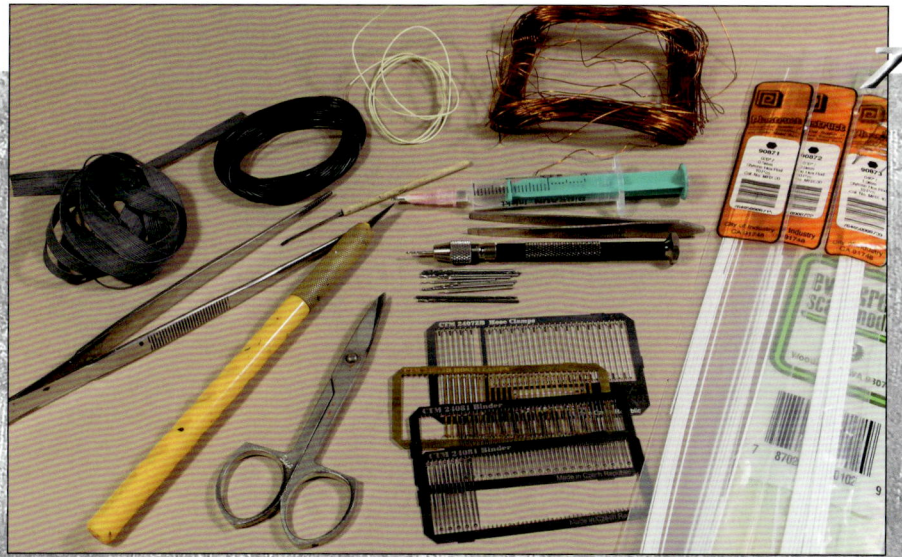

WHAT DOES THE WIRING CONSIST OF?

The model wiring (just like the real one) comprises the following parts: 1) Wires, hose and pipes, 2) Connectors and fittings, 3) Various relay and regulator valves, sensors, electrical boxes, 4) Cable ties and pipe fittings. Let's discuss them briefly.

Wires, hose and pipes

This group contains all the electrical wires and cables and all the hydraulic pipes and hose. The wires along the frame rails are organised in bundles and sometimes protected by sleeves. In the world of scale truck models there are multiple sources of suitable wires.

The primary sources are various telephone, TV or internet cables, coils and all kinds of electrical appliances. These provide a large amount of aluminium or copper wire, which can be used for both the cable and pipe representation with or without the insulation. The suitable diameters for models are up to 1mm. Except for the wires themselves, also just the soft plastic insulation slipped of the wire can be used to make soft plastic tubing used on modern vehicles.

Another useful material is that of small diameter rubber fibres. The most suitable diameter is roughly between 0.5 to 0.8mm. These are produced in different colors for various purposes and are very suitable for reproducing soft rubber hose.

A common material sold worldwide is nylon monofilament fishing line. This is also available in black and is very suitable for reproducing fine electrical harness on modern vehicles, and it often does not require painting.

Lead wire is commonly used by aircraft modellers. It is very soft and therefore easy to form into any desired shape. Multiple diameters are available.

Speaking of pipes and wires, we should also look at the materials used on real vehicles. Wire is wire, so in terms of the electrical

harness there is not much to say. It hasn't changed much over time except for its extent. Both the separate cables and also large diameter bundles can be seen on the real vehicles. Modern trucks also have various kinds of harness protection sleeves to keep the wiring dry and safe. Most of the hydraulic pipes, the high-pressure power steering hose for example, are made of rubber with metal end fittings and there haven't been any significant changes over the years.

Regarding the air lines the situation is more interesting. These were made of steel pipes until the mid-1980s (roughly). The steel pipes had straight sections with sharp turns, so they fitted precisely into the chassis and were connected by fittings and union nuts. Although some producers used galvanised steel pipes, these were always painted with the chassis color to protect against corrosion. Steel was replaced with vinyl pipes in the mid-1980s because of its weight and corrosion resistance. The vinyl pipes are flexible and therefore do not have to be pre-formed into a desired shape to fit. Another difference is that the pipes do not have to be painted, so on many vehicles the air circuits are in black as it is the most common example of vinyl used on trucks. The visual difference between steel and plastic air lines is significant and can be easily seen and shown on models in our scales.

Connectors and fittings
The fittings are discussed separately to emphasise the fact that in such a big scale, even these fittings, nuts, elbows and connectors are so big that they are worth making. Each hose or pipe has a fitting on each end, and each cable has its connectors and all of these should be visible on a model. The fittings and connectors can be created from various plastic profiles and rods, and are often available as precise accessories for model car builders in dedicated (online) shops.

Relay and regulator valves, sensors, electrical boxes
Fine little details such as various regulator and relay valves within the air system, and various electrical sensors and boxes in the electrical harness, are very important details that add the final touch to a model's wiring and piping. Just look into a truck chassis and you will see that it is busy with all kinds of valves and regulators. It is not just the wires and pipes, and almost none of these are available in model truck kits. Fortunately, the British company Kit Form Services (KFS) provides various types of cast white metal valves in 1/24 within its TQMT-3 Air valve set, which is commonly used by model truck builders all around the world. As the future of the KFS and their product range became uncertain around 2020, the Czech Truck Model (CTM) have released an array of products to supply modellers with with necessary parts. This activity resulted in CTM 24230 Universal air valve set, CTM 24234 Trailer air and electric couplings, an array of air fittings (CTM 24231 – CTM 24233, straight, elbows and tees). Furthermore CTM now also offers both the European and American style heavy duty batteries (CTM 24236 and 24237).

Pipe fixings, hose clamps and cable ties
Looking at the real vehicle, it is obvious that all the air and electrical lines have to be fixed properly. There are various types of supports

A great way to show there are more ways to go are the main pictures in this section. Page 32 shows a top view of an Iveco Stralis chassis where all the wiring was done after the chassis painting. This photo show the International Prostar chassis where the wiring was done prior to the chassis painting.

to which cables and hose are tied with cable ties or pipe fixings. If a rubber hose is used as a connection between two steel pipes, on the engine air intake for example, hose clamps should be used for proper sealing. 1/24 and 1/25 scales are big enough to show this on the models too. However these parts are rather small, but there are smart and use-friendly detail sets that turn this into real fun. A pair of sets is available by Czech company CTM (Czech truck model), which provide very fine photo-etched cable ties and hose clamps suitable for this purpose. If more robust fixings are required, mostly a piece of plastic profile will do the job.

COLOURS

Correct colours of wiring and plumbing on a model are very important. The colours may vary with the vehicle type and age, and with its use and maintenance. When building a model of a particular vehicle, it is definitely good to have an idea about its service life because it will help a lot during the following building stages.

As for the steel air pipes, these were always painted together with the chassis in the factory as well as during vehicle maintenance. This means the model chassis can be sprayed with one colour after wiring so there are no difficulties.

In the case of modern vehicles with plastic air tubing, it always depends on the particular production technology in the factory. Some companies paint the chassis components separately and the final chassis does not have to be painted after assembly, so the chassis may be grey with all the wiring and piping in black vinyl and galvanised fittings. This looks marvellous on a model! However, on some trucks the chassis assembly is sprayed at the end of the assembly line and therefore has one colour together with all the fittings and plastic pipes and cables. On some vehicles you can see a mixture of the two aforementioned options. Some wiring and piping may be painted in the chassis color and some may be fitted afterwards with no paint at all.

With old vehicles that might have been repaired and sprayed during their active service lives, multiple times, the situation is chaotic as nearly everything is possible here. There is an unlimited amount of colour variation and for old worn-out vehicles there are no rules at all. Reference photos is the only source of information you can rely on to find out what is common.

There are many colours of wires available. For some applications the natural black and dark tones are the best, and combined with the CTM cable ties cable bundles that need no painting at all can be created.

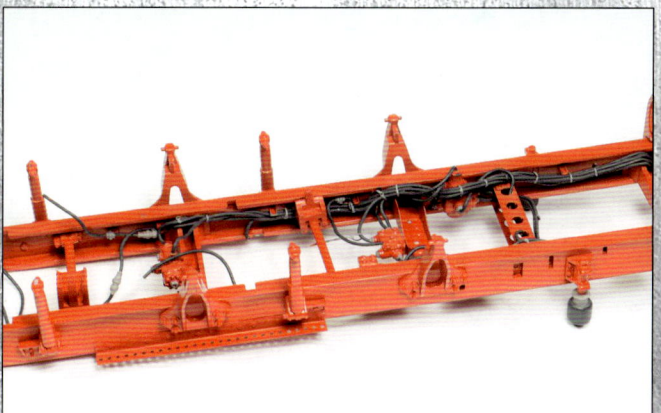

The complete wiring on the International Prostar was done prior to the chassis painting and all the air lines were later brush painted with Vallejo acrylics.

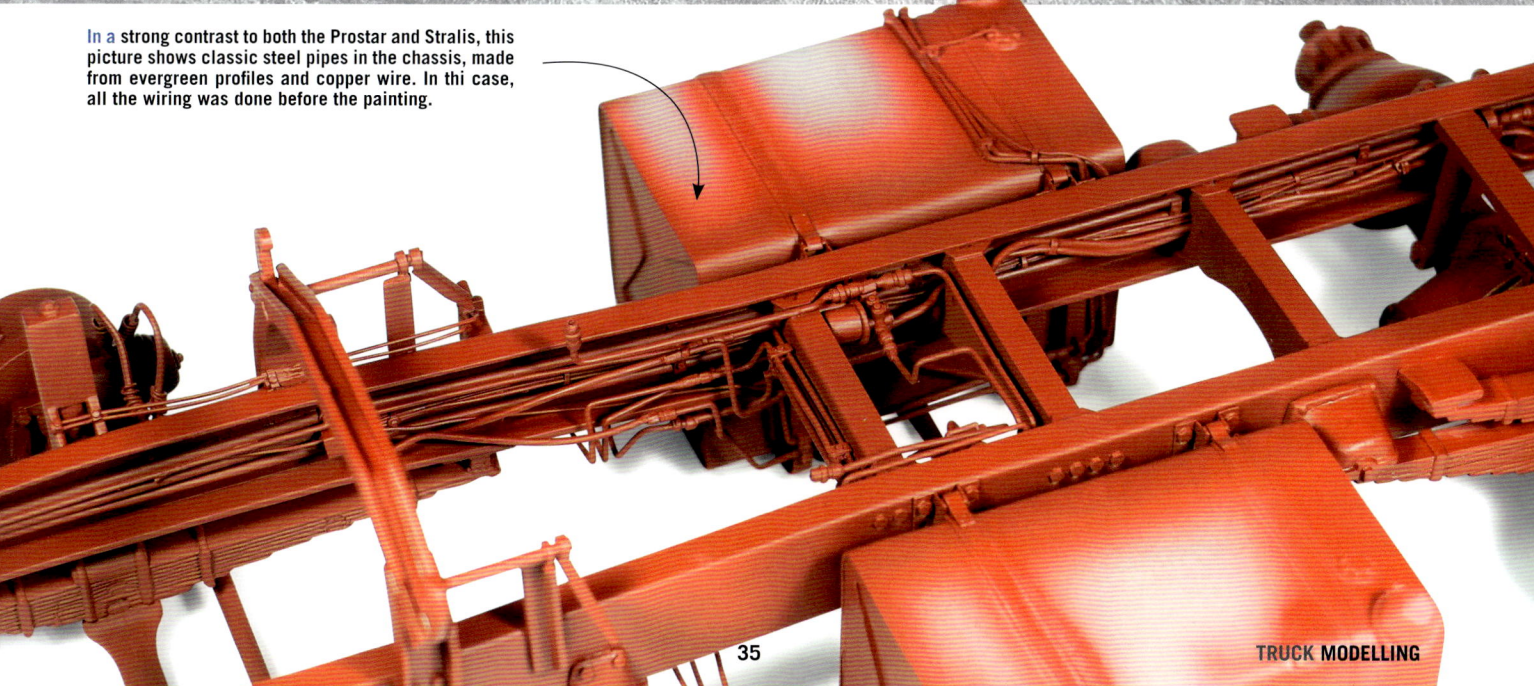

In a strong contrast to both the Prostar and Stralis, this picture shows classic steel pipes in the chassis, made from evergreen profiles and copper wire. In thi case, all the wiring was done before the painting.

Photo guide

3.2.2 WIRING IN PICTURES

A picture says more than a thousand words. Therefore, I have chosen a set of 30 images from my archive showing the basic air circuit components on heavy trucks. These should help you to learn more about wiring and be able to visualise what it looks like in various chassis areas. They also serve as elementary reference pictures.

1-2 Compressed air comes from an engine-mounted compressor. This air goes through a safety valve into an air dryer, removing moisture and excess oil. There are many various sizes and shapes of air dryer, but modern trucks have been using the same design for a few decades. It is a vertical cylindrical vessel with a rounded top, fitted on a rather complex valve assembly, which has a safety valve built in. Modern trucks often have a set of inlet fittings allowing an external compressed air supply (from a towing vehicle for example). The T-shaped handle in the first picture is a battery shut-off switch, while the other photo shows many cable ties used on air hose just above the spare wheel.

3-4-5 Once dry, the compressed air is stored in a reservoir (called a wet tank) from which it is then distributed via a four-way protection valve into the other reservoirs and separate brake circuits, a hand brake circuit and other systems. The four-way protection valve is often mounted close to the air dryer and separate air tank inlets. Older vehicles may not have this valve at all as it can be replaced by a series of smaller valves. There are more types of these valves but they look pretty much the same all around the world.

6 Another specific component is the trailer brake relay valve. The air brake foot valve is usually hidden underneath the brake pedal and controls the truck brakes. However, the trailer brake relay valve is often visible somewhere in the chassis and controls the trailer brake function. Its outlets are therefore linked to the trailer coiled hose as well..

7 An important advantage of air suspension is that it maintains a constant vehicle riding

TRUCK MODELLING

height. This needs a set of specific valves that monitor the vehicle riding height, and control the airbag pressure. They are usually mounted in the chassis and connected to the axle via an arm and connecting rod. This mechanical system is used on older vehicles. The latest trucks use electronic sensors and have no mechanical parts. Note the amount of cable ties used on both the cables and air pipes.

8 A large increase in the amount of various valves and wiring complexity on modern trucks has been caused by the ABS system in early 1990s. There are various ABS valves located on the chassis all around the vehicle. Note the characteristic protection sleeve around the cables.

9-10 Air tanks are important vehicle components and these are used for compressed air storage. Often they are fitted all around the vehicle. Note the light electric cable and the cable tie around the rear mudguard mount in the second picture.

11 The number of air tank inlets and outlets can be different, as well as their position. It could be on the tank ends or on the cylindrical wall. Besides the inlet fittings, most air tanks also have a drain valve located at the tank bottom, which allows condensation to drain. Mostly these are just simple spring-loaded valves, but modern trucks also have automated drain valves.

12 Brake chambers are essential air brake components. These are replicate well in most kits and adding air pipes to them ensures better detail. The large spring chambers are mostly fitted on drive axles (however a tag axle is shown in the picture) and have two feeds and an additional blow-off pipe Consider the difference between the fitting colors. The left-hand item was obviously changed after the chassis was sprayed.

13 Similar view shows how a spring brake chamber on the front steering axle is connected to the air inlet, via a pair of the soft rubber hoses with ends protected with a coil spring. The rest of the piping is made of steel.

14 The service brake chambers are much smaller than the springs and are located on the front vehicle axles and trailers mostly (however some European trucks have spring chambers even on the front axle) and are fed just by one pipe.

15 The chamber position can be different. This photo shows a MAN F2000 drive axle with a pair of vertically mounted spring chambers. The vehicle was produced in late 1990s and the increasing vehicle complexity (and extensive wiring and piping) is obvious on the chassis. Once again, note the amount of cable ties.

16 Another view showing the same area of a heavy MAN TGX tipper. The spring chambers with slack adjusters and horizontal brake cam shafts are clearly shown. Obviously this vehicle has drum brakes.

17 This view shows a Volvo FH drive axle spring chamber located under the frame rail. The chamber axis is parallel to the axle axis. This chamber arrangement is more common on a vehicle with disc brakes. A pair of the chamber inlet pipes are visible. The vertical cylinder on the left is one of the suspension air bags. Note the thin air bag inlet pipe and the pipe and cable fixings.

18 Another view showing modern Volvo FH chassis end. There are loads of pipes and cables and even a skilled model builder probably has no idea about their purpose. Note the various wire and hose diameters making the chassis rear end very busy.

19 This image of a 2012 R series Scania again shows one of the suspension airbags, its feed and also various air lines and cables. See the cable ties again.

20 Another view of a 2012 Scania tractor reveals extensive wiring and rather complex air valves. These modern systems are so intricatr that scaling them down needs a modeller to stay on top of things. Note the various valve and fitting colors. Obviously the wiring of the real vehicle was installed after the chassis was sprayed.

21 Although it may seem rather simple, even modern trailer wiring can be complex and not so easy to replicate on a model. This is a modern Schmitz container chassis (produced before 2010, so it is not one of the latest) and the air system complexity is obvious. Note the different air line, valve and fitting colours. Again, everything is secured by a vast amount of ties.

22 Modern trucks also have various electrical boxes (Iveco EuroStar shown in the picture). Their purpose may not be obvious, but that is not a problem for a modeller. Add some cables and take it easy. Note the cable protection sleeves and many cable ties used on the bundles.

23 Another view of the EuroStar chassis shows the borderline between the sprayed and unsprayed part of the wiring, as it was made in the factory. The upper part of the rear cab suspension console was obviously left unpainted with the chassis colour.

24 This view of a MAN TGA chassis exemplifies the extensive wiring array. This vehicle has a special fleet color and was sprayed with cream paint after assembly. The complex wiring with loads of cable ties is obvious.

25 In sharp contrast with modern vehicles is

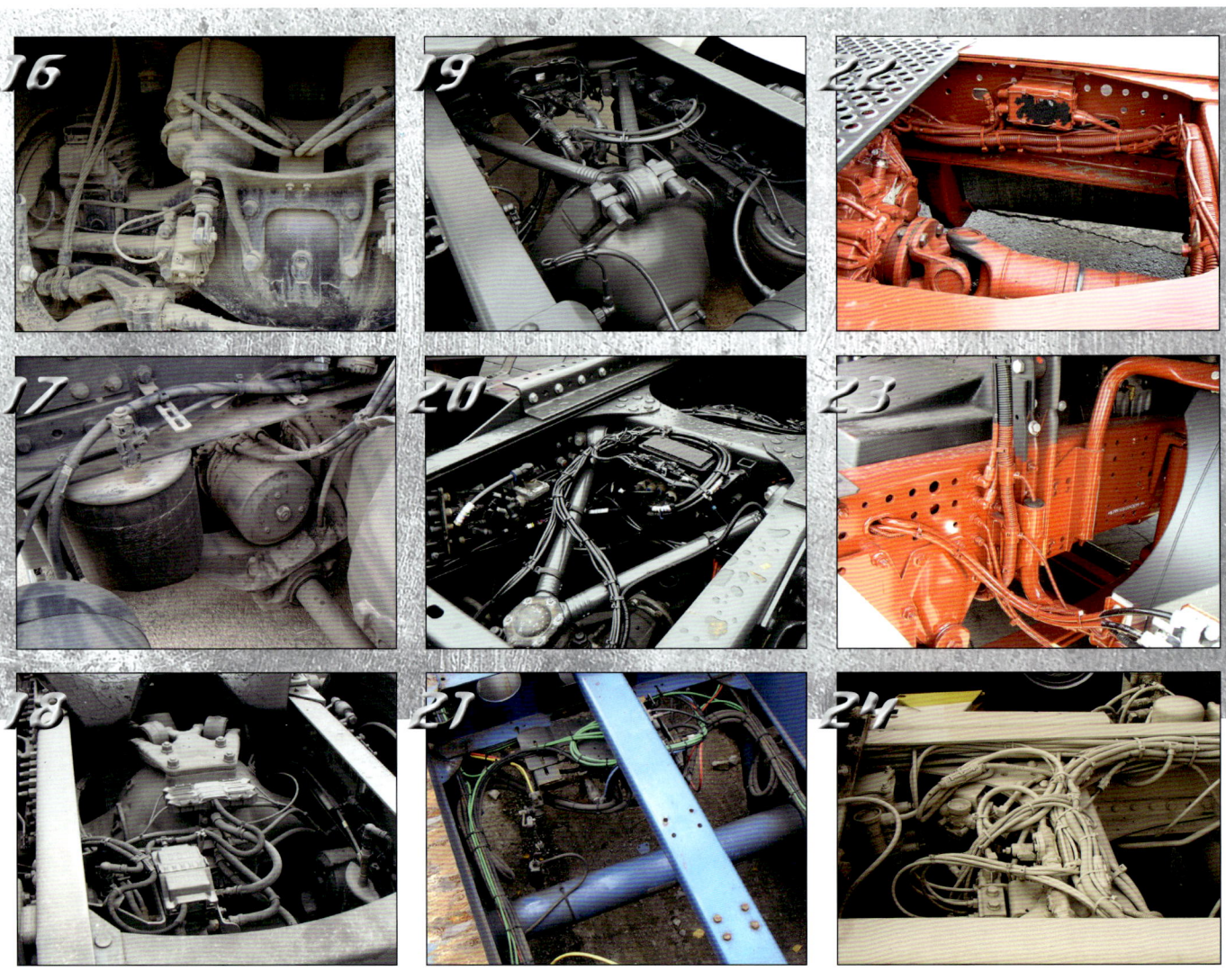

3. TRUCK DESIGN

this Scania LB141 chassis, with just a few steel air pipes and a hydraulic hose. The 197's vehicles were simple and robust.

26 Even the transmission has its wiring, as shown on this DAF CF. There are various air and electric lines required on modern gearboxes.

27 Looking into a modern vehicle chassis the various air and electric systems are rather difficult to be told apart. The picture shows a large aluminum air tank, a blue air dryer cap, a four way protection valve hidden behind the air dryer and probably a trailer brake relay valve on the left. A skilled mechanic could probably tell us more but not an average modeler. Still with a few shots creating a nice scale representation may not be an issue.

28 This Scania R730 chassis view shows just how visible the wiring is on a modern vehicle. The cable bundles are apparent, as well as the fuel tank pipes. The small plastic tank on the other side of the vehicle is an AdBlue container, as it has a blue cap. There is even the retarder cooling pipe visible just behind the catwalk.

29 This picture of a Peterbilt 359 chassis shows custom details and blue air lines on the chassis.

30 In contrast to modern vehicles, classic trucks used to have steel pipes - which are rather easy to tell apart from the plastic tubing via their long straight sections and sharp bends.

31 A great example of black vinyl air tubing is shown on this Volvo N10. Note the vast amount of air lines and valves fitted nearby. Although rather old, this mid-1980s truck features busy wiring areas.

I hope that this set of images will help you learn more about truck wiring and give you an idea about what different components look like. To start with, just use one reference picture of a particular vehicle area, and start adding one line after another and try and make it look just like the real thing with all the valves, fitting and fixing points. You do not need to know exacly where to each line starts and finishes; many wire ends can be hidden in dark corners on the chassis around the engine, or underneath the fifth wheel.

Photo guide

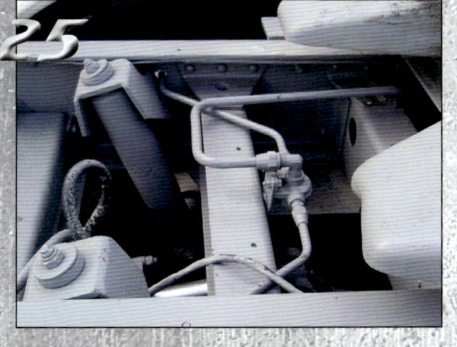

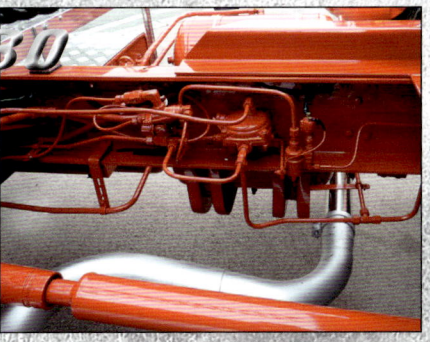

Truck MODELLING

4 A MEDIUM LEVEL

There is a large amount of theory around building models, involving tools, paints, painting, airbrushes and compressors. However, this is what you'll find in an average book on building scale plastic models, and most magazines keep publishing articles on these topics repeatedly (to cater for new readers), yet the basics haven't changed much in years. I therefore decided to not revisit these topics and instead, focus on content that is essential to every truck modeller and cannot be found elsewhere. This is why, here, we will deal with the kits, real trucks, wiring and model quality and authenticity.

PROJECT

4.1 INTRODUCTION

Now, it is high time we picked up a kit and see how it all works in practice. Most truck modellers are a little bored with Italeri, AMT and Revell kits. For this book's first build I therefore decided to choose something fresh and new: Moebius Models' International Prostar...a fully detailed kit of a modern, conventional American truck. I had a chance to obtain the prototype parts in December 2012, a few months before the kit hit the shelves, and I knew instantly that this kit represents what most of us have longed for. For us, this is a great start to impart the typical model assembly sequence, on a kit that needs no conversion at all. I prefer Prostar to Lonestar (the other kit offered by Moebius, based on the same set of moulds) because of the design. However, both kits are great, really do not need any extras and can be built straight from the box. I always enjoy adding custom details, though, so for this build I will use the CTM Prostar photo-etched detail set and add some wiring. I bought the Revell Prostar in the past, so am using the Revell kit. There is no change in the parts, just the decal sheet is different.

4.2 BASIC ASSEMBLY

Ok, so let's get back to our Prostar. When you open the box, always study the instructions first, look at the parts and see how they fit together, and if sanding and filling may be necessary. Think about painting the parts too, because not every component has to be painted separately and in some cases painting a whole assembly is a better option. Getting familiar with the kit instructions and parts prior to assembly may make your life easier. My other recommendations are: do not unpack the clear and chromed parts and keep them away from any dust and dirt for as long as possible (it prevents them from getting scratched). Put the decal sheet aside too and keep it away from moisture. Damaging any of these is quite easy and replacements are not easy to obtain.

The first building step in the instruction sheet shows you the parts you need, marked with numbers and letters where mostly letters stand for a runner, and number for a particular component so it is easier to find them within the kit. Sharp diagonal (wire cutter) pliers are the best tool you can use for this task. Cut each moulding gate that connects the part to the runner, and cut as close to the part as possible but make sure you do not damage the component itself. Often the moulding gate marks have to be cleaned further with either a sharp knife or a sanding sponge (or a file or abrasive paper) to remove any excess material and smooth what's left of the attachment point completely. In the next step you should watch out for any ejector pin marks that may be visible on the finished part. This is not essential on engine pieces (as most of them remain hidden) but very important on the frame rails for example. If there are no pin ejector marks left, the last operation of the part clean-up procedure is removing any flash or witness marks along the mould parting line. On some parts it can be scraped off easily; sometimes with a file or any other sanding tool. Sink marks may also appear on a part's surface where a larger volume of material hardens more slowly than those in the rest of the mould and shrinks, creating shallow depressions on the surface. These can be filled with putty and sanded just like ejector pin marks if necessary.

For good assembly, dry test-fitting is always handy to reveal any alignment issues prior to glue application. If no problems emerge we can start gluing the parts together. As for the glue, a standard modelling cement is what's needed. Made by many companies, they all do much the same thing – melt the plastic on the part contact surfaces, so they join together and become virtually one component as the molten material hardens. This works on plastic only and if joining painted parts, make sure the contact surfaces are free from paint. I got used to Tamiya Extra Thin Cement because of its thickness and fine application brush. It is so thin that capillary action forces it instantly into the narrow gaps between the parts, the moment the application brush touches the surface. To glue the parts this way you just press them together and brush the glue along the assembly split line, keeping the parts ma-

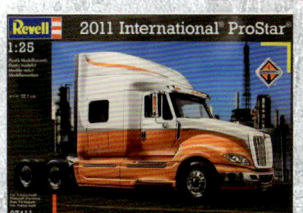

Kit: 07411 Revell 2011 International Prostar
Scale: 1:25
Accessories: CTM 018 International Prostar detail set, CTM 24092 US Tail lights, CTM 24072 Hose clamps, CTM 24081 Cable binders, KFS TQMT-3 Air valve set
Notes: A kit manufactured by Moebius models boxed by Revell

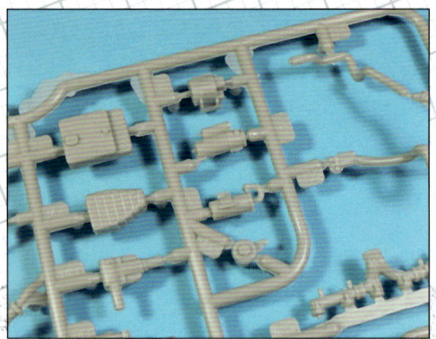
1. In most kits parts are numbered and positioned on sprues marked with letters.

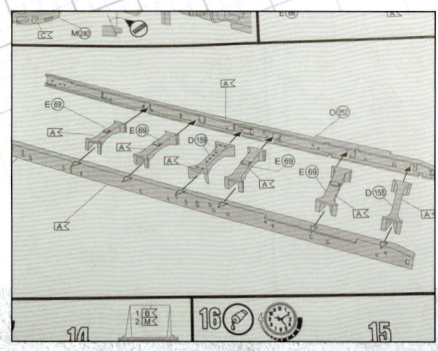
2. For each step the instruction sheet defines which part numbers are required.

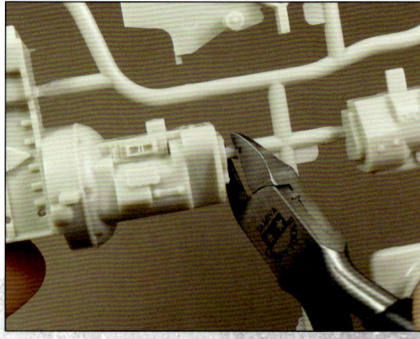
3. Side cutter pliers are the best tools for cutting parts from the sprue.

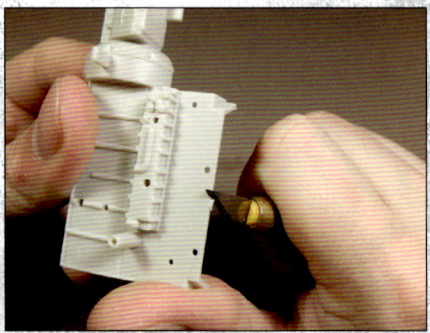
4. Once cut from the sprue, remove all the casting gates and flash, also remove any visible ejector pin marks.

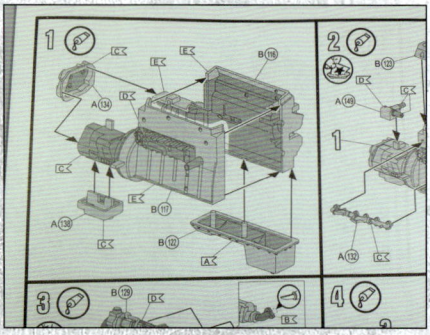
5. Some model parts consist of subcomponents (halves) to be glued together.

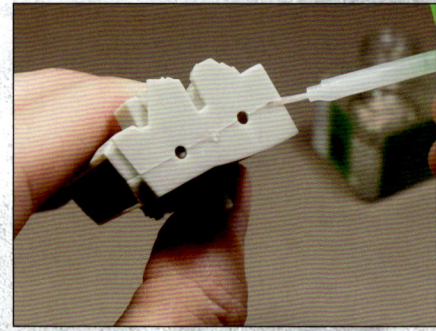
6. A thin glue is be applied with a brush applicator to bond the parts together.

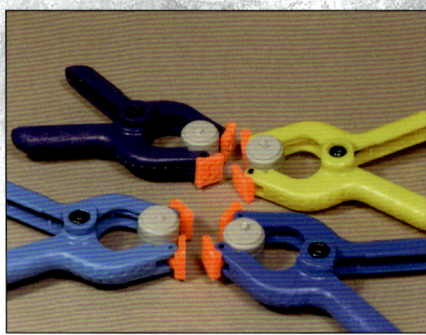
7. After that parts like these should be fixed together to secure their position before the glue dries.

8. On most of these assemblies the seam needs to be sanded and filled once the glue is fully dry.

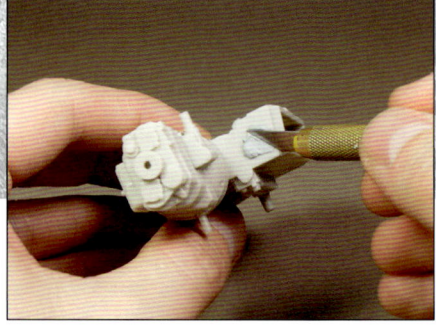
9. If required, a putty can be used to fill any unwanted gaps or part split lines. Once dry the filled area should be sanded again.

ted till the molten plastic hardens. The thinner the glue, the faster the small volume of plastic is melted and the faster it hardens; this is also the big advantage of the Extra Thin, as well as the fact that it leaves almost no marks on the surface. Common glues for plastic made by other producers are usually not that thin, and therefore have to be applied directly on the contact surfaces before the parts are pressed together. Most have either an applicator brush or an application needle and besides the different densities and application methods, they all work on the same basic principle. If more glue is applied, make sure you wait long enough before any sanding as the surface may sink while the plastic solidifies. To maintain proper assembly geometry, and to prevent mismatch between components, various clamps can be used to hold the parts together. Often just a peg is enough to do the job, but specialist modelling clamps are available.

As already mentioned, it may happen that a model part consists of sub-components, while the real vehicle part is just one piece of material (such as a suspension air bag) or the join between these parts does not generally represent a real join…and should not be visible (such as those commonly seen on model air tanks or fuel tanks). To remove these seams we use modelling putty. There are various types but basically, most are just standard one-component and two-component putties and each has its own pros and cons. It is always better to start with the one-component option (almost every modelling company makes it, just like the glue already mentioned) however, this is not good for applying thick layers. But this is not our case on the Prostar so a simple putty for plastic models will do the job. There is not a dedicated application tool, but for most cases a flat toothpick, knife

4. A MEDIUM LEVEL PROJECT

The engine block was painted, then some additional highlights were created by adding a few drops of white to the basic dark blue. On this the silver parts were glued.

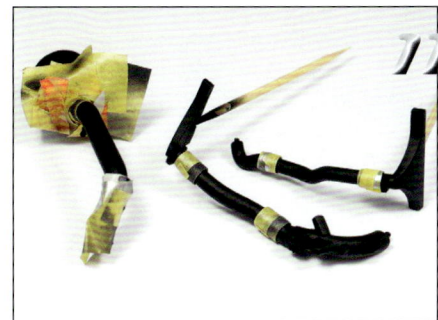

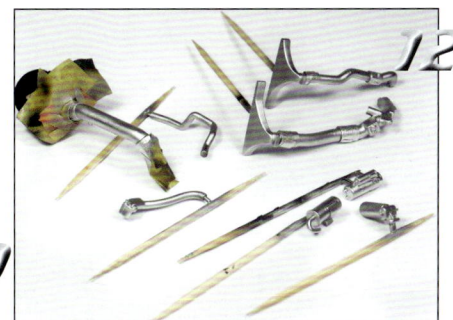

or scalpel blade is okay. For sanding, a general purpose tool can be used as mentioned: abrasive paper, any kind of sanding sponge or a file. Make sure you use the appropriate grade of sanding paper. Of course any paper can be used for the rough work (however I would not go below 200 for most modelling applications) but for finishing, the paper grade should be about 500 or higher (let's say to 2000, which is used on a surface before polishing and is very fine) otherwise there will be visible scratches on the surface even after painting, as the paint in general never hides any of these surface imperfections.

The three paragraphs above actually describe what has to be done with each model component or assembly. Cut out the part, remove any flash and/or witness marks, glue the parts together, use putty where appropriate and fill any unwanted gaps, sink or ejector pin marks. Sand the filled area smooth. Once finished, apply the base coat, then final paint and decals. Over and over, step by step you repeat this automatically till you get through the whole instruction sheet. In fact, this is what building models is about in any genre. It is not difficult but it needs time and practice. Your first model will not be perfect but that is normal. Neither was mine.

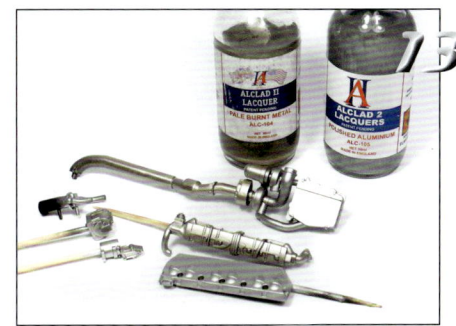

10. The engine has been primed and painted with Mr.Color paints. The dark blue was mixed in a medical syringe.

11. All the piping was first sprayed black and then the rubber hose parts were masked off using Tamiya tape.

12. Once masked the pipes were sprayed with Mr.Color silver.

13. To add more metal colour variations Alclad paints were also used. Flat aluminum was used on the rocker cover and Pale burnt metal on the exhaust manifold and turbocharger.

Note the colour variety of the metal parts. The darkest tones were achieved by spraying Tamiya X-19 smoke. The small decals come from the kit decal sheet.

4.3 ENGINE

Building the Prostar starts with the engine. In the case of truck models it is always either the engine or the chassis first, so what will be shown soon is a standard procedure. Most of the truck kits in 1/24 and 1/25 scales are designed in a similar way. Therefore, once you build one of them you virtually build them all. Each kit may have its own tricky areas but in general it all works the same way.

The Prostar engine is good and an accura-

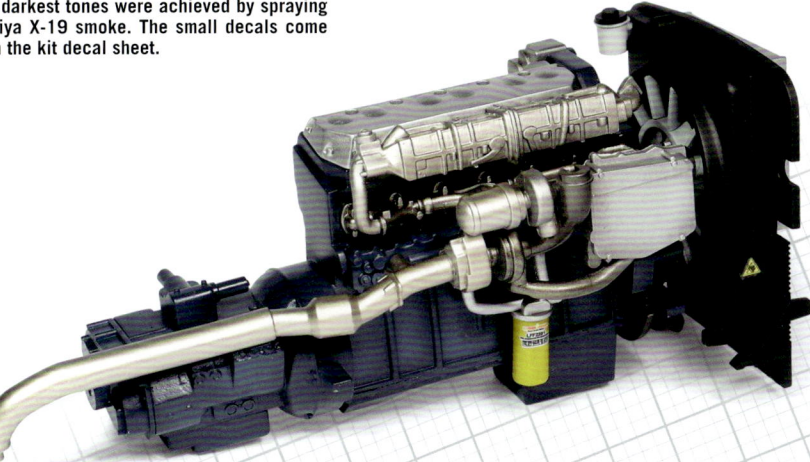

43

TRUCK MODELLING

> *The black plastic side skirts, the bumper and the red and white striping are the typical daily workhorse features. Such a vehicle calls for some fine weathering and a bit of rust that really bring it to life.*

te replica of the real thing – the Maxxforce 15 heavy duty diesel engine based on the famous C15 Caterpillar, produced in a joint venture with Navistar. The Revell decals and instructions wrongly describe the engine as the smaller 13-litre version but the Maxxforce 13 based on the MAN D20 is a completely different engine.

The engine assembly is rather straightforward. There was minor flash on some of my parts and the witness marks on most components are clearly visible and have to be removed. However, not a single ejector pin mark had to be filled or sanded and just gentle filling and sanding was necessary on the engine block...although this area is not visible on the finished model. There are numerous alignment pins on the parts so correct geometry is also not an issue during the assembly. The only change I made on the engine is closing the timing cover from the back, using thin plastic sheet to cover the hollow areas that did not look very good. Otherwise the engine was assembled as per the instructions.

4.3.1 ENGINE PAINTING

The real production engine block should be painted dark blue, (the blue metallic mentioned in the Revell instructions was used on promotional engines only) with some parts (the oil pan, the bell housing and some manifolds) in natural aluminium finish. To make it easy I sprayed the whole engine and transmission with Gunze Mr.Surfacer grey primer, followed by a few thin coats of dark blue mixed from blue, black and red colours and did not care about the pan or the bell housing as these will be barely visible on the finished model. I did not have any particular reference for the engine colour except for a few poor-quality photos. I simply added a few drops of black into the basic blue colour and kept adding more till the final shade was dark enough. A few drops of red were added to add the overall violet tone, but the painted block looked a little uniform to me. For a more interesting visual appearance I added a drop of light grey into the basic dark blue and sprayed highlights over the engine block structure (this technique is known as post-shading).

The Gunze Mr.Color paints (lacquer-based acrylics) I use are one of my favourite paint brands and the Mr.Surfacer primers are some of the best on the market. Using the original thinner with a few drops of Mr.Retarder solvent (or using Mr.Color Leveling thinner) they provide a pleasing, smooth finish and I got used to them as they are reliable and rather fool-proof. Their surface is also resistant to oil paints, which is handy during weathering. These paints have a distinctive odour, though, and you might consider them inappropriate for home use if you have no separate hobby room. In that case, water-based acrylics (such as Tamiya, Vallejo or Italeri) might be a better option. To protect your health, a spray mask should be used when working with any paints; please do not underestimate the dangers.

One thing that surprised me during painting was that some of the kit parts appeared to be greasy, and the paint did not adhere to them very well. I had not seen this on any plastic kit previously, (however it is quite common with resin parts) but after my experience I recommend you wash the parts in soapy water to prevent any issues.

The components with natural metal finish were sprayed with Mr.Surfacer black primer, followed by Alclad II lacquers. I used polished aluminium on the rocker cover, both the intercoolers and most of the pipes and small components, and pale burnt metal on the turbochargers, exhaust manifold and pipes. The black primer works better with Alclad pa-

4. A MEDIUM LEVEL PROJECT

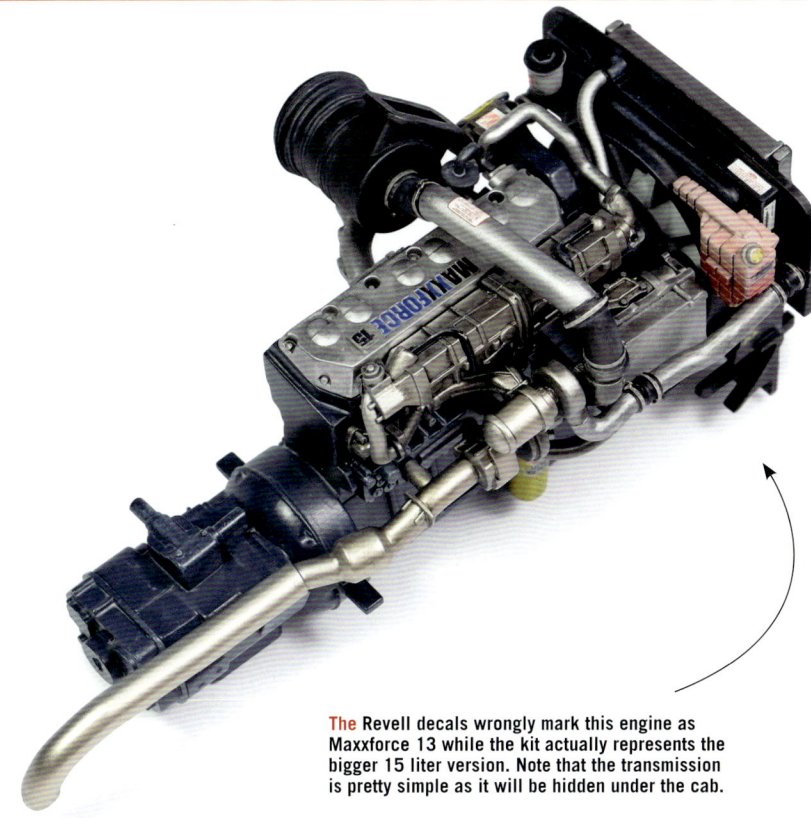

The Revell decals wrongly mark this engine as Maxxforce 13 while the kit actually represents the bigger 15 liter version. Note that the transmission is pretty simple as it will be hidden under the cab.

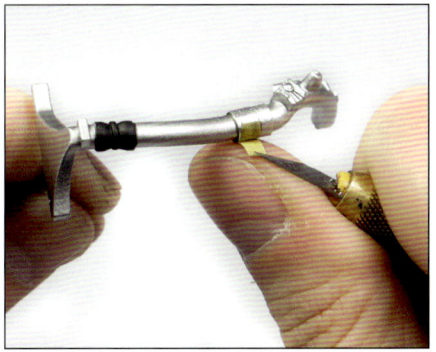

1. By removing the tape the black rubber parts are revealed. The careful masking ensures sharp paint edges.

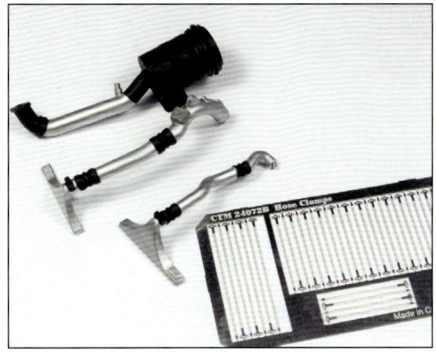

2. The beautiful etched CTM hose clamps are now added to all the connecting hoses.

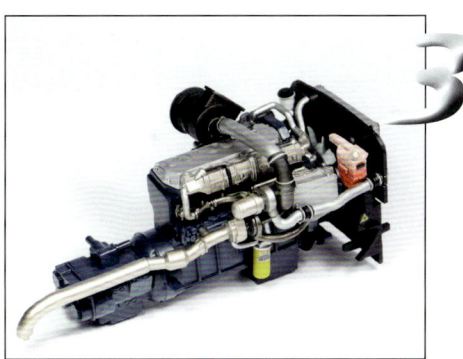

3. Once painted all the separate parts and subassemblies were attached to the engine block.

4. The cooler assembly is quite simple. I have masked the intercooler and painted it silver and left the remaining assembly in flat black.

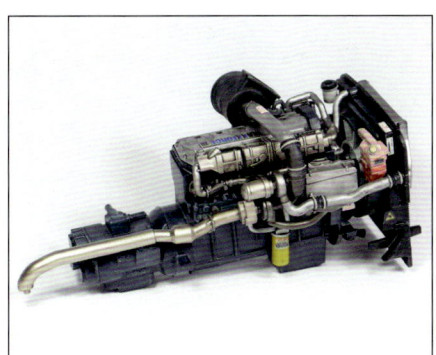

5. Note the red expansion tank. This nice little detail was painted with gloss white followed by clear red to simulate the cooling fluid level.

6. A basic cable harness was added to the engine which consists of 0.6 mm black rubber and CTM etched cable ties.

TRUCK **MODELLING**

ints than the standard grey version. Where a darker metal tone was required to add more colour variation, I sprayed the part with highly diluted clear acrylic Tamiya X-19.

There were initial masking demands with some parts. It is quite common that one plastic piece should be painted in more than one colour. In that case you can spray it the basic colour tone and paint the other details with a brush but this needs practice. You can also spray the part the basic tone and use masking tape to cover some areas, and spray the part with another tone. This is very handy when large areas are to be painted or where a sharp and precise borderline between the two colour tones is required…just like the black cooler assembly with an aluminium colour intercooler moulded as one piece. The masking tape I prefer is made by Tamiya. Using it is almost as easy as it sounds. Sometimes it just needs a little thought because there are always more options for masking and doing it one way may be much easier or faster than doing it the other way round, so think twice before cutting. When spraying, use just a decent amount of paint applied in fine coats to

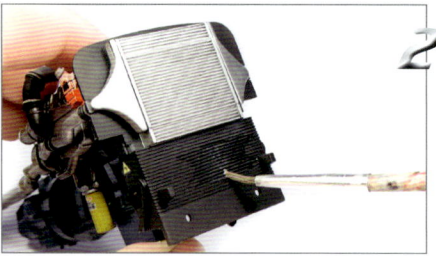

1. For weathering the 502 Abteilung oils and the AK Interactive odorless thinner were used.

2. The Abt035.Buff was used for a light wash, applied all over the engine to highlight the parts structure.

3. To reduce the shine of the bright metallic parts a few layers of Tamiya X-19 Smoke was applied with an airbrush.

4. Fine paint chips were painted over the whole assembly using the Vallejo acrylics.

5. Wiring was added on both sides of the engine to make the whole assembly visually more interesting.

TRUCK MODELLING 46

4. A MEDIUM LEVEL PROJECT

prevent the paint soaking under the tape.

The natural metal-finish parts and the pulley assemblies were attached to the painted engine block as per the instruction sheet, and other components such as fuel and oil filters, starter motor, air intake manifold and filter and expansion tank were added in the next steps. The decal sheet contains worthy engine data sheets for various components. More of these were added from a KFS engine and chassis data plate decal sheet to enhance the whole assembly. On the rubber hose, CTM photo-etched metal hose clamps were added. The expansion tank as well as the windscreen washing fluid tank were painted white. Then the fluid levels were masked with Tamiya tape and the tanks were sprayed with red and yellow Tamiya transparent shades to simulate fluid level in the tank, as the real tank is made of see-through plastic and the fluid inside is clearly visible.

4.3.2 WIRING THE ENGINE

As the Maxxforce is a modern powerplant, some form of harness is required on an authentic engine replica. I made a few generic bundles of thin wires, black rubber lines and the CTM photo-etched cable ties and attached them on the block as per the real engine pictures, and connected them to components such as the starter motor, alternator, air compressor, fuel pump and fuel filters. This was enough to simulate all the wiring as well as the air, oil and fuel lines all around the engine block. I did not pay any attention to the transmission as this will be fully covered by the cab.

4.3.3 ENGINE WEATHERING

Since the early stages I knew the engine would look relatively new…therefore, no rust or oil leaks were applied. The weathering consists of just a few basic steps. The engine block post-shading was highlighted by a dark oil paint wash. Light dust wash was applied over the lower engine and transmission area where dust may collect. Gentle light-colour dry-brushing was applied all over the block and selected pipes, and the light aluminium surfaces were treated to a few layers of black and dark grey filters to reduce their shine. Finally, just a few chips were hand painted with Vallejo acrylics on the cooler, intake filter and engine block. We will discuss some of these techniques later so do not worry if you are not familiar with them. It is just a regular part of my work and while this model is intended to be basic, I still could not resist as the few basic weathering tricks really brought the engine to life.

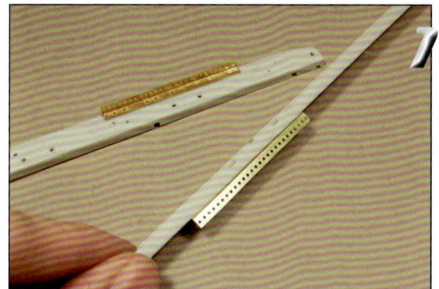
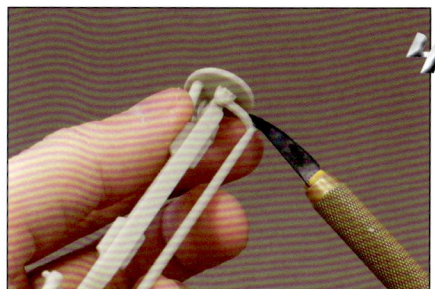
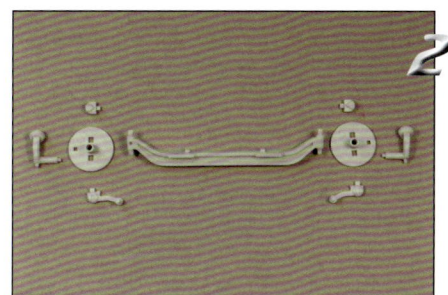
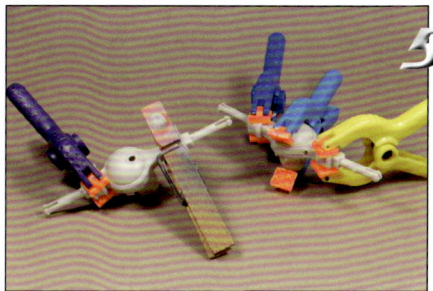

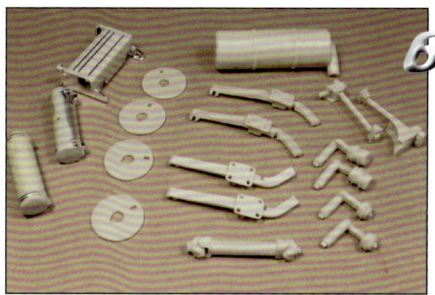
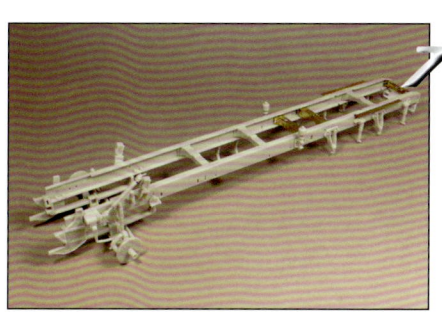
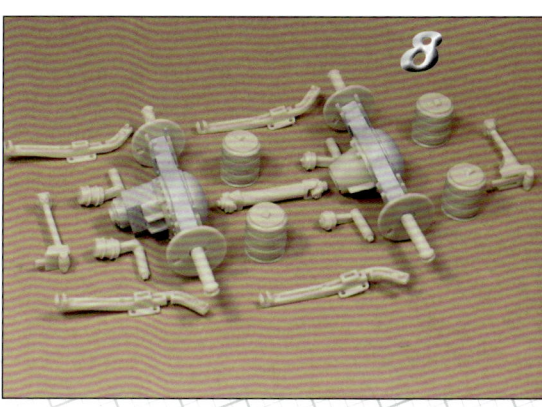

1. The frame rails were cleaned and fitted with etched fifth wheel mounts.

2. The front steerable axle represents a classic assembly included in most truck kits. The steering is fully functional but the assembly requires some specific steps.

3. The most critical step of the axle assembly is heat forming all the working pivots. For this a heated scalpel tip can be used.

4. To form the pivot slowly press the heated scalpel blade against the pivot tip. The trick is to create a collar retaining the connecting rod eye in the correct position and create a workable joint.

5. The drive axles are typical parts that always consist of two halves. These were cleaned and fixed together while the glue was drying. Afterwards no filling was needed.

6. All the chassis and suspension related components were cleaned and prepared for the assembly.

7. The complete frame assembly with the front axle fitted. Note the three rear photo etched cross members adding a bit more realism to the rear end of the vehicle.

8. The drive axle suspension is well detailed. It allows to keep the air bags separate for easier painting till the very late assembly steps.

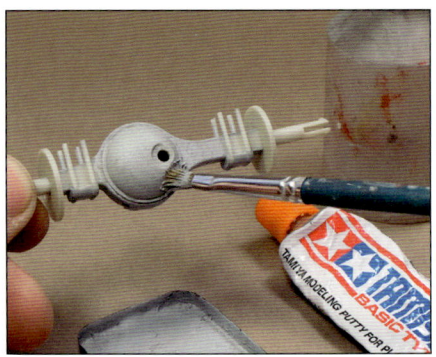

1. A rough texture was created on the axles using Tamiya putty thinned with acetone, applied with an old brush.

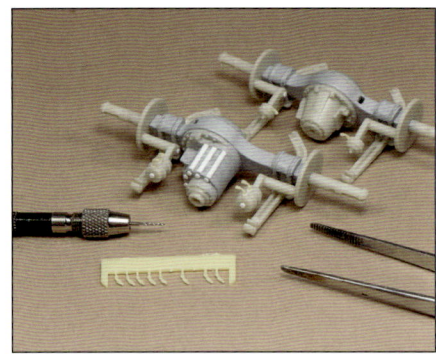

2. The first wiring step is adding various fittings to all the affected parts such as the brake chambers.

3. The KFS white metal air valves were used. These were again detailed with fittings made with punch and die sets.

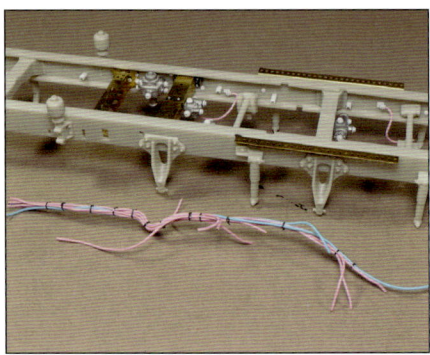

4. Each rail bundle was assembled and shaped separately outside the chassis.

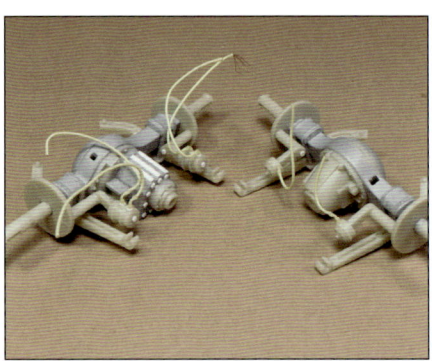

5. The separate components were fitted with inlet pipes which were linked to the air valves once installed in the chassis.

6. Once the bundle was attached to the chassis each of its carefully prepared ends was attached to the particular valve or component outlet.

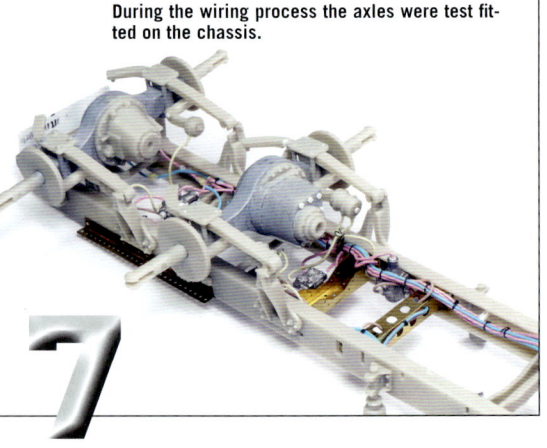

During the wiring process the axles were test fitted on the chassis.

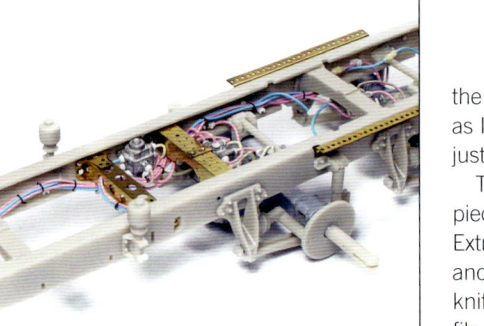

8. The wiring adds a lot of realism to the chassis and provides many nice details for painting and weathering.

4.4 CHASSIS AND WIRING

The chassis is another traditional assembly you will face during building every model. There are a few kits that have the chassis part number reduced to just one or two but most of the model chassis assemblies look more or less like the one on Prostar.

The kit comes with a pair of frame rails and cross-members that fit between them. Cutting the parts from the runner and removing the flash and witness marks was discussed in the previous chapter, and has to be done on most of the components here too, but I must admit that the Prostar chassis is very well moulded. The only thing worth mentioning is that of the ejector pin marks inside the frame rails. While those in the front and mid-chassis section are not important (and you need not care about these) those in the rear should be removed as they can be seen clearly in the chassis behind the cab. Again, this was rather straightforward as I just scraped it all off with a sharp knife in just a few minutes.

The rear suspension airbags come in two pieces each, so I glued these with Tamiya Extra Thin Cement. I let them dry overnight and removed the split line seams with a sharp knife, while the grooves were neatened with a file. It all went perfectly and there was no need for further filling and sanding.

4.4.1 DETAILING THE CHASSIS

Although I would normally assemble the chassis straight from the box, I had something special for this model. I was supplied with a prototype CTM chassis photo-etched metal set for the Prostar kit. Although the set contains all of them, I used just three PE cross-members that can be seen clearly on the finished model; I left the remaining examples in kit plastic to keep the chassis robust. As the detail set also included the fifth wheel mounting rails, I removed the plastic versions from the frame and fitted the fine PE parts too, which enhance the model's look and ensured sharp chassis detail. But for a basic model these are a

4. A MEDIUM LEVEL PROJECT

> The chassis rear end featuring the rear etched chassis cross member. Note the realistic part thickness in strong contrast to the plastic parts.

little more advanced so let's leave this topic aside. The plastic sheet, on which the rear lamps are mounted, is slightly out of scale on a model so I simply replaced it with a thinner version.

The frame has to be robust as it represents the basic model support to which all the following parts will be attached. At the rear of the vehicle, mostly the rearmost cross member is the only reasonable lifting point of the model, so make sure this area is strong enough. The correct geometry is essential to prevent misalignment issues later during assembly. Therefore, you should be very precise and keep both the frame rails straight and the cross-member perpendicular. The rails contain square and rounded holes, and as we build an out-of-box model all will be used for various chassis components.

If you drop a fuel tank, a spare wheel carrier or any other chassis components on some of your models, make sure you fill all the frame holes that won't be used.

The front axle assembly is a tricky step due to its moving parts. It does not matter if you build a Moebius or an Italeri kit, as the component design is very similar. Here (more than anywhere else) precise work is required to clean the parts and assemble them as precisely as possible to maintain proper wheel geometry. Attaching the wheel hubs to the axle beam is critical in terms of the amount of glue to be used, because any excess adhesive can result in poor steering function.

There is a special technique used here to create movable joints on most of the arms and rods. Instead of any glue application, the pins are longer and the instruction sheet suggests a heated tool (a knife tip or screwdriver) to be applied to the pin end to increase its diameter and secure the connecting rod eyes in their position. I use a scalpel tip because it is very thin and does not require a long heating time; therefore, just a few seconds in a lighter flame are enough to heat it. Once red hot you can slowly apply the knife over the pin end (not too slowly, as the temperature of thin steel reduces quickly) and press the tool gently to melt the plastic and create a tight pivot joint. This task is not difficult, but it does require practice. I recommend you to try this on a piece of sprue to make sure you have it all under control when working with the real parts. Any damage in this area is very difficult to repair. The rest of the front axle and suspension assembly is straightforward…you just clean them and attach the parts to the chassis. What is very smart in the Moebius kit is that the leaf spring witness marks go along the edge of the part, so little neatening is required. Most kits have it in the part centre, and this often demands significant cleaning-up time.

REAR AXLES ASSEMBLY

The drive axle assembly consists of many parts, but a great advantage of the Moebius kit is that the air bags are separate. These can be painted on their own, which is very handy as they should be rubber and aluminium

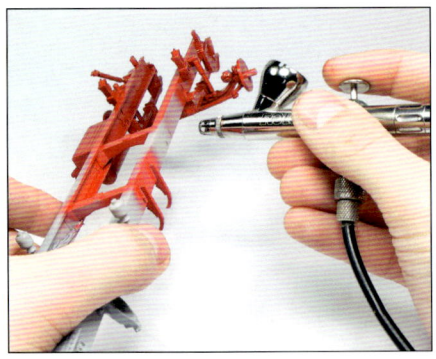
1. Once primed with Mr.Surfacer the chassis was sprayed with Mr.Color gloss red.

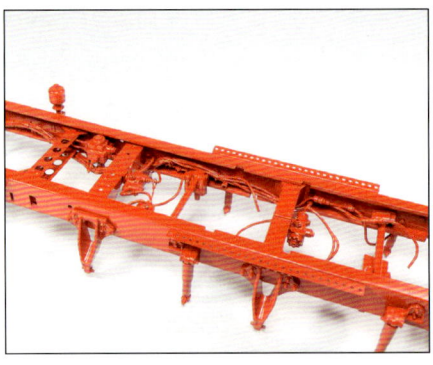
2. As the chassis internals were already fitted with wiring the spraying required some time and patience.

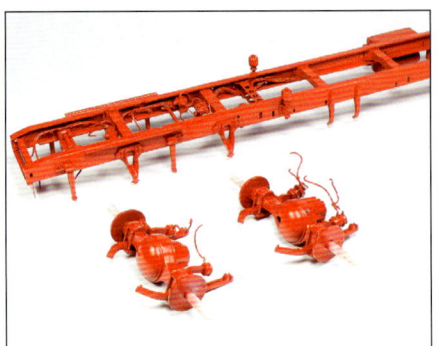
3. Spraying the axles separately made this step a lot easier.

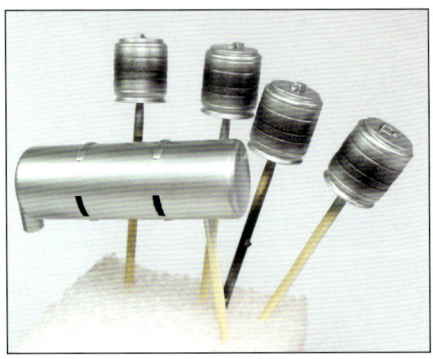
4. All the metallic chassis parts were primed with Mr.Finishing surfacer 1500 black and sprayed with Mr.Color 8 Silver.

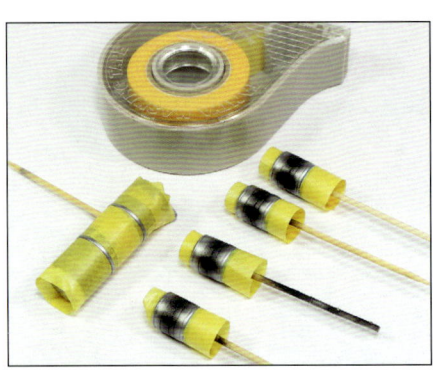
5. Again the Tamiya masking tape was employed here. The airbag bodies and exhaust silencer mounts are now ready for spraying.

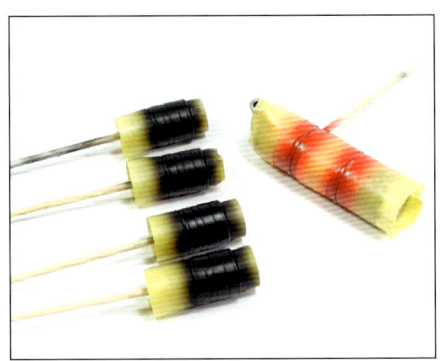
6. Using just a small amount of paint helps to keep this process under control resulting in a sharp and clean color edges.

7. When removing the masking tape always work slowly and be careful not to peel off any of the previous paint layers.

The drive axle mudguards and mudflaps were detailed with etched parts, painted and weathered. The vertical streaks were airbrushed using a highly thinned mixture of light dust paints.

regardless of chassis colour. The drive axles consist of two halves which have to be cleaned and glued together. I recommend fixing them together, as when force is applied to the join the molten plastic is pushed out and fills the whole area. If done properly there is usually no need to use putty on most parts. The rest of the assembly is rather straightforward, but make sure you do not muddle the parts for the front and rear axle; they look the same but are different and if you mix them (which I did), you won't be able to mount the axles to the frame properly. The completed axles were fitted with the brake chambers, suspension arms and brake drum covers (there is just a circular pad in the kit...no drum at all), and the only modification I carried out was that of cast steel texture, created with Tamiya putty thinned with a few drops of acetone.

No parts for the rear axles and suspension would be attached to the chassis yet, as there are two major tasks during which having these assemblies separate will prove very handy: painting and wiring. The less complex the assembly for painting the better. Being able to add wiring to the sub-assemblies prior to their mating also makes life easier.

The right moment to consider wiring can be different on various models. In most cases, attaching the axles to the frame is a good moment to think about it. At this stage you have most of the important parts already assembled (chassis, axles, engine) while access to important areas (brake chambers, chassis internal surfaces) is still quite good. Components such as various catwalks or a fifth wheel will block it soon. Now, the point is that when you study the real Prostar chassis, you will see many air pipes and wires. The chassis is so busy with cables and pipes that it is not easy to know the purpose of each one. But the funny part is that you do not need to know it at all. Just look at the photos and see where the pipes go from and to. If you go back to the chapters dedicated to real truck design and wiring, these will remind you that there are some elementary components linked together, and it is sensible to keep things in order here; the rest is just modellers' license and nothing else. In other words, the real vehicle pictures show the chassis busy with valves, wiring and piping and I want to have this on my model too. However, I am not going to waste time on replicating the wiring in all its details. I just need it to look right.

The general strategy was discussed in the wiring chapter and I will follow that on this model too. As the Prostar is a conventional truck, the cab is not tilting and there is nothing visible inside the frame rails around the engine. There is just one area worth spending some time on, though, and that is the frame behind the cab. Yes, you could bother with the whole frame length and add all the details under the cab, but as this should be a straightforward and simple build, let's stick with the easy route and do just what needs to be done. You won't see the difference on the finished model anyway. If you feel this is too complicated for you, though, just leave it out and follow my work on the model just after the wiring will be completed, as it does not have any significant effect on the later building stages. However, I recommend you try because I am going to keep this very simple and user friendly. If you follow my steps with patience and care, you will find out that wiring this model is like a walk in the park.

The first thing you will need are air valves and electrical boxes. These are usually missing in any kit and the only way to get them is either to scratch-build, or buy an aftermarket set. I used KFS metal air valves on most of my models in the past. They are discontinued now so I am replacing them with both the new KFS TQ142 and CTM 24230 resin air valves. The valves are resin castings and a sharp knife, or a file will do the job.

Another commodity you will need is that of fine wire. On a modern vehicle, a difference in diameter between an air pipe and an electrical harness protection sleeve can be neglected so for the Prostar I decided to use just one wire diameter, to keep matters simple. Furthermore, there is not much electricity required in the rear of the chassis so I will just add one line for lights and will not bother with any other electrical appliances. The wires I decided to use were fine and soft, and I got them from a broken iPhone charger. Now, if you compare the diameter of the wire to the diameter of the holes on the KFS valves, you will find out there is a problem, as the valve outlets are much larger. New outlet fittings were required and the easiest way to make them was by using

> *The Moebius kits feature a workable hood revealing the engine compartment details.*

a pair of punch and die sets…one for circular and the other for hexagonal parts. I made some rounded pads, fitted them over the large valve outlets with Superglue and on these some smaller hexagonal pads were attached to represent a fitting in which holes for wires were drilled. I chose just four valves from the KFS set, which were the best for this application and the model did not need any more. Obviously the KFS set will do cater for more models, not just one.

USING SUPERGLUE

Now to Superglue (cyanoacrylate). I just mentioned it for the first time in this build, and it is another adhesive commonly used when building models, as with other than plastic parts, traditional styrene cement does not work. For metal parts such as white metal castings, photo-etched or resin parts, cyano-type glue has to be used. There are various brands available all around the world and you can probably get one in a local store. As for the brands, I do not want to say it really matters but I have seen and used good and bad. Therefore, I stick with Loctite products, just to avoid trouble. I use both the liquid and gel, and both are handy. One short trick to extend their life is to keep them in a fridge when they are not being used.

The valves were ready for use so I picked their position in the chassis and fitted them with Superglue. Valve position matters, and it is good to keep them in a similar location to those as seen in real truck photos. It also makes sense to put them in places where they will not be covered with anything such as a catwalk or fifth wheel. Make sure you space them far enough from each other too, as it will make adding the wires later much easier.

The wires can be added separately one after another. This works best on classic trucks with steel pipes that have to be bent and prepared carefully for every single location. This takes time and much patience as such piping has a typical look. On modern trucks though, everything (air pipes and harness), is usually in soft black vinyl hose and protection sleeves, and look almost the same. That makes it all a lot easier. I used to add one wire after another, but this was a time-consuming operation I never really enjoyed. Doing this over and over and with the new material being available, I have started using a technique that makes it all simpler and faster.

The trick is that I assemble a complete bundle for each rail outside the chassis. This bundle contains an array of wires with ends along the whole bundle length, just where the various air vents or any other components are located. I usually start with the longest and keep adding a new wire for each single fitting, or connector, along the chassis length. This reduces waste significantly, and helps to save material. The bundle is tied together with CTM photo-etched cable ties (CTM 24081), which do not require any glue and not only that they keep the bundle together...but also look very realistic. Preparing the bundle takes some time, but it is not that difficult.

This operation is done after the chassis is assembled and fitted with the axles and all the air valves. At that moment you already have a very good idea about each pipe outlet position. Yes, some components are still missing. These will be attached to the chassis later and may also need a connection to the air, electrical or fuel system such as the fuel tank, trailer couplings or batteries. On the Prostar, all these components are hidden under the cab and behind the side skirts, so I am not going to add any wiring to them, but on other trucks it may be useful. You will see more detailed examples in the advanced builds later in this book.

Once the bundle is complete it can be installed into the frame. I have even used different colours for you to highlight the purpose of various wires. The blue wires will be connected to the air bags, the pink versions feed the brake chambers via the air valves and the differential locks (in the right-hand frame rail) and the light brown in the left-hand rail have no purpose and are just connected to the rest of the valve outlets. The longest light grey wire in the left hand rail will be connected to the lights at the very end of the frame. For supporting the bundle, a few mounts cut out of U-shaped Evergreen profile were fitted into each rail, and on these the bundle was secured with Superglue. Once aligned and fixed properly one after another, the wires were glued into the holes drilled in the components and secured with just a little drop of Superglue on the end of the wire, before inserting it into the hole. I did the same for both frame rails with just a pair of bundles, however to make matters more interesting, using another bundle or two with wires of different diameter would be a good way to go if you want to spend more time on detailing. Anyway, with even just a pair of bundles the frame behind the cab looks busy enough. Note that both the bundle front ends are hidden under a cross member beneath the cab. There was no point in making them longer, as it would not be visible at all.

With just four white metal air valves, a small etched fret with cable ties and a few cables, I was able to complete the most important chassis wiring on the model in just a few hours. Obviously the 'bundle' technique proves itself to be cheap, easy and a straightforward method of wiring the chassis without any deep knowledge of the particular vehicle systems; just a pair of chassis pictures was required to show the general arrangement on the vehicle. The Prostar kit does not need much more. We will just do something similar in the engine compartment later and that's it. Once the wiring is finished it is the right moment to start working on the chassis paint. With the chassis and following components ready (axles, air bags, chassis, battery box with air tanks, exhaust silencer) I sprayed

4. A MEDIUM LEVEL PROJECT

1. In terms of the assembly the few last chassis steps were simple and straightforward. The air bags and axles fitted perfectly.

2. Installing the engine assembly was a pleasure as well. Note that most of the lower engine details will remain hidden inside the chassis.

3. The thickness of the exhaust pipe ends was reduced and the parts were painted with Agama spirit based metal paints

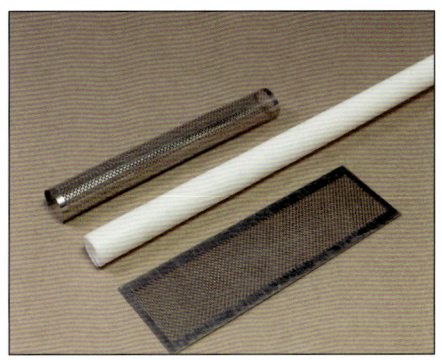

4. The exhaust heat shields are often provided in etched detail sets. These are flat in the original state.

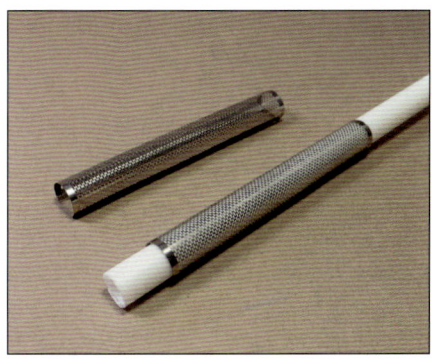

5. By rolling these parts over pipes of various diameters (starting with a larger, then smaller) the part can be formed into a cylindrical shape.

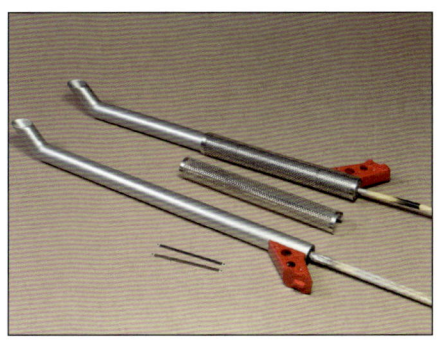

6. The finished exhaust stacks with the etched heat shields.

them with Gunze Mr.Surfacer primer (black on the air bags and silencer, classic grey for the rest of the parts). As rough sanding was carried out on the frame rails, the first primer coat revealed rough surface structure in some areas, and therefore fine sanding and another priming coat was necessary to clean the parts, as any surface scratches would be highlighted during the chassis weathering…an undesirable possibility.

The next step is final chassis painting; most Prostars come with a black chassis but my reference photos reveal that red was common as well. As the build in my next chapter is supposed to have a dark grey chassis, I wanted this Prostar chassis to be different and red was chosen as the final coat. I have already mentioned that painting the whole chassis assembly needs patience and is time consuming. However, the Prostar drive axle assembly made my life a lot easier and I could keep the axles and airbags separate, for easier painting prior to the suspension assembly. This is probably the smartest solution I have ever seen on a 1/24 scale airbag suspension. On most models, the chassis end is very busy and getting the paint into every corner here is not easy.

Gunze Mr.Color paints were used on the chassis, axles, air bags and the exhaust silencer, with a hint of Mr.Color Retarder (mild) for better spraying performance and a super-smooth finish. Both the air bags and the exhaust silencer were sprayed silver first; the silver areas were then covered with Tamiya masking tape and the rubber parts were sprayed matt black and the silencer mounts red.

The kit fuel tanks are provided with a shiny chromed surface, but each tank consists of halves, which would result in a join that would be visible on the model. Furthermore, the fuel tanks in my kit did not fit well and serious sanding and filling was necessary. Any clean-up operations damage the chrome surfaces of course and repairing them is not easy. You can either try to apply advanced chromed coatings (such as Alclad II lacquers) or settle for one of the silver or aluminium paints that may not look so shiny, but are easier to work with. As I wanted the journey to be simple on this model, and the fuel tanks are covered with side skirts anyway, I went for the second option and used the same silver as on the exhaust silencer. The mounting straps were masked with Tamiya tape and sprayed red.

Fitting the engine assembly into the chassis was straightforward. The prop shafts and exhaust piping were attached with just minor misalignment.

The kit fifth wheel is rather basic, but I did not want to spend time with complex conversion work. I just added a few bolt heads, a coiled airline and a few more details. The assembly was then primed and sprayed red, with a decent helping of brown as I wanted this area to be darker for future weathering. There always is much grease and dirt around the fifth wheel on working vehicles, and shiny red was not desirable in this area.

To finish the chassis assembly there were a few more parts to process. These took some time to finish because I wanted to use a photo-etched replacement from the CTM set. Note, though, that the exhaust stacks represent the same problem as most of the chromed parts. They come in halves that cause an ugly join, visible on the pipe assembly. The only thing you can do is remove the chrome, apply putty, sand the pipes and use one of the metal paints available. I have also reduced the pipe wall thickness as it was slightly out of scale. As I wanted a shinier result I did not use Mr.Color paint this time, but a Czech-made spirit-based Agama silver metallic paint, which can be polished after painting. Once painted, the pipes were attached to the mounts and fitted with the photo-etched heat shields. Comparing the original plastic part and the etched item, it becomes obvious why photo-etched parts are used on models. These provide precise details that cannot produced by injection moulding, and for various fine structures such as the heat shields or any kind of mesh, the metal parts win over plastic. However, working with the PE parts needs some skill so there are both pros and cons. A few more PE parts were used to replace the mud flaps, which are very thick and have no surface structure. While the heat shields required some rolling, the mud flaps can just be cut out to replace the plastic originals and this operation is simple. You can either rework the kit's plastic mounts for the rear unit, but I made my own using a piece of K&S aluminium pipe. For painting, matt black with additional dark blue tones was used on the mud flaps. A highly thinned mix of Tamiya XF-55 and XF-60 was used for light dust effects. All the tail lights on the rear chassis cross member, and the rear cab wall, come from the CTM 24092 US Tail lights set and look great.

4.5 CHASSIS WEATHERING

For some model builders, chassis painting would be over by now. Many modellers favour the appearance of a clean and shiny vehicle. However, I prefer the real-life working state where dirt can be seen on the vehicle, as well as paint chipping, rust or paint fading and oil stains of course. That is why I decided to apply them to this model, even though it was intended to be just a simple build. I have reduced the weathering intensity considerably, though, and what I did on the model was completed within just a couple of hours.

I do not want to wade too deep into weathering in this chapter. I would just like to mention the most common techniques and show examples, but nothing more as we will deal with the rest later during more advanced builds. Furthermore, all of these techniques have been described many times before and you can look them up on your own if desired. All I want you to learn here is that there are multiple techniques combined on models, which somehow follow each other and harmonise to provide great realism. The key is that model weathering is never just one layer of something. It actually starts with adding light and dark tones to your basic coat during

4. A MEDIUM LEVEL PROJECT

spraying, and is followed by the many steps mentioned presently. That is the only way to obtain a realistic result.

The techniques applied on this model are the following:

Colour modulation applied with an airbrush on large surfaces, and by brush for highlighting the details…after which the remaining chassis features were hand painted.

Dry-brushing, a traditional technique for highlighting details and edges

Dark wash (AK Interactive Streaking Grime and Odourless Thinner)

Chipping, hand-painted chips (fine brush and black/dark brown Vallejo colours)

Oil paint application, various tones (rust, dust, mud, grease and oil stains) of oil paints applied directly from the tube either in terms of streaks, or dots blended with the model surface.

COLOUR MODULATION

After the basic red coat was dry, a few more paint layers were applied to the chassis. The purpose of so-called colour modulation is to highlight some areas and elevate details with brighter paint tones on one side, and add shade into corners and lower areas of the vehicle on the other…and to add depth to the structures. This was done both with an airbrush and also hand painting on bolts, valves and small details. So I simply added a few drops of white to the original red chassis colour and sprayed the upper horizontal surfaces of the frame rails and cross members. Then I added red brown for darker tones, and sprayed the deep areas of the frame where shade was desired. Using a light red Vallejo shade, all the head bolts and other surface details were highlighted.

Once finished, some chassis details (including the wiring) were hand painted in matt black, silver and rubber black to bring extra colour to the chassis and make the assembly more interesting. This actually is not a part of the weathering but a painting process; as the modulation involves new layers of red applied with an airbrush, it made no sense to hand paint the details beforehand.

DRY-BRUSHING

This is a very basic weathering technique shown on the engine. It has been around for decades but is still in use and can be very handy. The principle is to highlight sharp edges and surface detail with lighter tones of the basic colour. This is done with a paintbrush that contains a very small amount of colour and is nearly dry

1. Painting chips using a fine point brush and Vallejo acrylics has become a very popular. However for a realistic result a lot of time and practice is required.

2. Fine rust chips were made from a mixture of Vallejo and Italeri paints.

3. Keeping the number and size of the chips under control is one of the most crucial parts of the job.

4. The engine received some traditional drybrushing with Revell and Humbrol enamels.

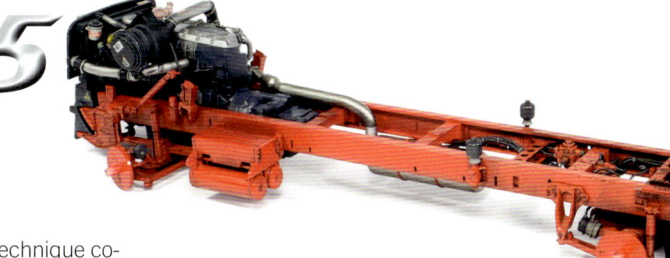

While the chassis front and rear parts are weathered, the central section is virtually intact as all it will be fully covered with the cab and the side skirts.

– that is where the name of this technique comes from. You just dip a brush into the paint but remove about 95% from the bristles immediately with a piece of cloth or tissue. With this brush you virtually slide over the model surface details and edges, that are slowly being highlighted with the remaining paint from the brush. This is being used over the surface details such as bolts, mesh and structures that are hard to paint, but worth highlighting.

Enamels work better than acrylics here (as their drying time is slower). The principle of dry-brushing technique is similar to wash – to highlight the surface details but in a bit different way. While the wash works in corners and gaps the dry brush works on the edges and sharp surface details and structures.

While for wash generally some darker paints are used for dry brush it exactly opposite as you always highlight the details with lighter tones.

WASH

If there is a basic painting and weathering technique that should be mentioned here it is the wash. It's a simple and effective way to highlight surface detail, and introduce definition around elevated feature, and in corners and recesses. The principle is to use highly

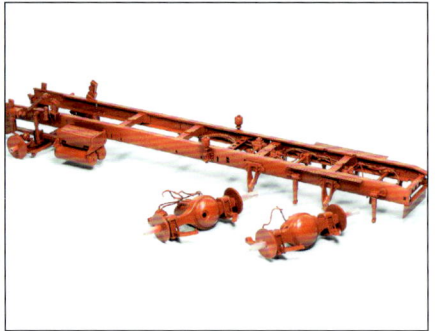
1. Once the chassis was sprayed with basic red the colour modulation could start.

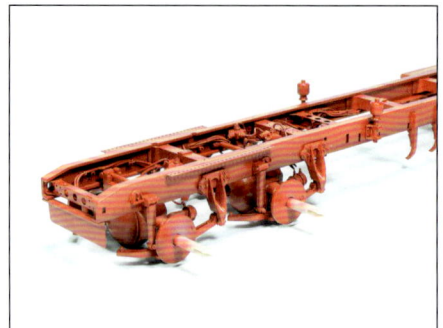
2. Note how the top chassis areas are visually different compared to the lower darker areas.

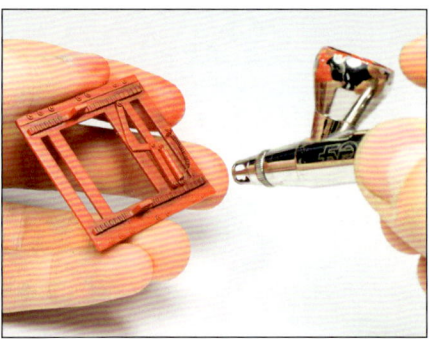
3. Where shadows were required (such as the area under the fifth wheel) a mixture of red and brown was applied with an airbrush.

4. The brake chambers, fittings and all the wiring were brush painted with Italeri and Vallejo acrylics.

5. Once all the details were painted, the airbags were attached to the suspension arms and the axle assemblies were attached to the chassis.

6. Oil paints (on the palette) together with AK Interactive enamels were used for staining the chassis.

thinned paint applied with a brush. This will collect around surface detail and in gaps, leaving the plain surface virtually untouched. Paint, thinner and a brush is all you need. However, enamel paints work as well but the most common wash is carried out with oil paints. The reason why modellers use oils for washes (and many other techniques) is that they dry slowly. It may sound like a disadvantage, but the fact that you can work with the paint for an extended period of time is the key point. You have a lot of time to manipulate the paint on the surface, remove excess or add more paint to reduce or increase the layer intensity and, most importantly, remove virtually all the paint from the surface if something goes wrong. Be aware that oils do not like enamels very much, so applying oil paint over an enamel surface is not recommended, and should be verified on a piece of plastic to prevent any model damage.

CHIPPING

The chipping method is a rather advanced technique that requires practice and excellent brush handling. Chipping is used to add chipped paint and scratches to the model surface. These are simply painted with a very fine brush and a good colour (Vallejo acrylics are most suitable for this), which may sound easy but actually is not and needs much practice before you'll be able to reproduce realistic results. The chips can be painted in various shades: old rusty chips, fresh metal colour damage or chips that did not fully penetrate the paint surface (therefore, revealing just fresh and clean original paint. To add depth, the chips are often combined. In addition, there are other methods of showing chipped paint. The hairspray method has recently been very popular and will be discussed in Chapter 6.

OIL PAINT APPLICATION

Applying oil paints features throughout the whole weathering process, for many reasons. While washes and filters are highly thinned mixtures, often the oil paints are applied directly from the tube or palette. Streaking rust, diesel and oil stains, dust and dirt or faded paint – all these can be portrayed effectively with oil paints. Applied on vertical surfaces in terms of streaks or rain marks, or on horizon-

7 Wiring the model before spraying the chassis ensured a clean overall result and the opportunity to brush paint all the details afterwards, a major challenge on this vehicle.

TRUCK MODELLING

MEDIUM LEVEL PROJECT

8. A dark red-brown wash from AK interactive enamels applied around the chassis bolts and details.

9. In a similar way a light dust wash was used on the engine block to highlight the casing structure.

10. The wheels and fuel tanks were fitted to the fully painted and weathered chassis.

tal surfaces, these can be blended either with a dry brush or a decent amount of thinner. An extensive oil paint method, known as Oil Paint Rendering, was described by Michael Rinaldi in his great Tank Art book series.

4.6 THE WHEELS

The wheels have always been one of the most important vehicle features for me. They can really enhance the model's look but also may seriously harm the overall impression. Fortunately, both the rims and tyres in the kit look pretty good. The latter are made of rubber so they do not need painting at all. The rims are chromed, which also indicated no need for painting, but I must admit that the items I had in my kit needed neatening and rough flash in some areas had to be removed.

I started with the rim assembly, followed by sanding the outer rim edges where the flash was most apparent. As I already knew the wheels would be weathered, I did not care about the shine and just painted it silver where the chrome was removed.

Weathering chromed parts in general is not easy due to their smooth surface and high shine. Even finding good reference photos may be tricky. However, with the wheels the situation is easier. The rims are made of polished aluminium that tends to become flat and stained (unlike chrome or stainless steel) if not maintained properly, and that can be seen on many vehicles.

I started with a fine coat of highly thinned matt clear varnish to reduce the shine. To add darker tones, a few drops of Tamiya X-19 Smoke were added to the varnish and Tamiya X-24 Clear Yellow was used to get that yellowish tone seen on older aluminium rims. Once the rims lost their shine and brightness, I started painting stains and scratches with a fine brush and Vallejo white and light grey tones. The front wheel nuts were painted dark grey. To add more colour accents I used 502

1. The original chromed wheels from the kit required some cleaning.

2. Sanding removed the flash, but during the process the chromed surface was damaged.

3. Where removed the chromed surface was repaired with polishable Agama spirit based paints.

4. The rims were stained with a few fine coats of highly thinned flat Mr.Color lacquer followed by clear Tamiya black and yellow acrylics.

5. As the tires are molded in black rubber the only thing they need is a mixture of pigments to highlight the surface texture.

6. Once fitted to the rims more colour variation was given to the tires using black soot and dark dirt pigments.

7. Further weathering on the neglected aluminum rims was simulated with Vallejo acrylics. Some fine dots and marks were painted all over the outer surfaces.

8. Unlike many other kits the wheels in the Moebius kit did not require any modification and except for some weathering these come straight from the box.

9. Fitting the wheels on the axles was a matter of seconds. The Moebius concept works nicely here.

TRUCK MODELLING

Abteilung oil paints (Buff and Basic Earth), applied directly from the tube and blended with a flat brush and Tamiya blending stick.

The tyres were treated with pigments applied in a dry state with a flat brush. I used more tones to reduce the uniformity, mostly black and light dust. As the tyre walls and thread have a good structure, the pigments help to bring it to life and make this part of the model more interesting.

Assembling the wheels does not require any glue and the tyres fit perfectly. Even attaching the wheels to the axles is straightforward.

4.7 THE CAB INTERIOR

Model truck interiors are great fun to build. Sure, many details of the cab roof and side and rear cab panels cannot be seen on the finished model, but still there is much embellishment that can be added to enhance the look. Furthermore, there are many ways to treat the various surface structures, such as leather or textile upholstery. Within this build we will focus just on the basics, and the only extra I will be using is the photo-etched dashboard by CTM, which is already painted and does not require any special technique. Further interior detailing will be shown in the next chapter.

Building the Prostar cab starts with the interior, which is of classic arrangement. The cab floor is a large flat part which has some lettering moulded from below (which is good to remove) and ejector pin marks that are large but shallow, so just need sanding where required. The seats and dashboard represent separate sub-assemblies.

The dashboard consists of three parts; filling and sanding is required as one of the split lines is just on top of the dash. All the gauges and controls are well moulded, and it's over these that the decals should be applied. The decal sheet also features the wood decking which is printed beautifully. However, straying from within the out-of-box format, I again used photo-etched parts here, as the CTM Prostar set features beautiful painted dashboard panels. To apply these, all the dashboard structure has to be removed…in this case by using my Proxxon hand mill. Working with painted PE parts is simple, but it needs patience as some are really tiny. The main dashboard panel consists of two layers, on which a gel cyanoacrylate was used, while the rest of the parts were just glued in the correct position once the dashboard was ready.

The seats are pleasing, and I consider these to be some of the best detailed items I've ever seen in this scale. The seat backrests required filling, for which my favourite black Superglue was used. The seat mounts come in halves, but there was no need for filling, just a minor clean-up operation once the glue was dry.

Once assembled, the seats and the dashboard can be attached to the floor plate together with the rest of the parts (a pair of side walls, a sofa in the sleeper area, the rear cab wall and the roof). What I did initially was only a dry test-fit as I wanted to paint the parts separately. I must admit that I am not sure if the Prostar cabs ever had this type of interior arrangement. Moebius simply took it over from the Lonestar kit but the Prostar bunk in

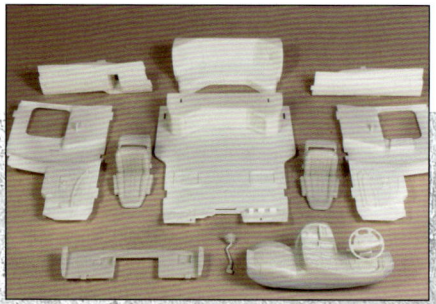
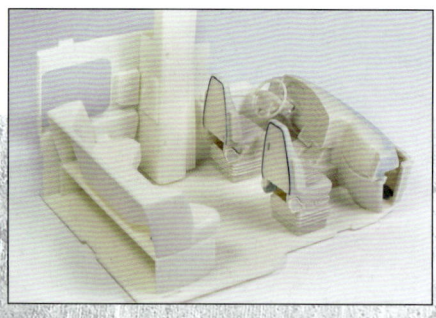
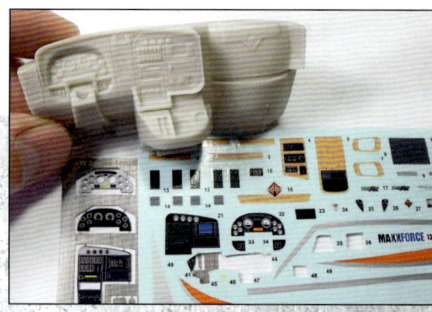

1. The interior assembly consists of large panels and separate seats, bunk, lockers and a dashboard.

2. Some filling was required on the seats and dashboard however the rest of the interior assembly was straightforward.

3. While the dashboard has some nice details molded and the kit decals are not that bad the CTM etched interior detail set is still miles ahead.

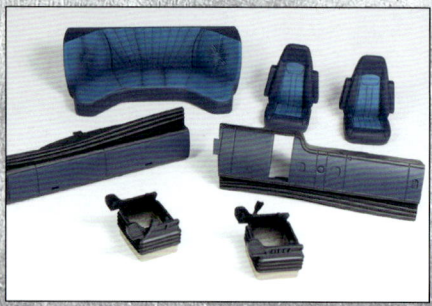

4. The instrument panels were sanded flat to allow an easy installation of the etched parts. The lower dashboard area was sprayed with dark grey, on the upper part the Tamiya XF-57 was used.

5. The seats, bunk and lockers were sprayed with Tamiya acrylics. The seat and bunk upholstery got some lights and shadows applied with an airbrush.

6. For the various parts in different color some careful masking was needed during the interior painting.

8. All the interior parts come straight from the kit. No modifications were required since only the front area is visible.

9. In the final step the interior parts are assembled into a shell which is later inserted into the cab from below.

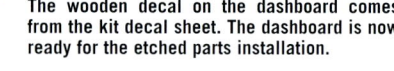

7. The wooden decal on the dashboard comes from the kit decal sheet. The dashboard is now ready for the etched parts installation.

the pictures I found did not look that luxurious. However, I did not do a thing with the interior and apart from the standard clean-up operations, everything was left in its out-of-box state.

Painting the interior was an enjoyable process. I did not follow the instruction sheet colours as all these leaned towards the luxurious Lonestar interior. I was looking for a daily workhorse look so I just followed some Prostar pictures found on the internet, with a grey and blue combination on the interior, beige dashboard and wood trim. All the parts were primed with Mr.Surfacer finishing black, then light grey was used on the interior side walls, dark grey on the floor and lower dashboard parts, while a mixture of blue tones was applied over the seat and the bunk followed by gentle shading. The interior roof and the dashboard top parts were sprayed beige. When airbrushing the door panels, seats and dashboard, simple masking could not be avoided and ever-reliable Tamiya tape was employed. In all cases I always use a few drops of Mr.Retarder Mild for spraying Mr.Color paints, as it improves their performance and surface smoothness significantly.

A great advantage of Mr.Color and Tamiya acrylic paints is that they dry very quickly. Therefore, the same afternoon most of the parts were sprayed, the decals could be applied too. The kit provides an extensive interior decal sheet. Although I did not use any of the control panels (as these were replaced by photo-etched parts) I used the wood decor for the dashboard and all the remaining interior decals. I appreciate the fact that there are even the smallest details such as the window controls for the door panels available. I always use both Mr.Mark Setter and Mr.Mark Softer with decals. Especially the Softer's use on the wooden dashboard trim was a must, to get the decal to conform to all the surface curves and details. Otherwise, the decals were pleasant to work with, worked fine even in cold water and no issues arose during their application. Spraying the decals with clear varnish is advisable and I always do this. The dashboard was sprayed with Mr.Color Super Clear varnish (to provide a high shine to the wood panels) and the remaining items received Mr.Color matt clear varnish. Once all the painting was done, the photo-etched parts were applied to the dashboard and other interior sections.

Final interior assembly was easy and straightforward. Once the roof was attached, the interior became a dark place and hid all the great details inside. Having the complete interior structure at this moment is very important for the cab shell assembly. For easier painting (and to avoid any construction issues) I always try to spray the cab shell as completely as possible. Most of the kit instructions do not show this but there are just a few model truck kits on which this cannot be done. To make sure this is a viable idea, it is always good to have the interior ready prior to the cab shell assembly, as you can easily use it for test-fitting and avoid any issues later.

4.8 THE CAB EXTERIOR

There are two ways in which cabs are designed in model truck kits. Most of the 1/25 products come with a single-piece cab shell that represents the cab external structure with a relatively simple interior, (which slides in from below) together with the cab floor as a tight fit insert. For most 1/24 models, a cab that consists of separate wall panels is more typical. The interior is mostly designed in a similar way where the wall panels, floor and roof are separate parts that are assembled together. While the one-piece shell usually does not require any filling and the cab assembly is rather straightforward, the multi-part cab provides more details on both the interior and exterior; but some filling usually cannot be avoided and the correct geometry during assembly is a must. The Prostar cab is a mixture of both. The cab exterior is a large shell to which the roof and the rear cab wall are attached. The hood is separate.

There were some ejector pin marks inside the hood that had to be removed, but nothing critical as these are shallow, with just gentle sanding being required. There is also a fine witness mark along the hood top edges that should be sanded off. The hood hinges are robust, but be patient during glue application as any excess adhesive can easily block the

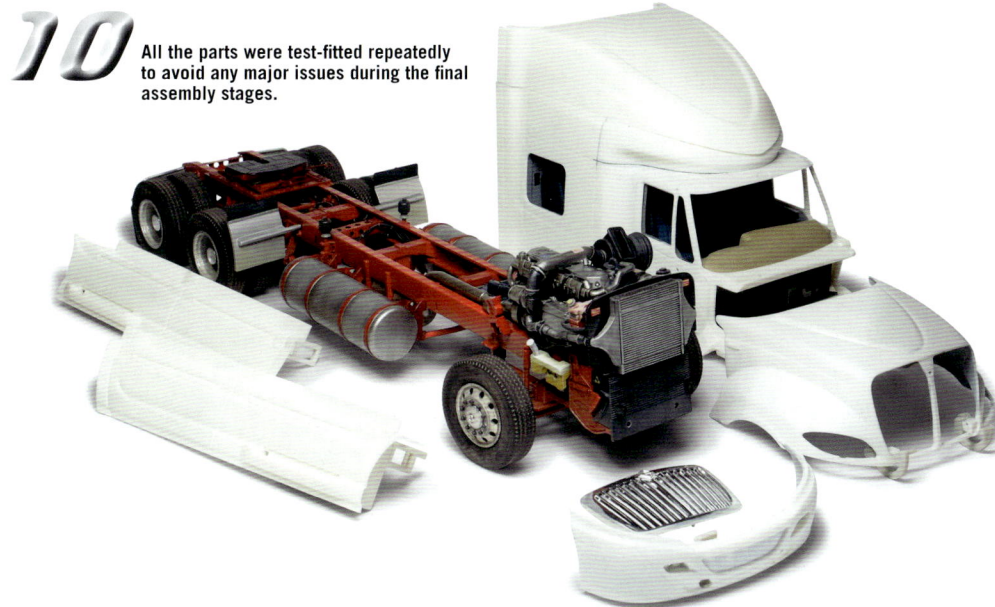

10 All the parts were test-fitted repeatedly to avoid any major issues during the final assembly stages.

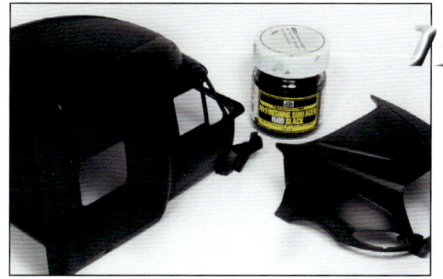

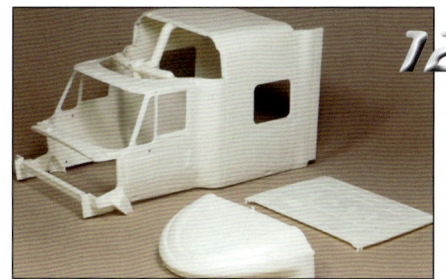

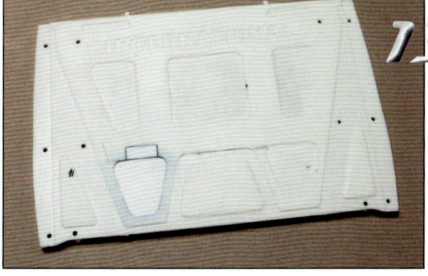

11. The hood's inner surfaces actually lack many details. The only thingä added was some structure using Tamiya putty and an old brush.

12. The cab shell comes in three parts only, so the need for filling and sanding is limited.

13. Some molded details (such as the susie bracket and vents) were removed from the rear cab wall as they come in the CTM Prostar detail set.

14. Finally some super glue was used to fill the gaps around the cab roof but the parts fit was not bad.

15. As black background is the best for spraying white the cab was primed with Mr.Finishing surfacer black.

16 After priming the cab was given a couple of coats of Mr.Color gloss white using the Mr.Retarder mild for the smooth and fine surface. Using this the Mr.Color paints behave nearly as the two component automotive lacquers.

hood tilting function. I did not like the large flat surfaces inside the hood so I applied Tamiya putty to simulate an insulation layer. This will help to make the painting and weathering in this area much easier.

The cab shell consists of the following parts: the main cab body, the firewall, roof, rear cab wall and the roof deflector that is separate, and does not have to be attached at all. I left the firewall separate because I would be painting and detailing it later. The major task was to paint the cab, as spraying such a large assembly is always challenging. The most important (for all model truck cabs in general) is to build and align the cab parts properly, and ensure the whole assembly is clean. Filling is usually required, but the more precise your work is the less putty you need. With the Prostar cab, the only tricky step is attaching the roof. The part fits well enough but patience and care is required here because any sanding of this join will be tricky…as it is located in a narrow gap and is hard to reach. Instead of standard modelling glue I used black Superglue, which provides more control and acts as both glue and putty. Any excess adhesive was removed easily with cyanoacrylate remover, and no sanding was necessary. Although the instruction sheet recommends attaching the rear cab wall after the interior is added, I always prefer to have the cab body as complete as possible, as spraying it as one part always prevents post-paint alignment issues where any sanding is almost impossible. Therefore, I have attached the rear cab panel but applied the glue just along its top edge, and leave the vertical edges free for easier interior installation after painting.

As I have already mentioned, there are still possible modifications on the average cab. I decided to add bits and pieces which are in the CTM Prostar detail set. The rear cab wall features a pair of ventilation mesh sections, which are available in photo-etched versions, as well as a pair of lights also supplied by CTM. Even the susie bracket is included in the PE set, so both the plastic vents and lights were sanded off and the rear cab wall pressings were rebuilt with thin plastic sheet prior to painting.

The Prostar cab is among the largest I've ever handled, and I can imagine that Italeri's Volvo VN can be even more challenging in terms of painting. I imagine that many modellers simply use spray can paint, but I always stick with my airbrush and just replace the nozzle set (I use 0.7mm for these large parts).

I quite liked the decal version provided by Revell; however, I wanted my model to be a proper working vehicle rather than a showpiece. Chassis painting and weathering were the basic acts and I already knew that the best backdrop colour for fading and dirt on the cab would be white. It took me a while to figure it all out but finally a friend of mine, Karel Krejčí, provided me the KFS North American decal set featuring classic American trucking companies. Among these I found the Central Freight Lines markings. This company runs a large amount of trucks in a white and green combination, and some modern Internationals are among them, though maybe not exactly of this type. However, I did not need any further reference pictures as all I sought was a little inspiration. The colour scheme I had in mind is based on a few pictures I found on the internet, and is probably not 100% correct but who can tell there hasn't been an owner-operator unit painted this way?

Therefore, white was the first to go on the cab after the primer. There's no doubt, though, that white is a tricky shade. Fortunately, the experienced guys have taught me that when spraying white, the best primer coat is black. I therefore used my favorite Mr. Surfacer finishing black again. Adding a few drops of retarder provided a perfectly smooth

1. Once the white coat was dry and polished the green stripes were masked on the cab. Patience was required here to make sure everything was symmetrical.

2. Fresh from the paint shop before removing the masking tape. Mr.Color green No.6 with a few drops of Tamiya black and retarder was used.

3. The finished cab and hood after removing the masking tape. As the masking was precise there were no major errors to repair here.

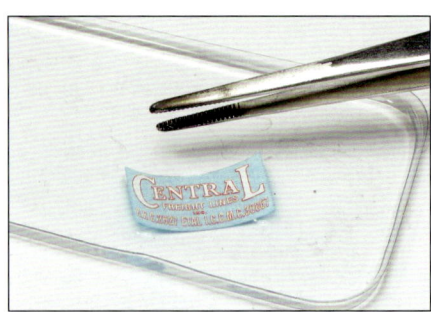

4. Working with decals is another part of building and finishing plastic models. The first step is to put them into a lukewarm water for a few seconds.

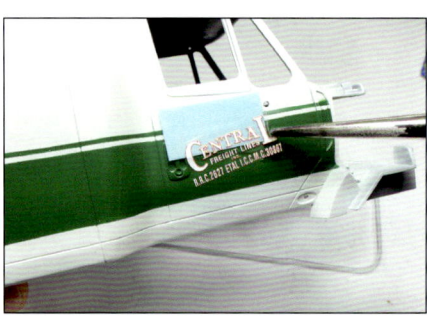

5. When released from the paper the decal can be easily placed on the cab surface using a pair of tweezers. Be very careful as the decals are easily damaged.

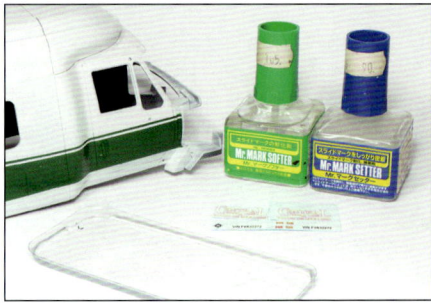

6. For better adhesion and softening of the decals (to let help them adjust to an uneven surface) some solutions were used. I am used to Mr.Mark Setter and Mr.Mark Softener.

4. A MEDIUM LEVEL PROJECT

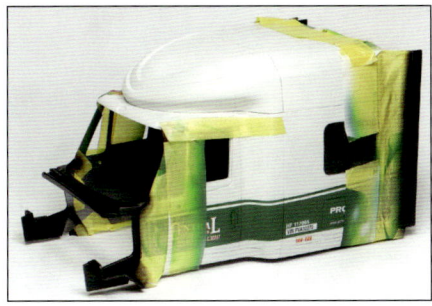
7. As the cab has some black plastic and rubber parts these were masked and sprayed flat black.

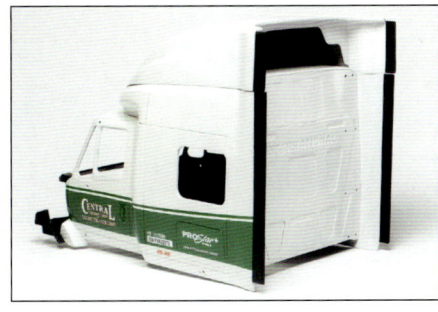
8. Removing the masking tape from the decaled cab needs all your patience and care as the cab surface may be now prone to damage.

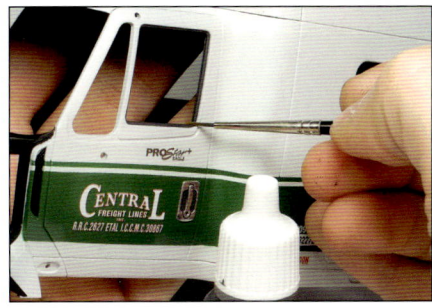
9. The side window rubber seals were haind painted with my favorite Vallejo acrylics.

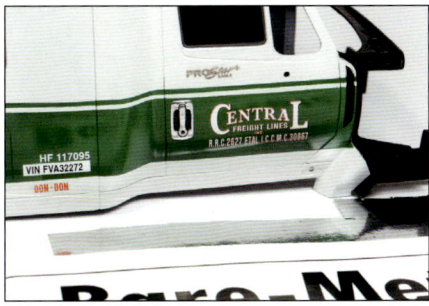
10. Bare-metal foil was applied to achieve a shiny metal surface on the cab door handles.

11. Three different black nuances were used on the cab windows. While the windcreen rubber was airbrushed, the side window rubbers were quite easy to brush paint. The smoke effect on the sleeper windows was made with Tamiya X-19.

12. Handling the clear parts is always a delicate task. Once damaged, any repairing is quite difficult.

surface that was just sanded gently to remove dust particles. I knew from my previous projects that there is a difference between building a perfectly clean, and a dirty white vehicle. While for the first, the white has to be bright but for the other, a bright tone may not be the best choice. So, for grimy vehicles I always prepare a 'dirty' white paint, which always consists of about 50 to 90 per cent white and the remaining percentage of grey or beige, to reduce the paint shine. For the basic paint I used an approximate 50-50 mixture of Mr.Color White (No.1) and Light grey (No.97). Again, Mr.Retarder mild was added to the mixture (the retarder amount I use is around 20% of the thinner volume). The thinner volume in the ready-to-spray paint mixture is about 70 per cent to keep the paint thin,

13

The very last step of the cab painting is sealing the decals with a gloss clear coat. The Mr.Color Super clear was used with a few drops of the Mr.Retarder mild.

1. The inner surface of the clear parts were also masked for a better protection.

2. The windows fitted the cab perfectly. Regular white glue is often used on them to stay on the safe side and prevent any part damage.

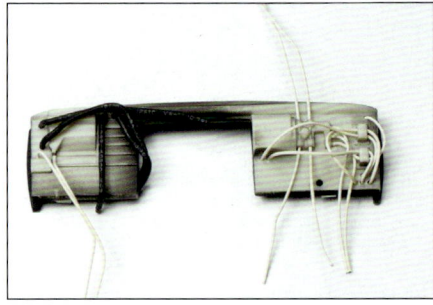
3. The engine firewall lacks a lot of details. To make this area a bit more interesting some wiring and hoses were added. .

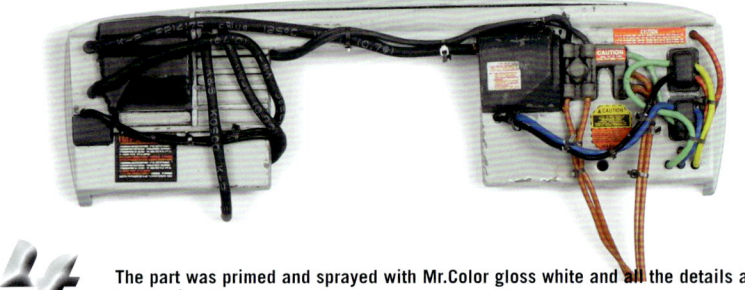
The part was primed and sprayed with Mr.Color gloss white and all the details and cables were hand painted.

and prevent any orange peel texture. The air pressure I normally use it about 1.8 bar and I always wear a face mask during such intensive work. Spraying such a large part needs plenty of patience and care. And it is always better to apply few thin coats instead of a single heavy layer. I have added a few fine layers on the cab shell, hood and the roof deflector and let the parts dry overnight. As the white layer opacity was not good enough in some areas (I usually work at night and the daylight always reveals some issues) I have added several more layers locally.

The next step was spraying the green stripes. I have already used masking tape in this book for a few smaller tasks, but employing it for the cab stripes is a major task and needs all your patience and care. All the areas have to be masked carefully, the tape edges must be clean and free of any dust and dirt, and the tape has to be burnished to the surface precisely to avoid any blurry contours. Precision is what matters here, as any errors are quite difficult to repair.

FINISHING THE CAB PAINTJOB

I used standard Tamiya tape to cover large areas and additional Jammy Dog 1mm tape for the thin stripe along the upper edge. The green colour is a mixture of Tamiya XF-70 and Mr.Color 6 with a few drops of Mr.Retarder Mild, all diluted with Mr.Color Thinner. When spraying over masking tape, I try to avoid any heavy paint layers that could get under the tape. A few thin coats are much safer, and ensure clean and smooth results. As for removing the tape, I prefer doing it sooner rather than later, before the pain dries and sticks to the tape itself.

I let the paint dry for a couple of hours and started with decal application. Although working with decals can be tricky, this particular case was rather straightforward as all the marking I was using were quite small and applied over a plain surface. The first, and most important requirement with decal application is a smooth and glossy base. A smooth surface improves decal adhesion significantly, so I always use gloss coat underneath. In theory no decal agents have to be used on a gloss surface, but using it means you will always be on the safe side. Using the paint retarder provided a shiny surface so once dry, I could start immediately with decal application. I cut the first door logo from the decal sheet and placed it into a shallow bowl filled with lukewarm tap water. The decals were ready within a minute. Tweezers were used to place the decal on the model and let it slide from the paper right into a drop of Mr.Mark setter, already placed on the door. I used the tool to position the decal properly and paper towel to absorb the excess water. The decal looked perfect, so I repeated the same process with all the remaining markings. It took some time, although no issues arose as patience and care were exercised throughout. I always work in steps, focus on every single decal and never put more than one into the water at a time. Work slowly and take it seriously, as you destroy a decal just once and replacements can be difficult to obtain.

Applying the decals was fun and took just a couple of hours. Before any further steps, I always protect the decals with a fine clear coat. I have used two layers of Mr.Color Super Clear, and polished the first layer with Tamiya 1,500-grade abrasive paper, to suppress the visible decal edges. The second lacquer layer applied over the decals blended them beautifully with the surface, with no edges visible.

When sanding or polishing the top paint or lacquer layers, you have to be very careful as the sanding might reveal some of the previous paint coats. On my cab, the white was exposed under the green stripe and on a few edges the black primer revealed itself. This is not a disaster and problems such as this can usually be repaired with further spraying and masking. In my case I had to mask the white lower edges of the cab, and later, some areas of the green fields.

CAB RUBBER PARTS

The last airbrush task on the cab involved the rubber cab fairings and the firewall area. All were masked properly and sprayed with Mr. Color flat black. Note that the masking tape use has both the white and green paint on it. I mostly used each part of the tape multiple times, and store it stuck on my cutting mat. This reduces waste and cost.

Although finished in terms of spraying, there were few more details to be added to the cab shell. First of all, the side window rubbers

4. A MEDIUM LEVEL PROJECT

were hand-painted with a brush and Vallejo Dark Rubber acrylic. The handles were more difficult, though, as I wanted them in chrome although some vehicles have them in black plastic or even in the cab colour. Using Alclad lacquers on such small details is challenging and time consuming, but there is another option that works on similar parts – Bare Metal foil. It is an extra-fine self-adhesive metal foil, which adheres to raised surface features brilliantly. This can be used for various chromed trim or window frames found on classic cars. It is also suitable for chroming fine surface details such as logos. The foil is very thin and has limited elasticity, so the depth of the detail on which the foil can be used is limited. This was also the case with the handles, which are embossed heavily and the foil is not flexible enough to cover them completely. I cut out a piece of foil slightly larger than the handle itself, pressed it over the handle with a piece of cloth and used a toothpick to burnish the foil into the depressions. A fresh scalpel blade was used to cut the foil around the handle and the recesses where the foil was torn were painted with flat black. It all took less than ten minutes per handle, which is much faster than using Alclad and the result is very convincing.

The clear parts were the next step. Working with windows is another demanding part of the hobby and needs all your patience and skill. Remember that, as with decals, you'll damage the windows just once and replacing them is difficult. Any scratch is hard to remove and there is no way for cracks to be repaired. Clear parts are very brittle and you should handle them with care. Any cutting or cleaning, therefore, has to be done very carefully. Just like the rubber parts on the cab, the clear part rubbers on the door triangular windows were hand-painted with Vallejo Dark Rubber. Using Vallejo colours on window rubbers is great, because any excess paint can be removed easily from the window using a sharp toothpick. As I wanted to reduce the transparency of the sleeper side windows, Tamiya X-19 Smoke was used. The windscreen frame to be painted black are quite large areas. I did not feel confident in painting this with a brush so I used Tamiya masking tape over the windscreen and sprayed the frame with Tamiya flat black acrylic.

Fitting windows into the cab parts also demands patience. Many people keep having issues with achieving clean results on windows. At first I would like to say that I do not find the standard modelling glues that suitable for working with clear parts in general, as they can very easily damage the parts. In modelling there are special adhesives designed for working with clear parts (such as Humbrol Clearfix), while standard water-based white glue works well here too, as it becomes clear once dry. These glues have one common attribute, and that is they are harmless to clear parts; particularly important when working with windows as any excess glue can be removed without damage. What I do, though, (but this requires practice) is that I fix windows with Superglue. I do not use any standard clear cyanoacrylate, as it leaves white marks (known as fogging) on the window surfaces, but rather the black Loctite 480. There are also special kinds of Superglue used for working with real glass, which should leave no white marks either. Anyway, no matter which cyano glue you use, your work has to be precise as the risk of damaging your windows is high - so I can't recommend this for inexperienced modellers.

The old KFS data plates used on this model are not available anymore. As this product was phased out CTM has released two separate decal sets (CTM 24243 and 24244) that contain all sorts of data plates and various instruction and safety signs.

What is very important in each kit, and can make your life easier, is how the windows fit into the cab. In many old kits the parts' fit is poor and this can cause trouble. However, my experience with the latest kits (MENG's Ford F350 and Moebius Prostar) is that they have improved significantly. The clear parts' quality in the Prostar kit is great and they fit perfectly, so just a small amount of glue was required to fit them in the correct position.

Once the windows were fitted to the cab I could insert the interior into the cab shell. It was quite easy, although I had fitted the rear cab wall and fixed it along its top edge previously. The interior fits perfectly and was secured in its position with a few drops of Superglue.

A large part of the cab that remained untouched until now was the cab firewall. It contains heavy wiring and piping on the real vehicle, while in the kit this is a relatively simple part. I Googled some International cab pictures, showing firewall details, and decided to add fine wiring in this area. As when wiring the chassis, holes were drilled into the part, into which one wire after another was glued using cyanoacrylate. The wired part was sprayed with black Mr. Surfacer followed by Mr.Color gloss white. Once dry, all these wires were painted with various Vallejo acrylic shades, as the real vehicle also features much colourful cabling here. CTM photo-etched cable ties were used to organise the wiring into separate bundles. The large diameter hose on the left-hand side of the part were sourced from a local hobby show and added after painting the part. They have excellent white print on them, which looks realistic, although it's somewhat out of scale. To add even more detail, warning signs were added from the KFS-50 Generic chassis data plates decal set. The part was sprayed with a flat clear coat to blend the decals with the background, fine chips were hand-painted with Vallejo acrylics and a generous amount of black wash was applied around the details. The finished part was attached to the cab. It took some time to create all these refinements, but this is exactly the type of detail that brings a model to life.

4.9 CAB ACCESSORIES AND EXTERIOR PARTS

Although all of the large vehicle sub-assemblies were finished, there were a few more details to be added on the cab.

I must admit that I loathe working with mirrors, and this always relates to the necessary neatening of thin mirror brackets…and for most kits, the mirror surface has to be produced convincingly somehow. The Prostar mirrors were exactly the opposite. There was just minor cleaning-up required and the chromed mirror parts looked fantastic. The sun visor fitted the cab perfectly, while the clear mar-

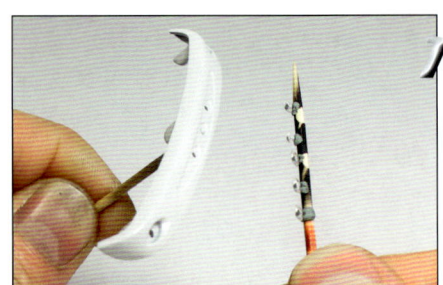

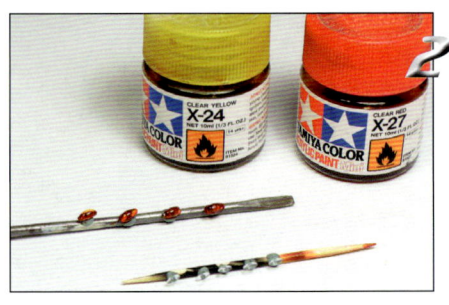

4. A MEDIUM LEVEL PROJECT

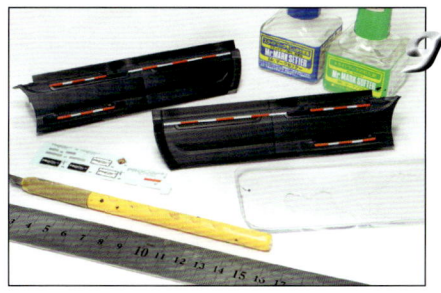

8. The vehicle side skirts were primed and sprayed black, and vertical rain marks were applied with an airbush as well.

1. The cab parts such as the mirrors and the sunvisor were assembled and painted separately.

2. A mixture of Tamiya red and orange clear paints was used on the marker lights.

3. As the chromed surface of the grille was damaged in my kit I had to repaint the part using Alclad Chrome II. Therefore the part was primed with Mr.Color gloss black.

4. When applied on a gloss black surface, the chromed Alclad makes a nice and shiny metallic surface.

5. On the hood a fine etched logo was applied.

6. The lights in the Prostar kit are some of the best I have seen, with a nice chromed background.

7. The clear light parts fit the hood perfectly and needed no glue at all!

9. The red and white stripes come from the Revell decal sheet and were applied using the Mr.Color Setter and Softer solutions.

10-11. Installing the bumper and side skirts on the chassis was a simple task. Note how they cover the fuel tanks and all the chassis details under the cab.

12. The etched steps from the CTM detail set have a fine structure and a realistic sheet metal thickness.

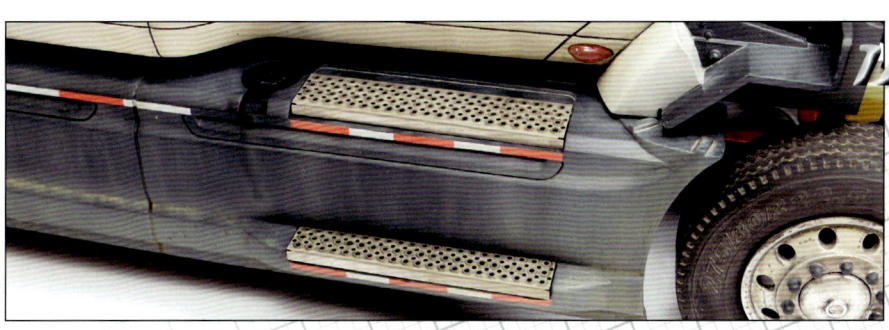

ker lights were tiny but looked great painted with Tamiya acrylics. On the cab and hood, fine photo-etched parts from the CTM detail set were applied with Superglue. One of the finest PE details was the hood logo. Handling these such very fine components is tricky; I came around to using a toothpick with a small ball of Tack-It, which works great with these diminutive parts. The photo-etched susie cable support fitted on the rear cab wall, as well as the vents, come from the CTM Prostar detail set. So does the number plate frame fitted with the kit decals, used on both the front and rear of the truck. The windscreen wipers were sprayed black and added to the windscreen frame. Although most of the kit wipers are too thin, and photo-etched replacements would be preferable, the Prostar parts look good enough.

The hood grille is chromed, but as on most parts the chromed plating was damaged during clean-up of the part. As this should be one of the shiniest sections of the vehicle, I decided to use Alclad II Chrome lacquer on it. The chromed surface was sanded away (it reduced paint adhesion significantly) and was primed with a few layers of Mr.Surfacer finishing black. Once dry, the part was sprayed with gloss black and polished with Tamiya polishing compounds. Avoiding scratches in the paint is vital, as the Alclad reveals even the finest surface defects. On the gloss surface, a few fine layers of Alclad II Chrome were applied. This lacquer comes in glass bottles and is pre-thinned for spraying, so you can use it directly. Although the gloss Alclad should be applied on special primers to provide high shine, I was more than happy with the result as my model was not meant to be a show truck, and the Alclad sprayed on Mr.Color paint looked just about right. Taking the classic Alclad used on the engine parts into account, polished Agama paint on the exhaust, Bare Metal foil on the door handles and now the Chrome Alclad on the grille, this model actually demontrates all of the most common ways of creating a natural metal finish on scale models.

The grille in the kit comes with fine photo-etched mesh, which is the first PE part that has ever appeared in 1/24 or 1/25 plastic kits. The mesh looks great and fits the grille perfectly. Superglue was used for attaching the grille to the hood, where a fair amount of force was necessary to align the parts properly. Speaking of the hood, I have to say that the main lamps are another beautiful part…moulded beautifully with chromed background and clear lenses. Both the parts fit the hood perfectly and look fantastic. I must admit, these are probably the best-looking 1/24 or 1/25 scale lights I've seen on a model. I used Superglue for fitting the background parts, while the clear parts did not need adhesive at all!

The bumper and chassis side skirts were sprayed black, with post shading in various tones of light grey, and dust tones to make these parts more interesting. The red and white reflective striping decals from the kit sheet were applied, and sprayed with flat clear Mr.Color varnish. These provide a great touch, especially when building such a workhorse. Another good detail is the cab steps from the CTM set. These look very realistic with their holes and thin walls, and fitted the side skirts perfectly. Once dry, the side skirts were attached to the chassis with Superglue, followed by the rear quarter fenders and mud flaps.

What is important when adding parts such as side skirts or bumpers to the chassis, is to think about any future model manipulation or even fixing points for transporting the model to shows. Just for lifting a model, you need to have parts or points which can support the whole subject's weight when you need to lift it. This may not be an issue on an aircraft or tank build, where the whole model is formed from a solid shell; however, as you have already seen, truck models have a quite complex structure and are rather heavy. Therefore, you need to make sure (as I have pointed out previously) that the frame is robust enough and all other parts such as the bumper and side skirts are attached properly, these can carry the weight of the model.

The exhaust pipes were attached to the frame rails and fitted perfectly to the manifold that goes into the exhaust silencer. I also completed the wiring by adding the remaining two air lines to the front axle brake chambers, and wires to the front lights in the hood and bumper. The Prostar PE detail set features a pair of catwalks. I used just one but omitted the other, as it would cover the chassis details.

The last step of the build was the cab installation. There are four mounting points on the chassis and I must admit that I had to lower the front example by a couple of millimetres,

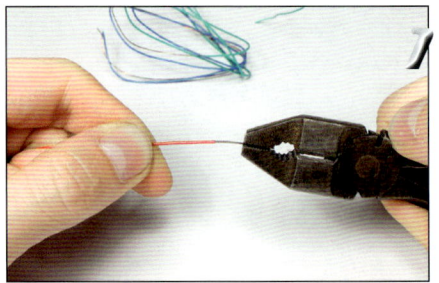

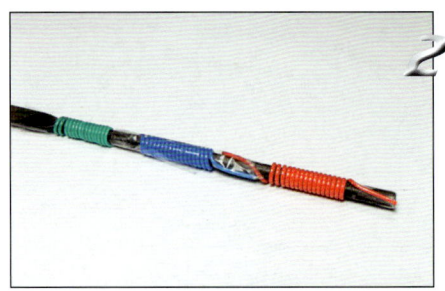

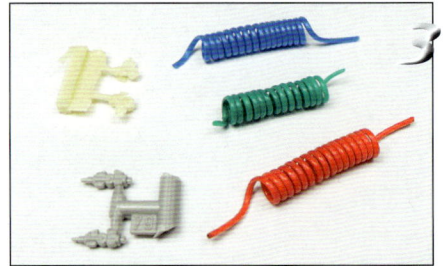

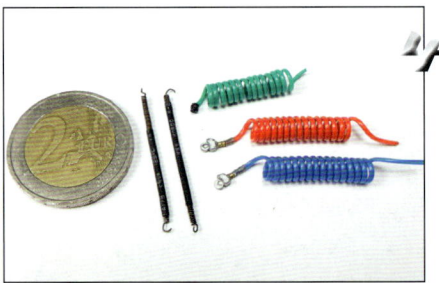

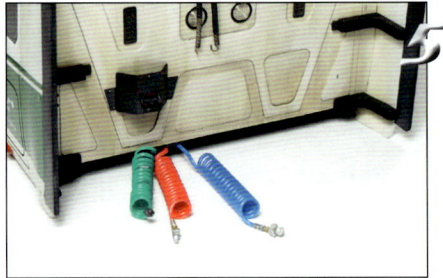

1. The first step of making the susie coiled cables is to strip the insulation from its wire.

2. Now wrap about 15 coils around a 4 mm rod and fix it with office tape. Put it into boiling water, cool down and carefully remove the tape and set the cable free.

3. When using correct material the insulation keeps the coiled shape but is flexible like the real cable.

4. The couplings were sourced from the Italeri 720 accessories set. Note the fine coiled springs, reinforcing the hose and cable ends.

5. Once finished these cables can be attached to the cab. As they are soft they can be arranged into virtually any position on the cab wall.

6. Czech Truck Model now offers their CTM 24234 Trailer couplings and electric plugs and sockets to detail your model as the trailer couplings are not included in model kits.

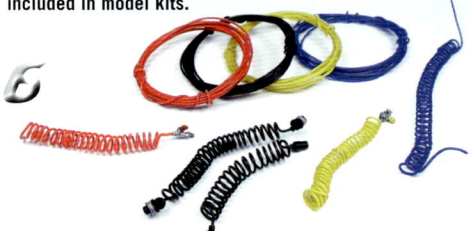

7. During a solo drive the cables are always secured in some way. Hanging them on the rear cab wall gives an opportunity to add extra detail.

to ensure the cab was level. I used a two-part glue instead of standard adhesive, as it provides strong but flexible joins and I wanted the cab to be the main lifting point. Once the front mounts were lowered, the cab sat on the frame properly and the hood matched the cab lines perfectly.

4.9.2 SUSIE COILED CABLES

What is missing in every kit, and is an essential detail that should be added to almost every truck model, are the coiled susie cables. You can find them on every tractor and making them is not difficult. Furthermore, the susie bracket is something you can actually find in most kits, so it is just the wires that are missing. I will show you how I do it on my models.

All you need is a piece of wire and the air and electrical couplings. The latter can be found in the Italeri accessories set (no. 720) and are fairly realistic. Just keep in mind that Italeri provides these parts coupled, so for a tractor you actually need to cut the part in half. The wire that can be used for the cables is available in the same accessories set, although there are many other ways of representing them. I do have a box full of various coloured cables, of different diameters, so every time I need any I just search for the right example… and mostly I do not even have to use paint.

My reference photos of various Prostar tractors show three lines for the trailer, of which there is a green electric line, one blue and one red for the air. I therefore found the appropriately coloured wire in my spares box

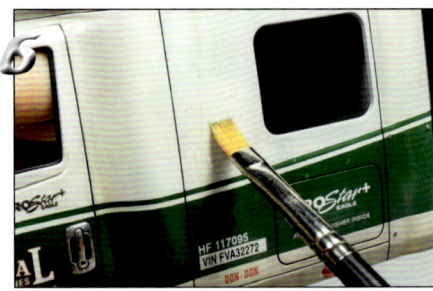

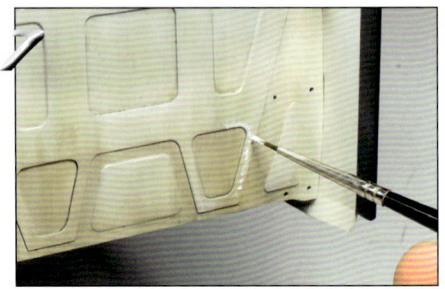

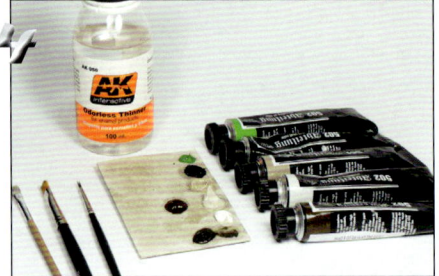

1. Weathering the cab is a story of its own. At first some rain marks and dust effects on various panels and along the panel lines were sprayed.

2. As the rear cab wall always gets dirtier and is rarely cleaned properly, some heavier dirt layers were applied here.

3. The panel lines were highlighted with a black oil paint wash.

4. For the next step, generally known as fading, oil paints related to the cab colors were prepared on a cardboard.

5. Using a fine pointed brush or a toothpick, fine paint dots were applied on the cab surface.

6. These dots were then blended with a flat brush using almost no thinner.

7. To highlight the rear wall structure a white oil paint was applied along some of the sharp edges using a fine tip brush...

8. ...and blended with a flat brush creating nice highlights emphasizing the cab wall.

9. To reduce the shine of the coiled cables a fine layer of Tamiya X-19 followed by a Mr.Color flat clear coat was applied over the entire area.

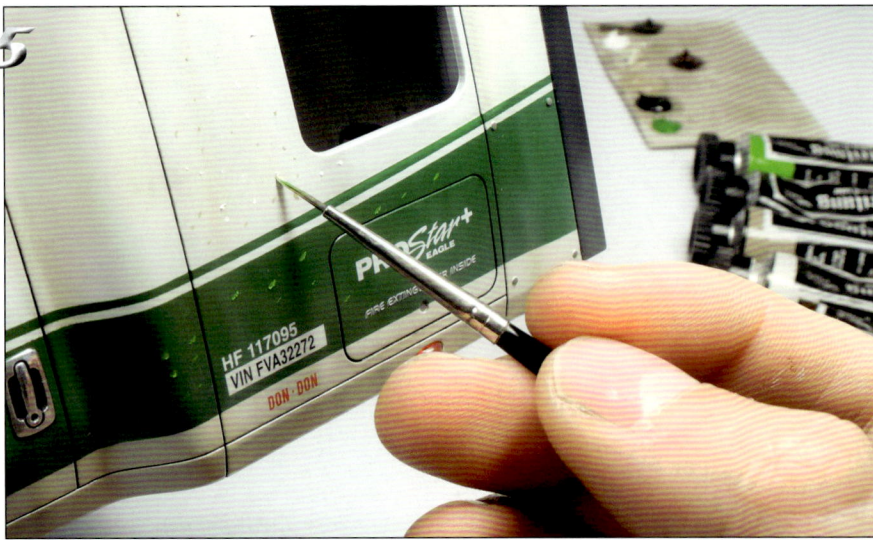

to make the coiled cables. For this there are two ways to go. In the past I just wrapped the wire around 3.5 – 4mm rod. What you get is actually a very softly coiled spring, which keeps its shape and looks just right. It can be formed into any shape and used on a model in any position, one end fitted with a coupling and the other attached to the susie bracket. The wires do not need to be very long. The cables usually have approximately 15 loops.

The other method is more difficult but provides more realistic results, in my opinion. The first step is to strip the insulation from the wire, and from then on it's the insulation that is worked with. Again, I wrapped it around a rod and secured it with tape, as without this, the inner wire is soft and does not maintain the coiled shape. I did the same for all three wire colours – 15 loops with short ends. While wrapped around the rod, I put it all into boiling water for a couple of minutes. I let it warm up, then removed it from the pot and chilled it with cold water. Repeating it three times, I ensured the current coiled shape of the wire insulation was preserved properly. When the tape was removed, the part kept its coiled shape and was more flexible compared to the

4. A MEDIUM LEVEL PROJECT

coiled wire. This provides good, soft cables, which can be arranged easily and realistically.

I employed Italeri parts for the air couplings, shortened them and used one of the remaining examples as a plug for the green cable. Once the couplings were glued to the cables, I hand-painted them using a metallic shade for the air couplings and dark grey for the plug. I also added a very fine metal coil around the cable end, next to the air couplings, which are used as a reinforcement on the real air hose. I made it by wrapping extra-thin wire around a pin. To hang the cables to the support bar on the rear cab wall, a pair of spring hangers was made from wire and a piece of insulation.

As the susie cables looked good, but were too clean and shiny, I applied a few dark filters over them. The finished parts were attached to the rear cab wall using the hanger and the photo-etched cable holder.

4.10 CAB WEATHERING

The cab and hood were weathered in a few steps and a similar process was used on the bumper and side skirts. Initially, fine vertical rain marks were applied with an airbrush on the cab walls, using a highly thinned mixture of white, grey and dust colours. Thin dust filters were added along the lower cab edges. The paint I used was highly diluted, and you

have to be really easy on the airbrush trigger as the paint layer has to be very fine and transparent to look realistic. This was done prior to the window installation.

Once dry, a black oil paint wash was applied into all grooves on the cab sides. This provided pleasing contrast and gave the cab a more realistic appearance.

The next step was oil paints and the so-called fading method. This is based on applying fine dots of oil paint on the model's surface. The colour is either related to the surface layer (lighter or darker colour of the basic surface) to provide light and shadow, or to a general dust and dirt patina to add more weathering

TRUCK MODELLING

> *The modern and simple look of the Prostar used as a daily workhorse stands in strong contract to classic American trucks with loads of chromed parts and traditional look.*

layers supporting the initial airbrushed coat. I have therefore used white and light dust tones on the cab, and green over the green cab areas. These paint dots were blended with the basic surface using a flat brush, with minimal thinner (I use Odorless thinner from AK Interactive) using a vertical motion of the brush on the cab walls.

White oil paint was used to provide highlights on the rear cab wall structure. It was applied along the edges using a fine-tipped brush and blended with a dry flat brush. This provided depth to the wall structure. Once finished, I let the cab dry for a few days (oils dry very slowly). The rear cab wall weathering followed, with a thin coat of Tamiya X-19 Smoke to darken the lower areas. In the next step, oil paints were used to add more vertical streaks. Another layer was made with highly thinned oil paints, applied using a 'speckling' method to create dirt and oil splatters, as these often

4. A MEDIUM LEVEL PROJECT

form on the rear truck cab walls…creating interesting visual effects. Finally, a fine flat clear coat was sprayed all over the area to reduce the paint shine. Oil paints and AK Interactive enamel weathering products were also applied along the lower edge of the side skirts, to add another layer of dust and dirt.

CONCLUSION

The Prostar is a great new kit that many of us were waiting for. Even I must admit that I really enjoyed building and detailing it… however, modern North American trucks are not necessarily my cup of tea. The kit fitted very well and I can hardly complain about anything, given the fact that injection moulding has its technological limits. Speaking of the Revell version, I would say that another livery or two would be beneficial on the decal sheet, as the shiny show truck s version may not be everyone's choice. If there is a kit that should be recommended to someone who is new to the hobby, and would like to try building an American vehicle, the Prostar (or Lonestar) kit should definitely be his or her first choice.

The model weathering goes down to basics. The Prostar is a relatively new vehicle so I did not feel any need for adding rust or significant paint chipping. Nor did I apply heavy dust and mud layers, and portrayed the vehicle in a normal working state that can be seen on the road every day.

I have really enjoyed the CTM detail set. Although I did not use all the parts this time, I can hardly imagine building this truck without at least the photo-etched heatshields, mud flaps and cab steps. The painted dashboard looks far better than the original decals, and the PE chassis parts brought the building to another level (for which I would like to apologise as it was well beyond what I would call out-of-the-box), but the details of the chassis are simply stunning. It looks so great that I did not use any chassis catwalk, as it would cover most of it.

TRUCK MODELLING

5 DETAILING YOUR

TRUCK **MODELLING**

5. DETAILING YOUR MODEL-FIRST LEVEL

MODEL-FIRST LEVEL

The previous chapter presented a model built almost out of the box. I agree that it cannot be considered as a pure OOB build, as I simply could not resist adding extra details here and there, which finally made the model more complex that intended originally. In any case, the point is to keep the model detailed but you can't let the complexity prevent you from finishing it.

5.1 INTRODUCTION

This chapter should represent a step forward in terms of detailing and reworking your model. Therefore, above standard building processes, I will provide you with additional information about different types of after-market parts, basic scratch-building materials and converting kits in general. What may seem like a small step (such as attempting a simple conversion) is actually something that may take years for a modeller to prepare for… and there is no point in trying to add every little detail on your first model. I always recommend doing this in steps; learn the ropes slowly and always keep the basics in mind.

Conversions are common in the world of 1/24 scale model trucks, for various reasons. It is natural to try and extend the narrow range of available vehicle modifications, by simply changing the number or configuration of the vehicle axles or modifying the cab size (from a long-distance version to a day cab, for example). Many of these conversions are followed by rebuilding some chassis components, such as the fuel tank size or even replacing the engine with another. Many conversions also take place where the kit parts are incorrect or not detailed enough. Here, all the Volvo FH kits are a great example as these are generally one of the most frequently converted models. Not only that, the basic kit is fairly inaccurate in many ways, but these trucks are very popular in three-axle configurations, while there is just a two-axle unit available in the box.

The problem with conversions, though, is that there is no general guide. Each project is unique and needs different actions. Some conversions may be rather easy when the kit parts are replaced by an after-market component that fits perfectly. In other conversions, even major scratch-building may be involved and this cannot be described by any generic guide. It's akin to painting. You can read about the techniques, you can appreciate paintings that others have produced, but there is no exact rule to guide your hands.

Do not forget that all the points about the kit parts and their assembly from the previous chapter are valid for any model. It makes no sense to use expensive after-market on models that bear witness marks or areas that require further sanding or even filling. All these actions should be part of every modeller's build regime and they should always be kept in mind

5.2 AFTERMARKET PARTS

For detailing and converting models there is an array of after-market parts available, from various specialised manufacturers, but many are intended just for experienced modellers. Using after-market parts is mostly the first way to go when converting your model, and they may make your life easy. However, the quality can vary between various producers and sometimes scratch-building may also be a viable (and cheaper) option. The basic types of parts available for model trucks are resin, and photo-etched or cast white metal parts. Let's briefly describe their characteristics.

RESIN PARTS

These components are low-batch castings made using silicone moulds. This technology is quite different in comparison to the high-pressure injection moulding used to pro-

TECH SPEC
Iveco Stralis

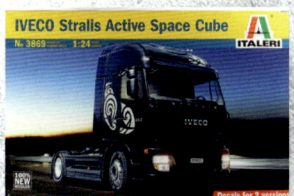

Kit: 3869 Italeri Iveco Stralis Active Space
Scale: 1:24
Accessories: MT&P 100101 Super single front wheels, CTM 019 Iveco Stralis detail set, CTM 24106 and 24108 US Front lights, CTM 24017 Radiator mesh, CTM 24049 Wheel chocks, CTM 24072 Hose clamps, CTM 24081 Cable binders, CTM 24075 Reflective boards, CTM 24076 ADR boards, KFS TQMT-3 Air valve set, UK Modellbau roof AC unit (UK-26), Plusmodel 446 Pet bottles, decals printed by decalprint.de
Notes: One of the best 1:24 scale truck kit on the market

TRUCK MODELLING

ducing mass-market plastic kits. Resin has its pros and cons and is the most common material used for producing after-market parts. It can provide outstanding, sharp detail and low wall thickness, with no draft angles necessary. Its drawback is that if not cast properly the parts contain various sizes of air bubble that have to filled and sanded, which is both tricky and time consuming. Depending on the production technology used, different companies provide varying degrees of quality. As for sanding, drilling and cutting there is no difference between resin and plastic. However, as standard styrene cement does not work with resin, either cyanoacrylate or two-part epoxy adhesive has to be used. Painting resin is also straightforward, but washing the parts in lukewarm soapy water prior to painting is advisable, for removing any remaining mould release agent. As resin dust is harmful, everyone should protect their respiratory health and wear a safety mask when cutting or sanding resin.

PHOTO-ETCHED (PE) PARTS

PE details are made of thin sheet metal (brass mostly) and often represent the most accurate accessories on the market. The production technology is very precise and allows even the finest details that other technologies are not capable of…but the material thickness is limited and is usually around 0.2mm. Therefore, PE parts are often combined with resin castings to cover all the bases. Any three- dimensional subjects built from PE have to be made by bending/folding, which is the most common operation when working with this medium. Cutting the parts is not as easy as with plastic, but as the material thickness is relatively slight, everyday tools such as knives or scissors can still be used, with care. Painting PE is simple and does not require any special treatment, and for gluing, again use Superglue or two-part epoxy. As PE parts often depict small details, and etched assemblies are quite brittle, their use is recommended purely to experienced modellers.

METAL PARTS

White metal castings are, in some ways, similar to resin parts and are sometimes used for fine details, or front axles for heavier models (such as those using resin cabs and engines that are significantly heavier than plastic versions). The materials used are soft alloys that can be machined, cut, sanded or drilled easily with standard modelling tools. Painting these parts is simple and does not require anything special. For gluing, cyano or epoxy glues can be used.

CTM recently introduced a new range of front diecast axles that provide a robust replacement of kit plastic axles that are very brittle and sensitive to model weigh increase due to extensive use of resin parts. These axles are available in both 1/24 and 25th scale.

3D-PRINTED PARTS

A technology that has changed to hobby in the recent years is the 3D print. Not only that it allows individuals to create their own 3D model and have it printed but it is also used by aftermarket companies to produce the parts they sell, not just for the masters. It is understandable that there will be more and more 3D printed parts around in the future. The most suitable technology for our purpose is the parts from SLA (stereolitography). These parts need to be cured with an UV light after printing and also washed with isopropanol or a similar cleaner. If done properly the parts then behave as a form of resin. There are different types of materials used for printing that differ not only in colour but also in physical properties (some are brittle, some are flexible) but they can be cut, sanded, painted and glued in the same way as resin parts.

5.3 SCRATCH-BUILDING MATERIALS

In addition to after-market products, there always is the option of making the parts yourself. Furthermore, the item you need may not actually be available as an after-market item. In this situation, a need for raw material arises. Fortunately, there are traditional companies supplying modellers with everything they need. Two big names are Evergreen and Plastruct. Both offer a wide range of high-quality styrene plastic sheets of various thicknesses, and profiles of many shapes and sizes. Without these, any scratch-building would be much more difficult. There are other sources where plastic sheet and basic profiles can be obtained, however the quality may be significantly lower and the standard glue for plastic models may not work with them.

If there is one thing I would like highlight, it is that Plastruct produces a small range hexagonal rods, which are great for making nuts, bolts and plumbing fittings. I often use them on my models together with both resin bolts, and those I make using my punch and die set.

Various profiles, both rods and tubes, are also available in other materials such as brass or aluminium. The most common supplier is K&S Precision Metals. In particular, the aluminium tubes are great for exhausts or hydraulic pistons. They have thin walls and can be polished to a high shine very easily.

5. DETAILING YOUR MODEL-FIRST LEVEL

1 Resin represents the most common form of after-market material. These castings come in many forms and colours.

3D-printed items are also becoming more common.

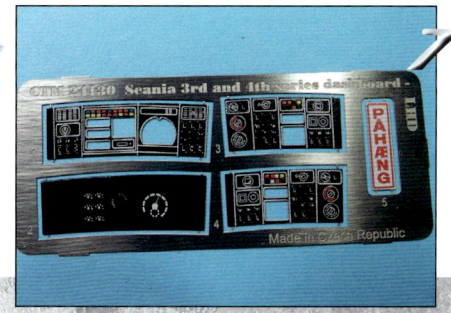

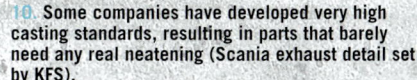

2 In most cases scratch-building involves Plastruct or Evergreen profiles.

3 Hexagonal Plastruct profiles are the cheapest and easiest way of making bolts for detailing your model.

4 Where metal surfaces and thin-wall pipes are required, K&S tubing is a great way to go.

5 Photo-etched (PE) metal parts represent super-fine details such as various grille meshes, as well as all kinds of badges.

6 A modern way of making vehicle lights is by using photo-etched parts with polyurethane lenses, to provide a 3D effect.

7 Another area where precise PE parts are useful are for finely printed items such as dashboard panels.

8 Typical aftermarket sets are various suspensions such as this american 4 spring Reyco suspension from CTM with complete axles.

9 Resin casting allows low-batch production at acceptable costs. A great example of this approach is this beautiful but limited Rába six-cylinder diesel engine set.

10 Some companies have developed very high casting standards, resulting in parts that barely need any real neatening (Scania exhaust detail set by KFS).

11 A popular combination of products for any truck project: CTM air valve set and various CTM fittings for plumbing and wiring.

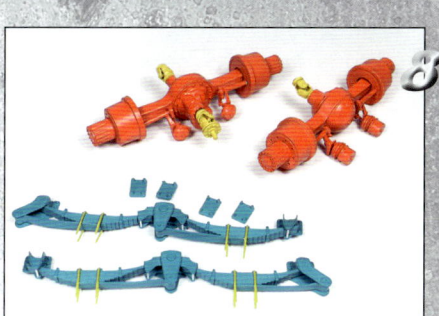

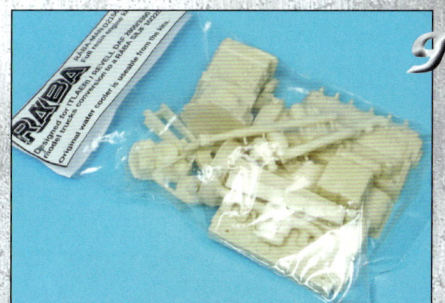

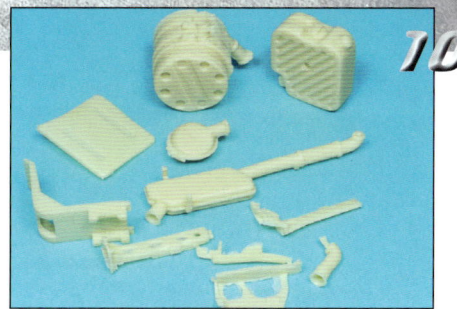

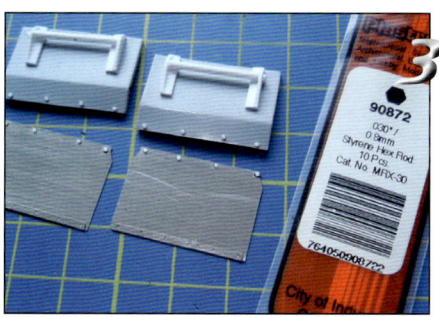
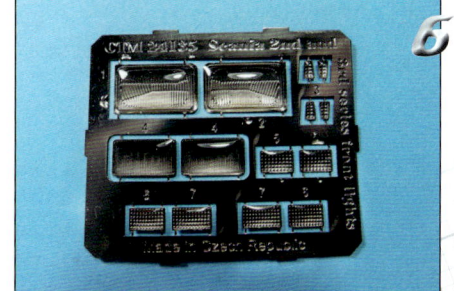
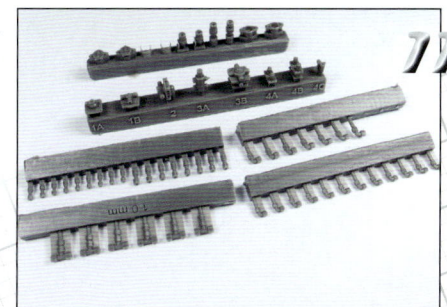

TRUCK MODELLING

5.4 A SAMPLE BUILD: ADVANCED LEVEL

5.4.1 INTRODUCTION

As a North American truck was built in the previous chapter, it is now Europe's turn! The Iveco Stralis kit was a straightforward choice, since the very early stages of this book. It's not just that I like the vehicle design, but the kit itself is brilliant too. It does not need much to make a good model and with a few simple conversions, it can be turned into a highly detailed replica of the real vehicle. Detailing and using additional parts is what should be highlighted in this chapter, as building the standard kit, as you will see, is just a repeat of what was done and written about the Prostar...just in a slightly different form.

The Stralis kit was introduced by Italeri in 2014 after many years of promises. It immediately became the best-detailed truck kit on the market. However, despite the box stating 100% new moulds, the wheels are the old items. This is the only negative comment about the kit, as the detail is fantastic and even the decal sheet provides a great choice of realistic liveries.

As we talk about conversions and detailing here, there is a shortlist of what I wanted to change on the model from the outset. There is a good, detailed photo-etched set by CTM that caters for both the exterior and interior of the truck. A friend of mine, well-known German truck modeller Guido Kehder, supplied me with a few detail sets for the Stralis that he made himself on his own CNC milling machine, of which I decided to use the well-detailed drive axle wheel hubs. To complete the model, modern injection-moulded European truck wheels and a resin roof AC unit were purchased. Common material for wiring was prepared, as well including the good old KFS metal air valves, CTM 24081 PE Cable ties and CTM 24072 Hose clamps. The CTM 24049 Wheel chocks, CTM 24075 ECE R 70 Reflective boards and CTM 24076 ADR boards were used to add classic modern European truck features. CTM 24017 etched radiator mesh was used on the coolers.

The livery was clear to me way before I started building the model. There is a trucking company in Děčín, Czech Republic, founded by Mr. Jiří Viktora in the early 1990s, who operated Liaz trucks till the closing chapters of their existence. When production at Liaz ceased, the vehicles were, successively, replaced by Iveco trucks. I have always loved this company because of their clean vehicles in a special blue-green tint, and once the Stralis kit was out I immediately had the decals produced for one of their Stralis trucks. These were drawn by fellow modeller Jan Moštěk and printed by decalprint.de.

5.4.2 WHEELS AND WHEEL HUBS

I started with wheels, because in conversions the wheels and wheel hubs are the most frequent topic; I've written many articles about truck models and in all of these, it's guaranteed that wheel hubs are addressed.

The reason for this is that all the Italeri kits have generic runners with rims and hubs. Although the differences between rims in certain periods and countries could be ignored (Italeri offers different rims for US and European trucks), the wheel hubs (wheel centres in other words) of different vehicles have a very specific shape...the differences are significant and cannot be generalised. In January 2016, Italeri introduced a new type of 1/24 wheel (both rims and tyres, set No. 3909) which have the hubs moulded separately. For most kits, though, this came too late and the new rims' shape is also far from ideal.

Fortunately, after-market producers are aware of the wheel hub issue and many hub types are available, mostly in resin. Wheel hubs have recently appeared in some PE sets as well, providing the end cap details. A majority of the hubs provided are drive axle versions, and the differences are significant here, while the difference in front axle and trailer wheel centres can often be ignored on truck models.

5. DETAILING YOUR MODEL-FIRST LEVEL

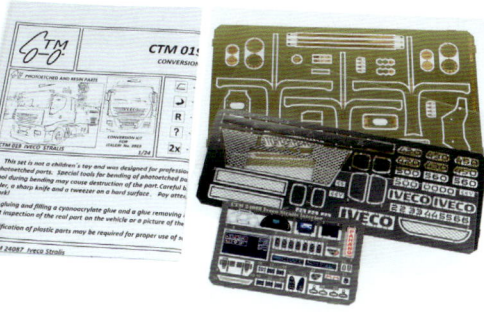

1. The basic way of improving the Stralis kit was defined by the content of CTM's Stralis photo-etched detail set.

2. The classic Italeri drive axle rims with wheel hubs, which are far from the ideal shape.

3. The inner drive axle rim has a moulded pin for the outer rim.

DRIVE AXLE HUB CONVERSION

Since the early 1980s, Italeri has provided three basic wheel types on European trucks. The first were the accurate five-hole 1970s-style rims moulded with Volvo hubs - supplied mostly with fine-threaded two-piece plastic tyres. Later, a set of generic wheels with rounded holes and drive axle reduction hub appeared, which was mostly available with relatively rough drive axle-pattern tyres. The early 1990s brought brand new rubber tyres with fantastic detail, realistic highway pattern and modern European rims with oval holes. These new rims had a different type of drive axle hub, which was of a smaller diameter and a relatively universal shape…but were too long for modern axles.

Reworking these hubs became, let's say, a basic step in wheel conversion. These 90s rims are fine for many modern trucks. The biggest issue is the hub length, and that can be changed easily. However, the generic shape is not perfect and still far away from some designs (such as the very specific Scania hubs), but it will do its job on most trucks and will look far better than the original without any need for resin replacements.

The first step in converting the wheel is the same, no matter which particular wheel hub you want to use. The rim central hole has to be drilled or cut out for, which a 10mm drill is very handy, but a scalpel can also do the job. The spare wheel rim can be used as a stencil here. The separated hub now has to be shortened to about a half its original length, and glued to the inner rim. The axle shaft also has to be shortened.

If you are more demanding, resin hubs will probably be your choice. These are available for most well-known truck manufacturers, either separately, together with a disc brake or even a full axle and suspension conversion. All the hubs are designed to fit Italeri rims, on which the hub has to be removed (as described previously). Furthermore, the axle shaft

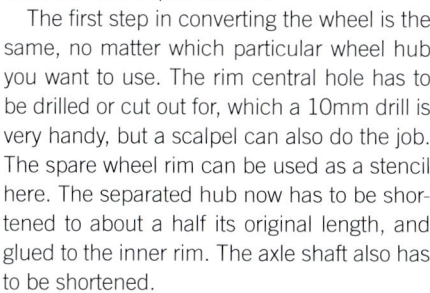

4. An array of the European style rims supplied in the italeri kit: five-hole rims with Volvo hubs (left), early generic (centre) and late generic European rims (right).

5. During the conversion, the pin from the rim should be removed entirely.

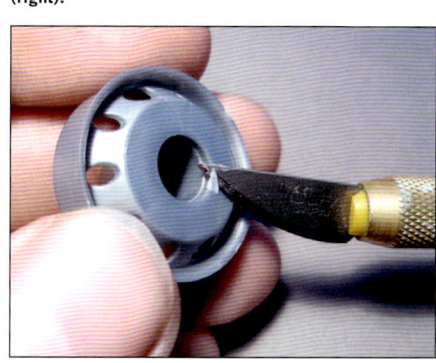

6. Now cut out the hub section from the outer rim using a scalpel. A 10 mm drill can be used eventually.

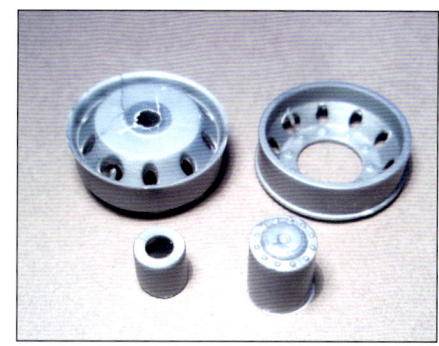

7. The inner and outer rim with both the pin and hub removed. The hub can now be shortened or replaced with a resin one.

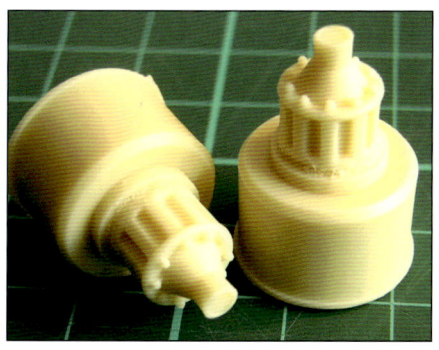

8. An example of the resin Scania drive axle hubs, which could be used as a replacement for the unsuitable Italeri parts.

9. The same Scania hub installed on a modified Italeri axle; the nearby item is the Heller Scania 141 part for comparison.

TRUCK MODELLING

> All the fine details such as the photo-etched wheel chocks or hand-painted fittings on the air system bring the model to life.

length has to be modified or cut off completely. Patience and care are required here, to maintain the correct geometry of the axle and wheels.

There are also a couple of injection-moulded plastic hubs available in the Italeri accessories set No.3870. Unfortunately, the wheel hubs provided are far from anything in reality and can hardly be used, as either the diameter or overall shape of these hubs is wrong. What is beneficial in this set, are the modern trailer axle rims with wheel hubs, and drive axle rims moulded with a hole that just needs a hub to be added, allowing you to avoid that tricky cutting and hub removal operation when converting a standard kit rim.

Although hubs can be a problem and need attention, the rims and tyres in most of the kits are much better. There are many wheel types and versions available in both 1/24 and 1/25 kits, and if you do not look at the hub details most of them are decent representations of the real thing, and there is a lot to choose from. Within each, scale wheels can be used from different kits to make your model more interesting, and even for some 1/25 kits, using 1/24 wheels does not look bad, despite not being absolutely correct. By combining different truck rim parts, a modern super single rim can also be created, which fits the wide 1/24 Italeri trailer tyre and the 3909 Italeri wheel set even contains new super single tyres with rims. Various wheels were offered by Italeri in many accessories sets, and the rubber tyres were often sold separately too. So, it really is up to you whether you need something extra, or you can just make do with what you find in the plastic. For those mad about wheels (like me) there are plenty of beautiful after-market parts available.

IVECO STRALIS WHEELS

In the case of my Iveco I wanted to replace both the rims and hubs. I am quite sensitive about wheel details and I am very picky in this area. Therefore, I only rarely use the wheels from the kit (which actually proves the quality of the Prostar wheels, as in the previous chapter as I did not feel any need to replace them). The truck I wanted to build had super single wheels on the front axle. I therefore purchased the conversion set from Model Maker Shop, which contains a set of modern aluminium super single rims with tyres and a Scania wheel hub. All these parts are in beautifully designed injection-moulded plastic, and the set also provides accurate real rubber super single tyres. I liked the Austrian set so much that I wanted to have it on my model, although the real vehicle has ordinary steel rims. I used the rims out of box but the wheel hub was modified to look a more like the Iveco hub. The drive axle outer rims are resin castings based on reworked old Italeri rims, which have modified holes and removed wheel hubs; the inner rims are standard Italeri old rims with the pin for the outer rim removed. The drive axle hubs are true jewels (Vielen Dank, Guido!) and working with them was a pleasure. They fitted my rims perfectly and look fantastic. The rear tyres are standard Italeri items.

My intention was to build a clean vehicle. I therefore only sprayed the rims with Mr.Finishing Surfacer 1500 Black, followed by Mr. Colour Silver No.8, which seems to be one of the best silver paints on the market. The bolt caps on the front rims and bolts on the rear rims were hand-painted with a brush using my favourite Vallejo Dark Rubber grey. No weathering was done, except for a fine coat of highly diluted Tamiya X-19 Smoke, which was applied via airbrush to ensure a darker tone on the rim silver.

Compared to the original kit parts, the modified wheels look far better and provided a great base for an attractive and original model...tyres, rims and hubs always deserve attention and care. On various trucks in different countries and time periods, some specific wheels were used, which can be portrayed in scale terms to help your model stand out and be more realistic.

The original Italeri rim and the finished wheel for my Stralis, with the resin rim based, on the early Italeri wheels and a fully detailed CNC milled wheel hub.

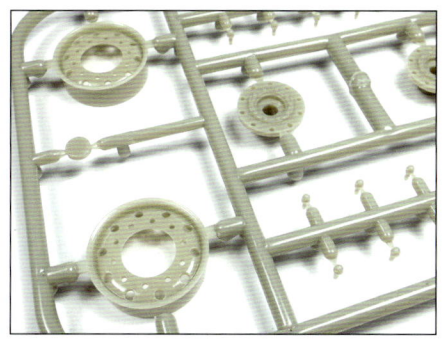

2. Injection-moulded plastic rims from Modelmakershop were used for the front axle.

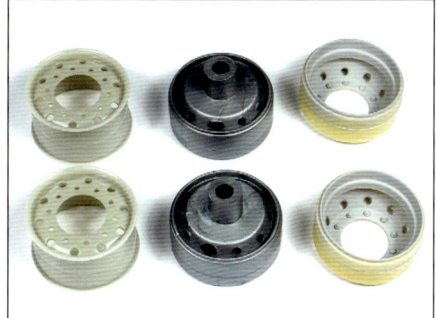

3. A complete set of the Stralis wheels. Note that the pin on the inner rear rims was yet to be removed.

4. All the parts were primed with Gunze Mr.Finishing surfacer black and sprayed with Mr.Color Silver No.8.

5. Tamiya X-19 Smoke was used to create shadows and depth.

6. The front rim bolt caps were supplied as separate parts, which makes their painting easy.

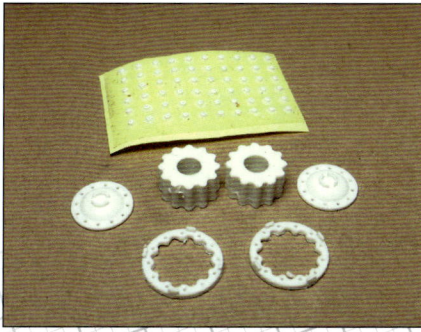

7. The drive axle hubs are CNC milled parts supplied by Guido Kehder.

1. All the components consisting of more parts (fuel tanks, air tanks, air bags) were assembled at first...

2. ...and therefore were ready for filling and sanding anytime the instructions demanded their use.

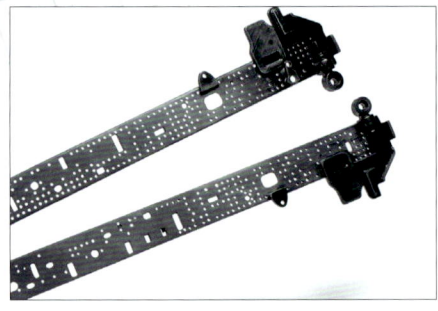
3. All the holes in the frame rails were drilled out.

4. For the fifth wheel, mounting rails and a photo-etched drilling stencil were used.

5. Once the frame was assembled it was primed with Mr.Surfacer, followed by my own mixed dark grey.

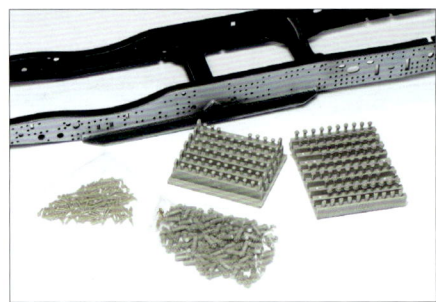
6. Resin bolts and rivets were employed for detailing the chassis.

> *When detailing and converting models, having various types and sizes of bolts available is always handy, as they help with adding another level to the authenticity.*

5.4.3 THE FRAME AND CHASSIS

The kit frame is unique among all 1/24 and 1/25 scale kits. It represents a modern component with a large number of holes, used for installing various accessories across version arrangements. For the first time, these numerous holes have been moulded in the frame rail, providing interesting detail. Since this was revealed, it has always been a big topic of discussion whether to leave the holes in the frame rails (moulded shallow and blind) and just highlight them with a dark wash, or drill them all (there are more than 100 holes in the frame rails!). I made my choice easily, as I saw a couple of models built with the drilled holes not only showing that it is feasible to do it, but also that it looks great. For comparison, I used a hand drill for one frame rail and my Proxxon drill for the other. Despite my doubts, using the electric drill was quicker and with no compromise in precision. It took just one evening to drill the holes and clean both rails and it was actually rather fun. Furthermore, the work resulted in probably the most realistic frame rails I have ever had in my hands. The procedure was not particularly complex, as the moulded holes guided the drill, so the work was quick and easy.

All parts were sprayed with Mr.Surfacer 1200 prior to assembly to reveal any scratches and other imperfections. Just a few more issues were discovered, which were solved by sanding, and once sprayed again and dry, the frame was assembled with Tamiya Extra Thin Cement.

Meanwhile, I assembled all the kit parts consisting of halves, requiring further cleaning and filling. Details such as the air tanks, brake chambers, fuel tank and air bags were glued with Tamiya Extra Thin and left aside for a few days.

BOLTS AND BOLT HEADS

When detailing and converting models, having various types and sizes of these components available is always handy, as they help with adding extra authenticity. When searching for bolts there are various choices.

The most precise, but usually also the most expensive way to go, are resin bolts, nuts and rivets provided by various companies in various sizes, covering the needs of model builders of all main scales. In such sets, various combinations of nuts, bolts and washers are available, for any number of applications. Superglue has to be used for these, which makes their use less than simple.

A limited amount of plastic rivets, nuts and bolts is also available. The most recent and accessible are probably those supplied by MENG Model.

Last but not least are the nuts and bolt heads you can make yourself, and two basic methods are available. First there are a few sizes of hexagonal rod available from Plastruct, which can be cut into separate bolt heads and glued with standard styrene cement, which makes this a cheap and simple solution. If more details are required, such as a washer and nut with a piece of bolt end, more parts have to be combined and here the process becomes more challenging and requires patience.

Another way of making your own bolts and rivets are with various types of punch and die sets, available for both circular and hexagonal shapes. I have shown this on the Prostar wiring in the previous chapter. This tool may seem expensive, but with just a piece of plastic sheet they give you an almost unlimited source of bolts. Again, in the basic shape they provide you with just a flat pad, so if there is something like a washer under a head bolt required, for example, this has to be made with combining more pieces of various pads or plastic profiles.

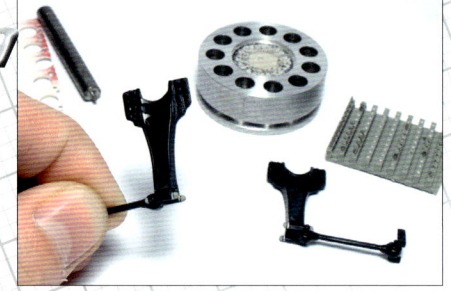
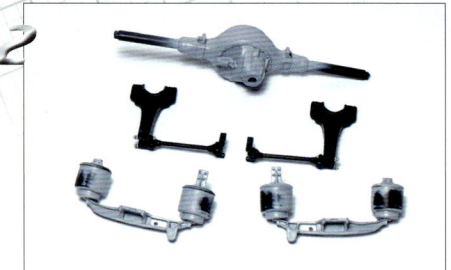

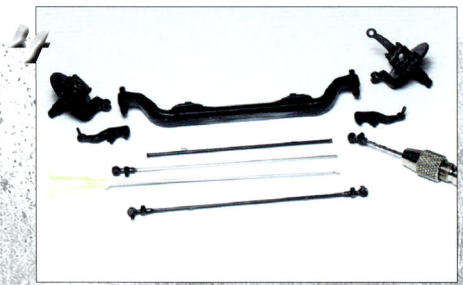
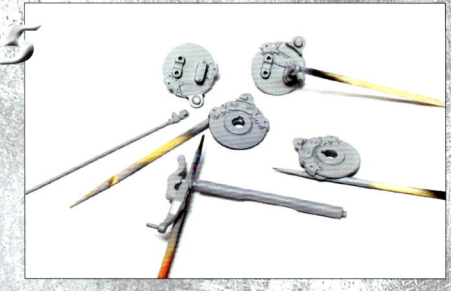

> *The battery box, exhaust silencer and the air intake filter assembly were detailed with a few parts from the CTM Stralis set.*

1. Resin bolts helped detail the rear axle suspension.

2. The rear suspension assembly is slightly different when compared to the Prostar, and the airbags are moulded together with the steel suspension parts.

3. The chassis parts prior to the assembly. Note the aluminium air tanks were painted separately prior to their installation.

4. The front axle exhibits classic assembly. The brittle tie rod was replaced with a syringe needle.

5. The brake discs come straight from the kit and have pleasing detail.

6. The discs were sprayed with Mr Color silver after priming.

SUSPENSION AND CHASSIS DETAILS

On this model you will see many different ways of using most of the bolts mentioned above. The first chance to use them here was on the fifth wheel mounting rails. I used a mixture of bolts and rivets just like on the real vehicle. Other opportunities for using the bolts were on the suspension parts and axles, however, in terms of moulding, the bolt detail on the Stralis kit is some of the finest I have ever seen on 1/24 scale trucks. Compared to the Prostar, the Stralis detail looks sharper and more realistic.

The next step involved the air tanks. On the Stralis there are more avenues to take, as on some units all the air tanks are painted in the chassis colour, while others feature natural aluminium air tanks...and the latter was my option. Not only that, reference photos revealed them on my truck but they also showed another colour on the dark grey chassis to make it more interesting.

The painting of the chassis on this model, in contrast to the Prostar, somehow became a continual process. Once the frame was assembled I sprayed all the internal surfaces grey, and then some bolts were added. All the following components such as the suspension and axles were sprayed prior to the installation. There were reasons for doing it this way; the air tanks having a different colour, and the suspension assembly, on which the air bag painting is quite difficult after installation. In addition, painting the parts separately gives you more control of the painting quality, which is very handy on a model that represents a tidy vehicle. I also like to keep the additional details in different colours to make it all more interesting. Comparing this process to that on the Prostar reveals that there are more ways of painting the chassis, and sometimes one is more useful than the other. It's also the same for wiring.

A special consideration on the Stralis axles are disc brakes, as it's the very first time a model truck has them on all four wheels. They look great, so I decided to spend extra time painting them. I started with Mr.Color silver, onto which a few layers of Tamiya Smoke were sprayed. This created a shiny dark metal surface. In the next step the brake mechanism was hand-painted with dark grey and the parts were weathered with a mixture of black and dust pigments. The outer edges were painted with Lifecolour acrylics from the Rust and Dust set, providing diverse rust coverage. Otherwise, the axle and suspension build sequence is normal. Again, the front axle steering mechanism needs care and patience, but the overall process is nearly the same as on the Prostar. What I have seen on other Stralis builds (and I have followed this myself) is replacing the connecting rod with a piece of wire (a hypodermic needle in my case), providing extra stiffness to the mechanism. Both the front and rear brake chambers were detailed with fittings painted with Agama metal colours. All the parts were then attached to the chassis easily.

The battery box, exhaust silencer and the air intake filter assembly were detailed with a few parts from the CTM Stralis set, painted and attached to the chassis. The battery box has no bottom, so I enclosed it with a piece of styrene sheet. As some of the plastic parts (battery box cover and rear mudguards) are apparently much brighter when compared to the dark chassis, I mixed a special grey colour for them and used it on all these parts around the vehicle. While there is just one fuel tank in the kit, the vehicle I was building had two fuel tanks so I used another from a spare Stralis kit and cut it to length between the battery box and the rear mudguard. As the

5. DETAILING YOUR MODEL-FIRST LEVEL

1. Darker metal tones were made with a light coat of Tamiya X-19.

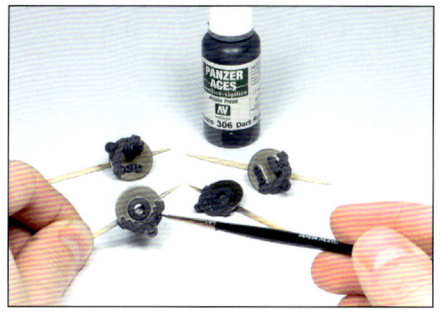

2. The calipers were hand painted with Vallejo dark grey.

3. The rust on the disc outer edges comes from Lifecolor's popular Rust and Dust set.

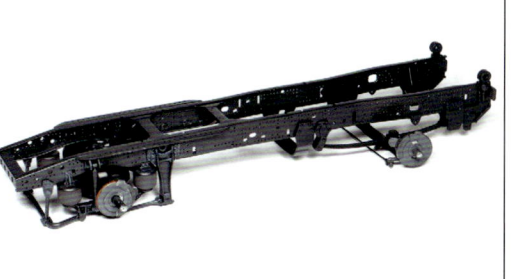

6. The frame fitted with axles and brakes. The air bags were hand painted and weathered with black soot pigments.

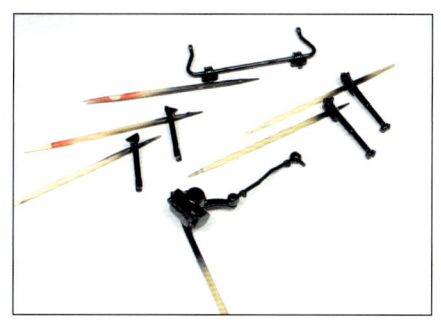

7. The well-moulded steering, shock absorbers and anti-roll bar were painted separately.

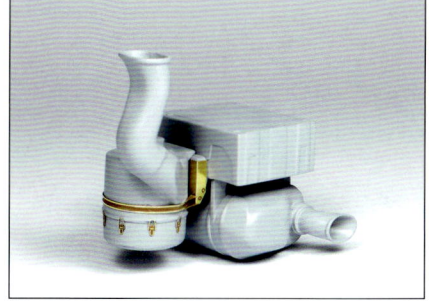

4. Once painted, the parts were weathered with a dark wash and pigments.

5. All the fittings were painted with silver and brass spirit-based Agama metal paints.

8. CTM photo-etched parts were used to detail the exhaust, battery box and intake filter assembly.

CTM detail set contains both the tank mounts and straps, I removed all the tank surface details. The tanks needed filling, and my favourite black Superglue was used together with plastic strips to cover the holes created by removing the mounts. I had to combine a pair of the CTM sets to get five tank supports for both tanks, and assembling them took time but the result is very convincing. From the same source comes a generic set of various weld sizes, which were added on the outer tank edges. Black insulation tape was used under the straps during assembly. Again, Mr. Surfacer and Mr.Colour silver were employed for painting the tanks, and the mounts and straps were painted separately. The mudgards were just cleaned and did not require any modifications.

The rear lamps are a great example of how rear lights are made in most kits…now, let's look at realistic painting. At first the background was sprayed with silver. This actually prevents the background and glue from being visible on the finished parts. The silver was followed by black, which represents the part outer plastic. In both cases the front clear part was masked with Tamiya paint. The next step is a little tricky and needs a steady hand.

Using Tamiya X-27 Clear Red and X-27 Clear Yellow (I mix my own orange from these two) I paint all the lamp sections. With the background painted silver, the clear colours give the lights realistic depth. I have also painted four photo-etched side marker lights fitted on the rear mudguard, these being sourced from a generic detail set. The lights fitted the mudguards perfectly, as well as the mud flaps enhanced with the CTM reflective boards.

The kit comes with a pair of wheel chocks. These represent a plastic version which has a quite complex structure in reality, and the scale version is not very convincing. I there-

TRUCK MODELLING

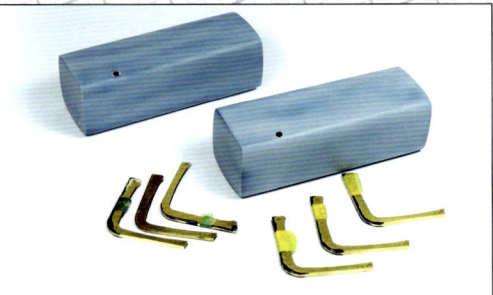
1. The CTM detail set provides realistic fuel tank mounts. The originals were removed and the tanks were filled and sanded.

2. CTM's detail set also provided the tank end cap welds.

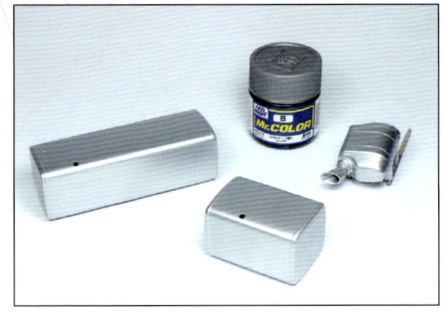
3. My favorive Mr.Color No.8 was used on the tanks and exhaust.

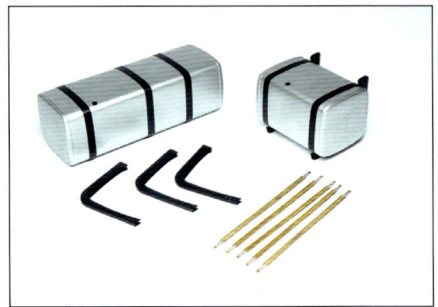
4. The mounts were painted separately, and separate stripes of black vinyl tape were used under the mounting straps.

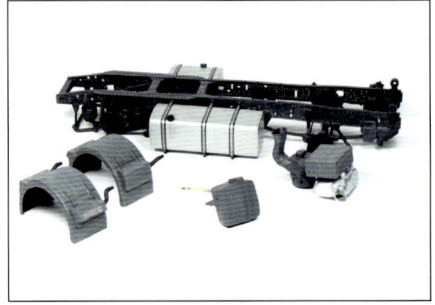
5. At this stage, basic oil paint filters were applied to the chassis and all components.

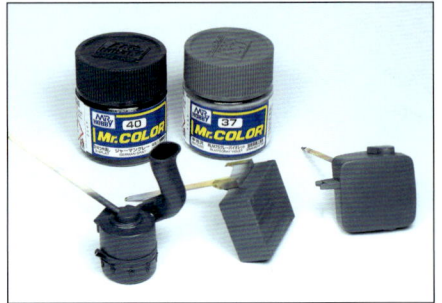
6. Note that more different grey tones were used on the plastic parts.

fore decided to replace them with CTM photo-etched wheel chocks, which represent the zinc-plated steel version. These chocks come with individual holders and the whole assembly looks just like the real part - and elevates this area to another level.

The susie bracket is moulded together with the cab suspension and transmission cover. It was detailed with fittings and a couple of wires, resin bolts and a PE working light lens. The catwalk, however, is a story all on its own. It is the most beautifully moulded part I have ever seen on a scale model truck. It is so fine that even the CTM detail set does not offer a better replacement. The fifth wheel and its mounting plate look great as well….no need for detailing at all.

WIRING

The wiring on this model was a post-painting operation. It was caused by the aluminium air tanks that were added only after the frame painting. I therefore used another approach than that you would have seen on the Prostar.

Once the chassis was ready for the air tanks' installation, all the other air circuit-related systems (brakes, suspension), as well as the electrical components (batteries) were already fitted on the chassis. As a first step, a bundle that leads to the battery switch positioned next to the battery box was assembled. Again, the ever-useful CTM cable ties were used for this, while the battery switch was scratch built. The bundle was then fitted to one of the cross members, and its end was hidden under the catwalk. Next, the air tanks received resin fittings and rubber wires. One after another the air tanks were fitted into the chassis and their hoses were brought tight together to form a pair of bundles, each running inside one of the frame rails from the back of the chassis towards the vehicle front. The

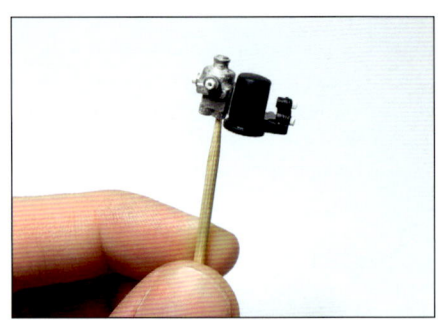
7. The chassis was again fitted with air valves. Most of them are based on KFS parts, detailed with fittings.

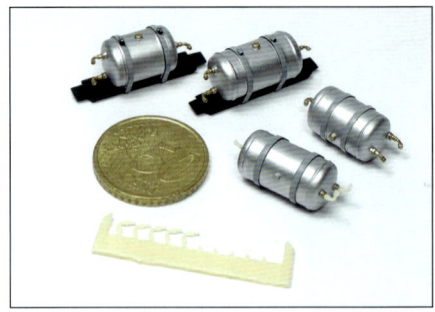
8. The first wiring step was to add the resin fittings to the air tanks. Note that all the details are painted in different colours.

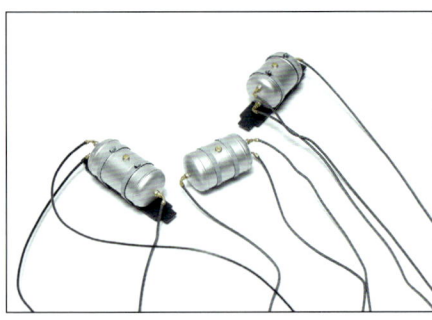
9. Each air tank outlet then received rubber fibre, tied into bundles and fitted into the chassis.

5. DETAILING YOUR MODEL-FIRST LEVEL

1. The rear lamps were painted in three steps. At first the rear area was sprayed silver. Clear outer surfaces were masked with Tamiya tape.

2. In the next step, black was applied over silver. Thanks to this the light internals appear silver.

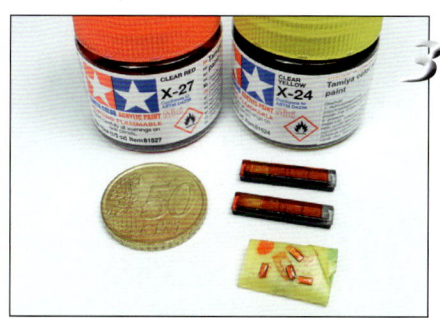
3. Once the masking tape was removed the clear parts of the lamps were hand painted with Tamiya clear acrylics.

4. The fuel lines were made of a few rubber and vinyl fibres and tied with CTM photo-etched cable ties.

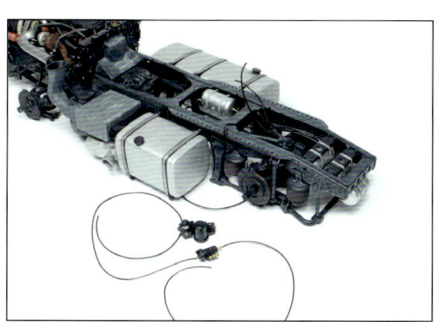
5. The air valves were painted, fitted with wires and installed in the frame.

6. Note how much is actually hidden by the fifth wheel, under which no extra detailing is really necessary.

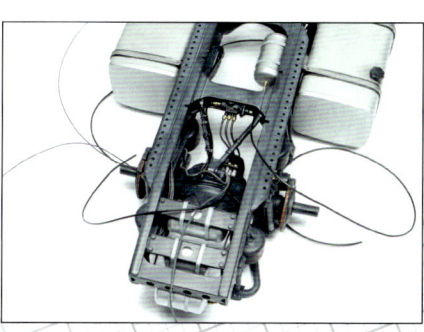
7. One after another the cable ends were attached to the components, such as brakes and air bags.

TRUCK MODELLING

ends of these were hidden under the fifth wheel. Two KFS white metal air valves were rebuilt, detailed with resin fittings and one was coupled to an air dryer that comes from the Stralis kit. One of these was fitted on the frame rail under the fifth wheel and linked to the brakes, while the other was fitted in front of the fifth wheel and its outlets were linked to the nearby air tank. Two generic bundles were also added where the chassis did not look busy enough, and their ends were hidden in dark corners. Following the real vehicle's arrangement, fuel lines were added to the large fuel tank, again with the housing and fittings. A couple of scratch-built ABS valves were fitted outside the frame rails near the front wheels, and were linked to the front brakes and their chambers.

Although almost wired completely, this operation was straightforward, easy and just a few valves were required for overall authenticity. As all the wiring material used was black rubber and wire, there was no need for any painting except for the valves, which were painted in the chassis colour and the fittings picked out in silver and brass. Compared to the Prostar, there was no extensive hand-painting required, but as all the parts were assembled on the finished chassis, precise glue application was the key to success.

5.5.1 THE ENGINE

Next comes the powerplant. In comparison to other kits, the Cursor 13 available in this kit is of a decent standard. It has a well-moulded structure on the engine block and the transmission. However, there is also a significant number of parts that are too simplified. Some of the pipes are hollow and have no detail moulded underneath. The intake filter outlet pipe is pretty poor, and I spent time rebuilding it. On the whole the engine is good, but does provide extra detailing opportunities. I collected reference photos, posted them on the wall in my hobby room and followed them during the whole engine building and painting process.

The cases were assembled as per the instructions, primed and sprayed dark grey, and all the individually painted details were attached to these. The radiator and the charge cooler are good but still deserved PE radiator mesh, which again comes from CTM. All the water and air pipes were detailed with connecting hose and photo-etched hose clamps, which may be challenging but bring

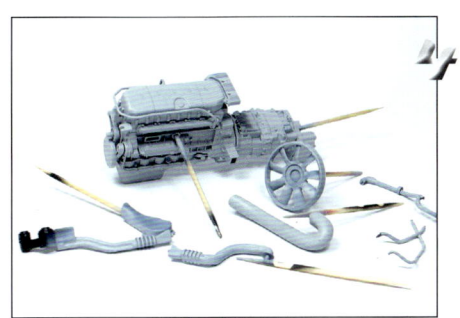 

1. The engine halves were glued and allowed to dry overnight.

2. The transmission cover and susie bracket were detailed with bolts and fittings.

3. I have collected a set of reference photos of both the real and model engines, which helped during the detailing.

4. Most engine parts were just cleaned and primed. However, the main intake pipe was hollow and needed filling.

5. The block and transmission cases are well detailed and look authentic.

6. The rubber hose on the cooling circuit and air inlet pipes is made of black vinyl tape and CTM photo-etched hose clamps.

7. The engine's right-hand side was fitted with a new power steering fluid reservoir, scratch-built fuel filter and wiring.

the engine details to another level. The turbocharger was replaced with a resin item and a new oil filter was scratch built from Evergreen profiles. New details on the right-hand side of the engine were added: the stop and start buttons assembly, fuel filter and power steering oil reservoir, and some resin fittings, hoses and wiring. A spiral pressure air pipe was made of a lead wire. As the transmission in the kit is fitted with a hydraulic retarder (which actually lacks many details) I added a cooling pipe, visible at the gearbox rear cover. It is made from a piece of Evergreen rod and detailed with hose clamps. Unfortunately, there are no decals on the engine and I really missed the typical Cursor sign on the rocker cover. But I did at least add generic warning signs from the KFS decal sheet and the Iveco sign comes from the kit decals.

5.5.2 WEATHERING

As you may have noticed from the photos of this model, I was painting all the parts continuously. I actually painted the chassis at a very early building stage and added even weathering to it at that moment, and every single component was painted separately before being attached to the chassis. The weathering, however, represents a prescribed set of steps and can be explained separately. The first thing is that this truck represents a relatively new vehicle. With that in mind, you may end up with just grey tones as there is no space for any rust, and the result could be somewhat dull. So for artistic purposes, rust tones were applied locally.

The very first step was carried out quite early on. Right after painting, dry-brushing was used on details such as bolt heads and sharp edges to highlight them, as the whole assembly looked quite dark…and the light blue Humbrol enamel I used highlighted the details perfectly. Once dry, I followed with light dust tone oil paints along the outer vertical surfaces of the frame rails, as a basic layer for the forthcoming weathering steps. It was quite easy, as at this moment no other components blocking the access. A few light grey filters were applied all over the chassis, axles and suspension to provide random effects and more tones to the uniform base coat. The complex parts and assemblies (such as the battery box assembly, fifth wheel, susie bracket) were weathered separately prior to their installation. Again, this was done mostly with light dust oil paints. I use a fine brush for painting vertical streaks, which were blended using a flat brush once the oil paints were drying. I mostly used just oil paints from a cardboard palette, which helps with removing the oil (and reducing the drying time) and blended them with a dry brush with no thinner at all.

Dust filters were applied all over the engine and transmission, although most of the surfaces are covered with other parts so I did not spend much time on this. The exhaust manifold was painted with Vallejo and Lifecolor acrylics, with extra pigments added for tonal variation. An interesting fact is that the exhaust

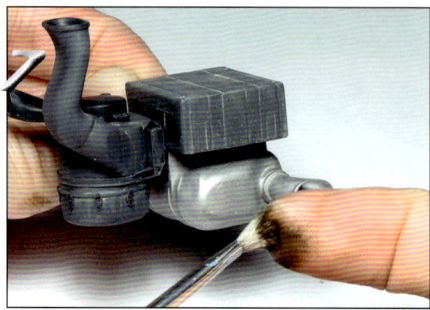

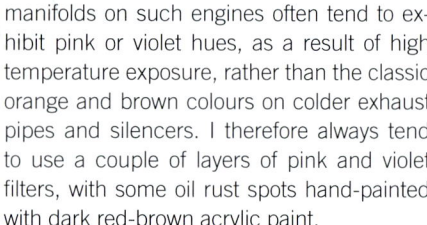
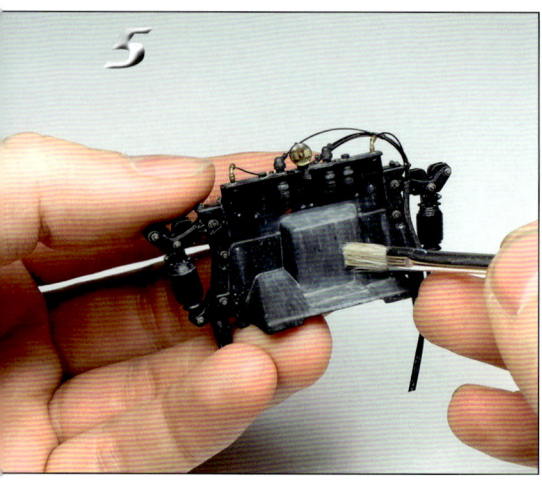

manifolds on such engines often tend to exhibit pink or violet hues, as a result of high temperature exposure, rather than the classic orange and brown colours on colder exhaust pipes and silencers. I therefore always tend to use a couple of layers of pink and violet filters, with some oil rust spots hand-painted with dark red-brown acrylic paint.

Once the chassis was assembled and all parts such as fuel tanks, engine and mudguards were added, I went over all the surfaces, added more filter layers and a black oil wash to details such as bolts and fittings. On the chassis bottom and frame sides around the wheels and mudguards, dust tone AK Interactive weathering enamels were sprayed with an airbrush, creating a heavier dirt layer. The dust and dirt were applied using the speckling method, which provides fine and random effects; I repeated this with more dust and earth colours, as well as with black.

The final stage of the vehicle's weathering, which could be called oil paint rendering (a term described in detail by Michael Rinaldi), was done when the chassis was already on the wheels and all details were in place. Various oil paints were applied to particular areas of the chassis to add convincing rust tones, and enhance the visual appearance of the chassis. I have used rust tones, dark dirt and black. In some areas more concentrated dust was added with a fine brush and blended.

5.5.3 THE CAB AND EXTERIOR DETAILS

Building the Stralis cab is a pleasing contrast to the Prostar cab. While the latter has a non-tilting and almost one-piece shell cab, the Stralis has a classic 1/24 scale tilting cab that consists of separate panels. Tilting the cab provides access to the engine and reveals the cab bottom, which means details also have to be added to the floor bottom. Correct geometry and precise work is required here, as the cab position affects the model's overall look and proportions. Furthermore, the fit has to be precise here in order to prevent any cab tilting issues and part conflict.

THE INTERIOR

I must admit that during this build I have ignored the instruction sheet. Italeri suggests building the interior first, on which all the exterior parts are added one after another. But I always prefer to assemble the external cab shell first and spray it as one part. This ensures all the clean-up and assembly can be done prior to painting. This change in strategy did not have any effect on the cab exterior

1. Traditional dry-brushing highlighted bolts and details in darker areas.

2. Oil paints were used in chassis weathering, for both washes and filters. Note the cardboard pallete used to remove excess oil from the paints.

3. When applied, the filter is a highly diluted paint that consists of about 90 per cent thinner.

4. The filters were applied in many layers, creating soft color variations.

5. Vertical streaks were painted with AK Interactive enamels, left to dry for a couple of hours and blended with Odorless thinner and a flat brush.

6. The dust gathered on horizontal areas and in corners was made with AK Interactive enamels.

7. The speckling method was used for creating small dots of dust and dirt.

8. The rust on the exhaust manifold and turbocharger was cerated with Lifecolor's Rust and Dust set.

TRUCK MODELLING

5. DETAILING YOUR MODEL-FIRST LEVEL

1. Dust effects on the lower chassis areas were applied via airbrush, with highly diluted Mr.Color paints.

2. Once painted and weathered separately, all the components were attached to the chassis.

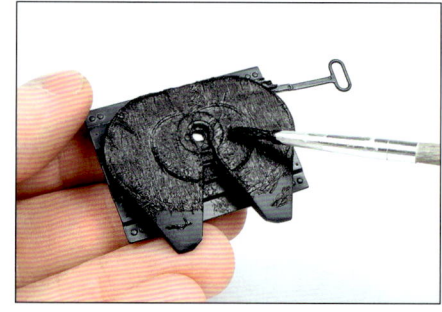
3. The grease on the fifth wheel is black oil paint applied with an old brush.

construction, but required a few modifications of the interior parts (trimming the floor front corners) and inserting the cab roof, dashboard, vertical walls and floor separately.

I started the interior with the floor part and its bottom. Not only were there large pin ejector marks visible (I covered these with circular pads made with a punch and die set, filled and sanded flat) but there are also many basic details missing. I therefore covered the whole area with Evergreen plastic sheets and built a pair of tool boxes. A rough surface texture was created by brushing thinned Tamiya putty, and the part was painted dark grey and weathered with oils and enamels, just like the mudguards.

Except for enclosing the hollow upper bunk with styrene sheet, all the interior parts were assembled as per the instruction sheet. The Stralis interior parts are well detailed… however, I have avoided detailing it as most of these refinements would remain hidden in the dark interior. All I did was to use all the CTM painted interior set parts. These cover the dashboard, but also other control panels around the cab including the vent meshes and seatbelts. The magazines and road maps were found on the internet, scaled down in Word and printed on a laser printer. The bottle of Coke comes from a 1/35 Plus Model detail set. Various Mr.Color and Tamiya acrylics were used on all these parts. I did not follow all the interior colours correctly, and rather used my own mixed tones. Dry-fitting of the interior components on the chassis revealed no issues.

THE CAB EXTERIOR AND DETAILS

The Stralis cab shell comprises four vertical walls to which the roof is attached. The front grille is moulded separately and provides the option of building it either opened or closed. Making a pair of hinges allows the grille to open, but I did not want to spend time with detailing this area. To assemble the parts, a combination of black Superglue and Tamiya Extra Thin was used to fix the parts quickly, but provide a strong join. No putty was required and everything fitted perfectly, which makes this probably the best cab in 1/24 scale. As no serious modifications were re-

5. DETAILING YOUR MODEL-FIRST LEVEL

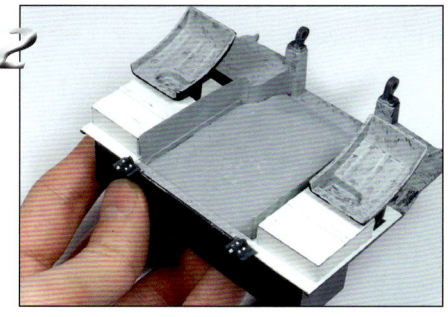

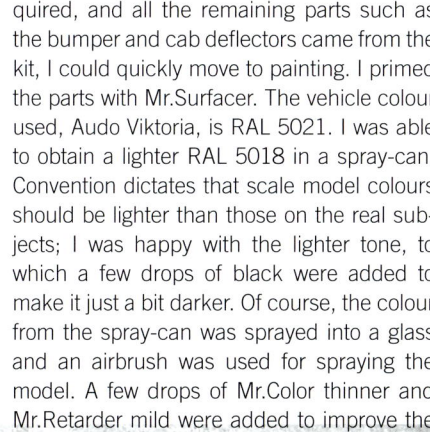

Test fitting of the interior shell on the chassis to verify the clearances under the floor

1. The cab floor had deep ejector pin marks, which were filled by plastic pads made with a punch and die set.

2. Openings in the cab floor were filled with plastic card, and insulation panels and tool boxes were added too.

3. The part was weathered with filters and washes mixed from AK Interactive enamels and 502 Abteilung oils.

4. The upper bunk is a hollow shell, so I enclosed it with plastic sheet and let the part dry overnight.

5. After basic cleaning-up, all interior parts were primed with Mr.Finishing surfacer black

6. All the interior parts were sprayed with Mr.Color light and dark grey.

quired, and all the remaining parts such as the bumper and cab deflectors came from the kit, I could quickly move to painting. I primed the parts with Mr.Surfacer. The vehicle colour used, Audo Viktoria, is RAL 5021. I was able to obtain a lighter RAL 5018 in a spray-can. Convention dictates that scale model colours should be lighter than those on the real subjects; I was happy with the lighter tone, to which a few drops of black were added to make it just a bit darker. Of course, the colour from the spray-can was sprayed into a glass and an airbrush was used for spraying the model. A few drops of Mr.Color thinner and Mr.Retarder mild were added to improve the paint spraying properties.

I am quite familiar with the decals made by decalprint.de, so applying these was straightforward. I cut out all the logos from the decal sheet and applied one after the other, using Mr.Mark Setter for all and Mr.Mark softer for those covering any gaps, to make sure they adhered to the cab surface properly. I let the decals dry for a couple of hours and applied a few fine coats of varnish over them. Again, I used aerosol varnish applied with an airbrush, as I was happy with the extremely quick drying time. I always use to varnish, sand and polish the cab until the decal carrier film disappeared completely within the clear coat layer, so I had to sand the cab surface gently a few times between spraying, which took me a couple of days but the result is great and very realistic.

Once completely dry I could also mask the black areas around the windows with Tamiya

TRUCK MODELLING

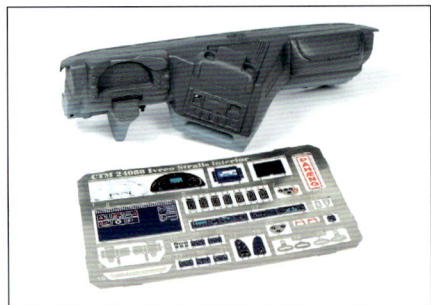
1. The dashboard was detailed with painted CTM parts.

2. For assembly, the dashboard was left separate until later.

3. To make the interior more visually atractive, magazine covers and road maps were scaled down and printed.

4. These were cut out and arranged on the dashboard and over the cab floor and bunk.

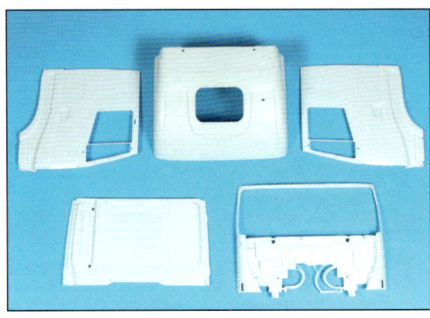
5. The cab exterior consists of separate panels.

6. The cab assembly revealed that the cab parts are so precise that no filling is necessary.

7. Custom decals were drawn by Jan Moštěk and printed by decalprint.de.

8. Once applied and sprayed with clear gloss varnish, the cab surface was polished with GSI and Tamiya polishing compounds.

9. Thanks to using acrylic paints, the cab was finished within a couple of days...including the decals, varnish and final polishing.

tape, and spray them flat black. Finally, just Mr.Finishing surfacer was used for this. Also sprayed were the door handles, windscreen wipers and all the mirrors, which were just cleaned-up and did not need any modification at all. Mirror glass comes from the CTM detail set. All these parts fitted the cab perfectly although the door mirror assembly needs care. None of the air horns I had available were close enough to those on the real vehicle, so I made my own using various parts from Italeri horns in my spares box. I sprayed them with gloss black and Alclad II Chrome. The roof AC unit was a one-piece casting and, unfortunately, full of air bubbles so just the basic clean-up and filling took a few hours.

The CTM detail set covers the grille and all the mesh and lettering. The top bar grille with Stralis letters was sprayed blue and the paint from the letters was scraped off gently, revealing the shiny nickel-plated letters. All the mesh fitted the kit parts perfectly and there was no need for any modification. The Iveco grille letters and door power rating numbering were attached carefully one by one with Superglue. A typical detail that Audo Viktoria vehicles carry on the bumper is a pair of boards...one for the ADR marking and the other for transport of waste. Both these came from the CTM detail set, the letter A was cut out of a Revell Büssing decal sheet. The number plates were drawn by my friend Karel Václavík (who is always helpful when I need something in Corel draw), printed on paper and covered with clear tape.

The head lamps are a distinct detail of the bumper. I decided to enhance them with photo-etched light lenses, which mostly came from the CTM set. The background was made with chromed Bare-Metal Foil. The light frames and indicator lights were brush-painted with Vallejo and Tamiya acrylics. The bumper

5. DETAILING YOUR MODEL-FIRST LEVEL

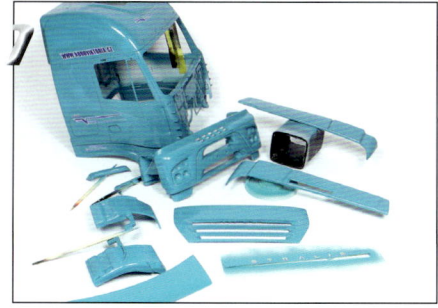

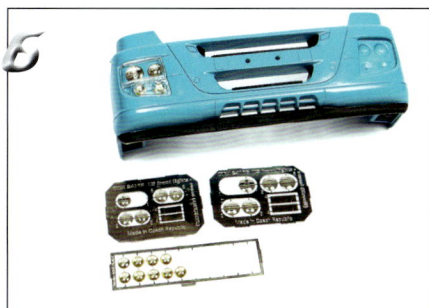

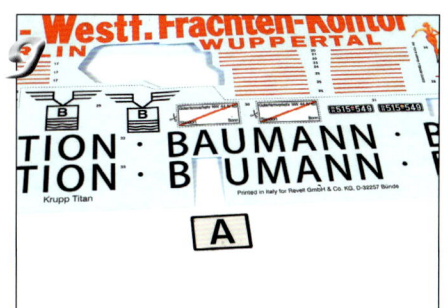

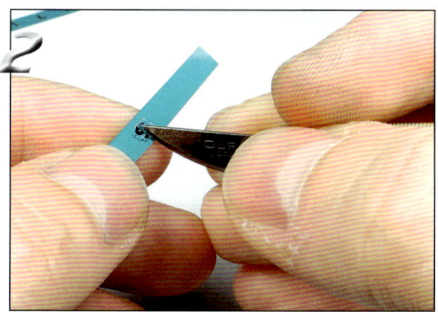

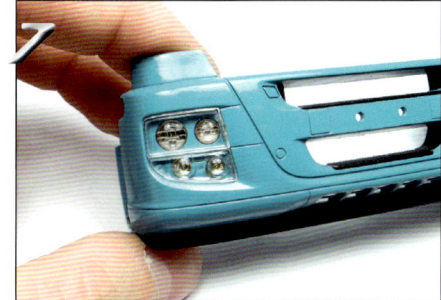

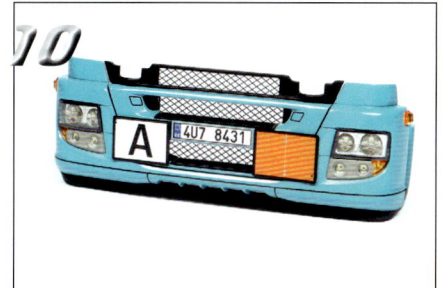

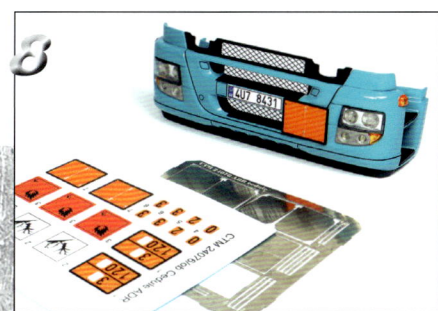

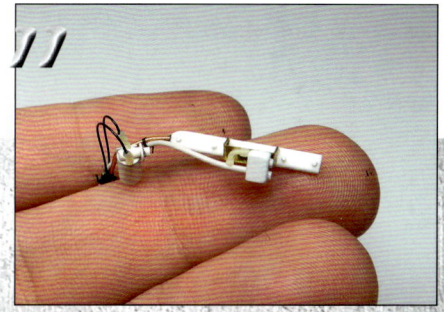

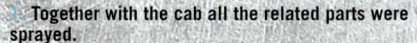

1. Together with the cab all the related parts were sprayed.

2. The upper grille's photo-etched strip with Stralis letters was sprayed blue without priming, and the paint was peeled from the letters using a sharp scalpel tip.

3. Although it may look like everything is almost finished here, there are still many things that can go wrong during the final model assembly. Patience and care is important here.

4. The finished grille parts, detailed with the CTM photo-etched set and ready for assembly

5. The window rubbers and cab plastic parts were masked with Tamiya tape and sprayed flat black.

6. The bumper was detailed with a mixture of CTM and Scala43 photo-etched light lenses.

7. The lights with PE lenses and clear kit parts during test-fitting

8. The ADR board comes from a separate CTM detail set, as does the example used for the 'A' plate.

9. The letter on the 'A' (A for Abfall – Waste in German) plate for vehicles carrying waste materials comes from Revell's Krupp decal sheet.

10. Finally, just a simple part such as the bumper was loaded with photo-etched details.

11. There are no upper mounts for the front wheel mudguards, so I made my own. The right-hand example was detailed with a fuel filter and cab tilting pump.

12. All the scratch-built components were always test-fitted on the chassis prior to painting.

TRUCK MODELLING

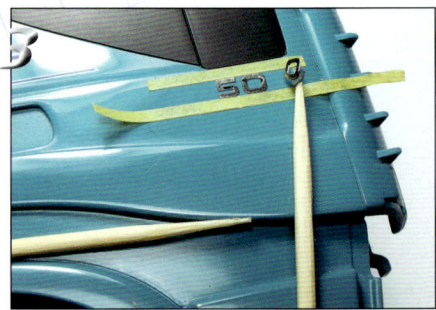
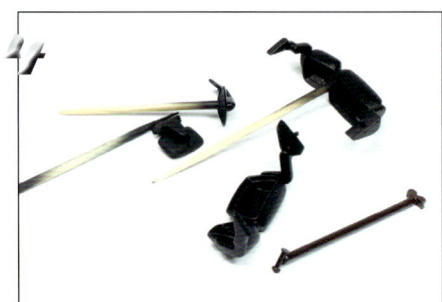
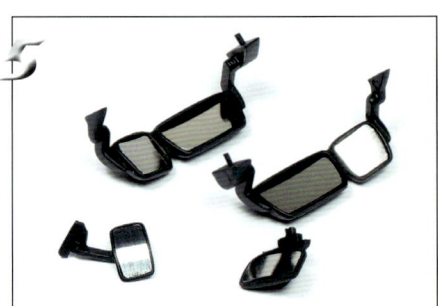

1. The complete cab exterior ready for assembly.

2. Water-based white glue was used during window installation to prevent any part damage.

3. Photo-etched power rating badges were applied to the doors, along with masking tape stripes used effectively as a guide.

4. For all the black plastic exterior parts, Mr.Surfacer finishing black was used as a top coat.

5. Working with mirrors was a pleasure, as CTM's detail set provides all the reflective surfaces.

6. The air horns are a mixture of a Scania items and horns from the Italeri accessories set.

5. DETAILING YOUR MODEL - FIRST LEVEL

> Although looking almost like an out-of-box build, the Stralis kit actually allows the modeller to focus on tiny details all around the vehicle, resulting in a highly realistic model

A Schmitz trailer was later added to the Stralis. A full description of that build is included in volume 2 of this book series.

internal areas were fitted with wiring for lights, and additional front mud flaps were made from a piece of aluminium sheet. Except for the bumper, a few more parts were processed during the cab assembly that actually belong to the chassis, and these were the front mudguards. Both were fitted with upper mounts that are not included in the kit. The right-hand mudguard carries the ad blue tank, and the upper mount was fitted with the cab tilt control and the fuel filter. The front wheel arches received black plastic extensions, cut out of a piece of Evergreen sheet.

Working with the cab glazing was fine. The clear parts are great and fitted perfectly. To avoid any damage, I used white glue on a fine brush to fix them. The interior installation was fine but what was unexpected was that I had to break the walls and floor apart, to allow all the parts to slide in perfectly. The rear cab wall details (intake and deflectors) are straight from the box; just the air inlet was fitted with PE mesh from the Stralis detail set.

A crucial step was installing the cab on the chassis. This fitted tightly and I highly recommend dry test-fitting to ensure there is enough clearance between the cab and bumper. To keep the cab in the tilted position I made a simple support bar. Finally, the area was detailed with susie cables, made the same way as described previously on the Prostar.

5.6 CONCLUSION

All in all, building the Stralis was an absolute pleasure. The kit has fantastic detail and its accuracy is great. Instead of correcting potential kit faults, I could focus on adding fine detail all around the model, which I really enjoyed. Although I prefer older vehicles, after finishing the Stralis I must admit there is much to admire on modern truck models.

6 PASSION FOR SU

Sooner or later, most modellers find their favourite topic among truck kits. European long-haul between the 1960s-80s became the one for me. Many great trucks from this period provide a constant flow of subjects I would like to transfer into 1/24 scale. Middle Eastern trucking has drawn a lot of attention recently, and one would never become fully dedicated to this era without building one of the well-known Astran vehicles.

> *As most truck kits come with engines, detailing them is a natural choice when an out-of-box model is simply not good enough for you.*

TRUCK MODELLING

SUPER-DETAILING

6.1 INTRODUCTION

I should point out that life would not be so easy without Ferdy De Martin's inspiring website toprun.ch and Ashley Coghill's book The Long Haul Pioneers…both providing a large amount of reference material.

Therefore, when the CTM photo-etched detail set for the Scania 141 was ready I immediately started building one. It was clear from the first moment that I am building one of the Astran units, and as this was meant to be a 4x2 LB141, the choice was pretty narrow because Astran operated just a few of these. Fortunately, all these vehicles are covered by Ashley's book and he kindly provided additional information anytime I needed to know more. The KJN 671P was my choice, as it provided extra details that cannot be seen on other Astran trucks; the stainless steel wheel trims and additional striping on the cab, and the bumper, make the model much more interesting.

As I really love these classic European trucks, I was going to add many details to the model. I was poised for serious scratch-building and was also ready for complex detailing of the engine, plumbing the chassis, and weathering, as the vehicles suffered much on their journeys from the UK to the Middle East. In other words, this model was meant to be far away from an out-of-the-box version. To do this, a large amount of reference material is usually required, but luckily I had a chance to take enough photos of various first-generation Scania vehicles at different model and truck shows around Europe. For detailing the engine and wiring the chassis, many detail views of various components were needed. Even the weathering stage requires photos to show various details of an ageing vehicle. In other words, for any project such as this, I typically prepare for months or even years before I cut into plastic, to ensure I have all the reference material covered.

Heller's Scania LB141 is a pretty old kit but is still very popular despite its age. Although some of the details are well rendered, and the cab fits perfectly, the wheels are poor and the frame concept calls for a replacement. The part quality on this kit varies from great to rubbish, and finally, around 50% of the original kit parts were used. However, I was quite confident with the CTM Scania LB 110-141 detail set as it provides great details including the grille, painted dashboard, a beautiful set of lights and many fine features that will give the model a much higher level of authenticity

6.2 DETAILING A TRUCK ENGINE

I started building this model with the powerplant. Different people like different things and it works for building models as well. During model construction, everyone finds one of the chapters their utmost favourite. For me it's engines…not just because I am an engine designer, but I'm generally fascinated by engines and I enjoy showing various associated details and painting techniques, making them the centrepiece of almost every model I build. Therefore, I would like to impart more of this in detail. Let's briefly go over all the main components and explore just how such an engine can be painted and weathered.

For this chapter there are two basic engines on which I'm going to present most of my work. It is a classic 14-litre Scania V8 engine built for the Astran Scania, a combination of both the Heller and Italeri parts, with many modifications and detailing, and a nearby competitor…a state of the art product on the six cylinder market in Europe in the late 1970's,the Volvo TD120C. The latter comes from the Italeri kit, but after much investigation and research (I do have the real engine in one of my trucks, so I know it very well) it was cut into pieces, fitted with components from Revell's 1/25 Volvo engine and prepared for casting, and later introduced as an exclusive resin set. On both these engines, basic components such as injection pumps, turbochargers, alternators or starter motors are shown, as well as other details such as pulleys, detailed manifolds, hoses with clamps and wiring. Most of these small refinements are resin castings based on converted and detailed

TECH SPEC — Scania LB 141

Kit: Heller Scania LB 141
Scale: 1:24
Accessories: CTM 022 Scania LB 141 detail set, CTM 14125 Scania LB badges, CTM 24123 Scania LB141 lights, CTM 24124 70's European tail lights, , CTM 24072 Hose clamps, CTM 24081 Cable binders, modified KFS TQ127x, TQ126x Split rim wheels, Italeri 764 Truck shop accessories, an array of low batch castings
Notes: One of the good old kits being reissued repeatedly

> The Heller Scania LB 141 is not a bad kit at all. Howeve,r looking at this Scania in detail reveals few parts from the original kit remained untouched.

engine parts from various model truck kits I had made for myself, to reduce time when detailing engines.

6.2.1 BASIC ENGINE COMPONENTS

I have already pointed out that most model truck engines share the assembly sequence and the differences are usually small. But I do not think there is a need for repeating what was shown in the case of the Prostar and Stralis. What I would like to add are comments on different engine parts, which might help you when adding details to them.

Engine block and transmission cases

The first step after a usual clean-up and basic assembly is focusing on the large parts. Nearly all of the main engine components are steel castings. Although kits show them all nice and smooth, I like adding a fine cast-steel structure as the sand-cast parts feature various surface imperfections. Although this is probably not perfectly in scale, it helps considerably during the painting and weathering stages.
I use either a thinned Tamiya putty or Mr.Surfacer for this, and an old brush, as it really suffers during the application due to the tapping motion. The more thinned the paint, the finer structure I get and this varies between large and small castings.

What is mostly missing on these large components are various sizes of bolts on the oil pan, around all the flanges and covers, and also most of the bolt bosses that are often moulded on the covers but not always used on each engine. Adding these technological features and the cast structure makes the parts look very realistic, and also provides the chance for painting as you get much more fine detail on which to apply dry-brushing and washes, for example. Many of the oil pans are also missing oil drain plugs.

Do not skimp on details for transmission, especially its rear end, as this is acutely visible on many trucks…especially if the catwalk is not fixed.

Cylinder heads assembly

Cylinder heads represent a complex component on which many fine details can be shown. Furthermore, the head with a rocker cover represents the very top of the engine and is always clearly visible. Starting from the top, fine small bolts can be added to the rocker cover and larger bolts to the head. In many kits, a simplified representation of the fuel lines is available but mostly just as surface ribs, which I recommend you remove and replace with wires. I also make separate injectors, to which both the feed and overflow pipes are attached.

Unfortunately, there are many other details moulded on cylinder heads, such as exhaust or water manifolds, which would look much better if produced as separate parts. This often does not look very realistic, but cut-

6. PASSION FOR SUPER-DETAILING

1. On 'vee' diesel engines the valley is often very simplified and provides space for detailing.

2. Out-of-box transmission cases call for detailing with bolts and bosses.

3. In addition, a cast steel structure was made on this Volvo gearbox using thinned Tamiya putty.

4. The large engine block is fitted with smaller parts such as the oil sump and clutch housing..

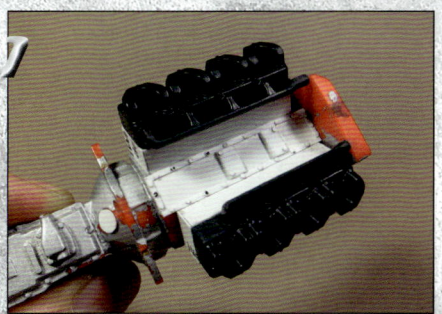
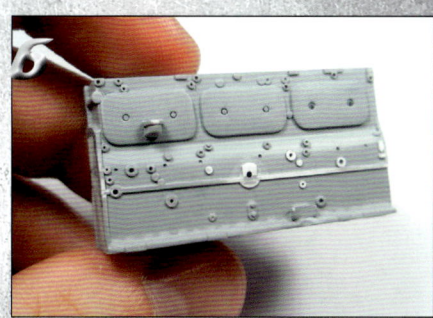

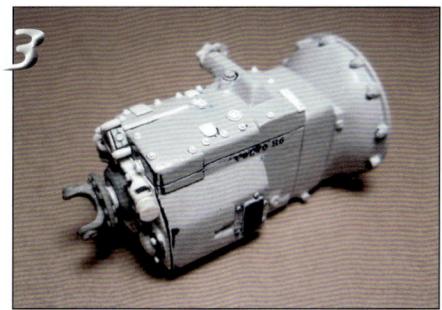
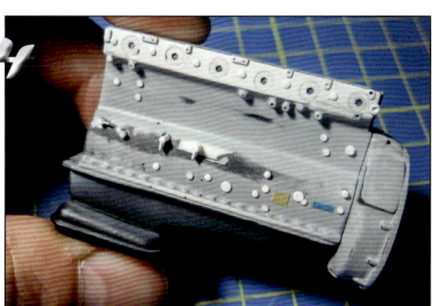

6. This Volvo six-cylinder engine block was detailed with all the bolt bosses as per the original part.

7. The cylinder head in the Italeri Volvo engine has all the manifolds on it. The part in the picture is based on the reworked 1/25 Revell engine and has the fuel injectors separate.

ting and replacing these items can be a time consuming activity so I do this only where I feel it would be worth spending the time. I did so on the Volvo as the head really lacks detail, while on the Scania the only feature moulded on the head is a manifold to collect cooling water, which is quite good and does not require cutting. In any case, you can always add bolts around the manifold flanges to make it look more interesting.

The high-pressure fuel pipes that feed the injectors are a crucial component of the fuel system, and are designed carefully. There are guidelines these pipes have to meet, and therefore you always see them carefully organised on the engine. They always have the same length for all cylinders to prevent any variations in fuel delivery, and have to be fixed properly as they are prone to vibration...so when adding these to model's engine, make sure the pipes are perfectly straight and with sharp turns and proper alignment.

Engine accessories

With regard to the fuel system, it should be noted that on many engine kits the overall number of parts is reduced, and some important details are just moulded on the block walls - although they would deserve being separate parts. This is often the case with an

The Scania transmission in the Heller kit is a great basis for detailing. In fact, just bolts and sporadic wiring was required.

TRUCK MODELLING

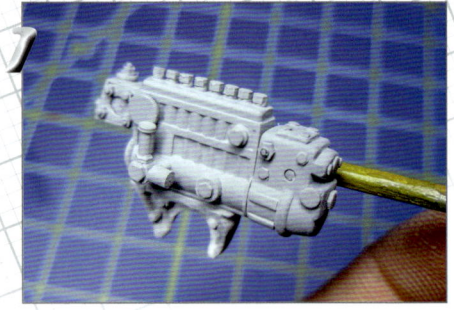

1. While engines have the injection pump moulded on the block, the Italeri Iveco TurboStar has it as a separate part. The example in the picture was rebuilt, detailed and prepared for casting.

2. Some engine components really call for wiring. All the fuel filters have external fuel lines and so has the Volvo oil cooler (RH cylinder in the picture).

4. Once the fuel pump is fitted to the engine it needs at least the injector feed lines. On a 'vee' engine the fuel pump is usually fitted in the valley.

5. In-line diesel engines have the fuel pump fitted on the block side. Note the external pump drive shaft.

Engine front end
The engine front end area is often simplified, as most of it is hidden deep in the chassis underneath the cab. Well, the first think you can always do here is to replace the belts driving all the accessories, as these are always too thick. Cut the separate pulleys from the belt and once installed on the engine, you can replace the belts with black insulation tape. Mostly there should be the following components mounted on the engine front end: an alternator, a water pump within the engine block, a power steering pump and air compressor. While the water pump may be hard to identify and the power steering pump is often dropped, the alternators and air compressors are included in most kit engines. Both can be detailed with wiring as these are crucial components of electric and air circuits, where all the wiring actually begins.

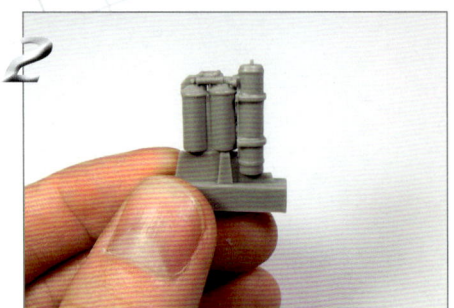

Radiator, air cooler and related piping
There is always a set of coolers mounted in the frame in front of the engine, which consists of the main water cooler and can be fitted with additional coolers for the intake air (intercooler) and possibly an air conditioner or oil cooler. The water cooler is connected to the block with a pair of pipes…upper and lower. These are steel pipes with rubber hoses and hose clamps on both ends. The hose and clamp details are often reduced on models, but with the latest PE accessories this can be solved easily. The fine photo-etched hose clamps are almost always tricky to work with, but provide outstanding detail.

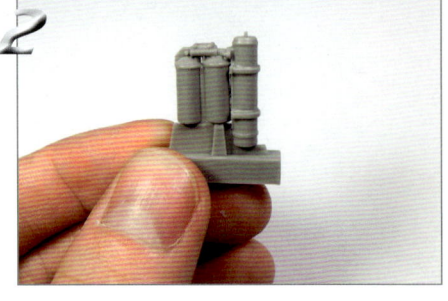

Rebuilding and detailing this Volvo engine was a demanding job, but once I assembled it from the finished castings I knew that once installed into a model it would make a real show-stopper.

The intake system starts with the intake filter, after which a turbocharger and an intake cooler with its pipes follow. All these are again connected with rubber hoses with hose clamps, providing lots of space for detailing, just like on the water pipes.

The coolers themselves also deserves attention. Often the front radiator wall can be seen through the model's grille, and not all have the structure moulded. For this fine-etched cooler structure, meshes are available. Most of them are provided in sheets from which a desired cooler mesh size can be cut..

injection pump and an alternator, or an air compressor. There are also numerous oil and fuel filters.

Modifying this always requires time and patience. Not only do you need to cut the particular component from the block, cover the hole and rework the block details, but you also need to create the new component itself. For this I had made a small engine detail set, which includes all the basic components that do not vary from vehicle to vehicle, and helps me with detailing every engine I build. This makes the whole operation quick and easy.

Keeping the various components separate is also handy because of painting. Many aluminium parts such as the alternator or injection pump are often left in the natural metal colour, and when reproduced on a model these small items provide useful and interesting colour variation to the engine assembly.

Exhaust and turbocharger
The turbocharger, exhaust manifold and all the piping with the muffler is a frequent topic when building engine models…mostly because of rust. However, many important details are missing here and they deserve attention.

The majority of kits lack all the bolts on the flanges between these components. As the turbocharger is fed with intake air, the

TRUCK MODELLING

6. PASSION FOR SUPER-DETAILING

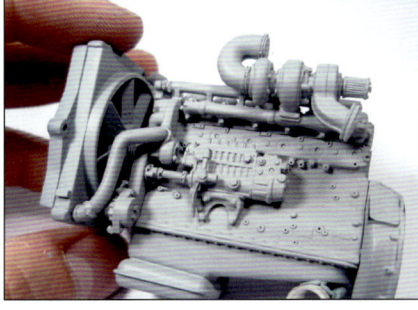

6. On every engine, the cooler is connected to the engine block with an inlet and outlet cooling pipe. These always have a short rubber connecting hose with hose clamps.

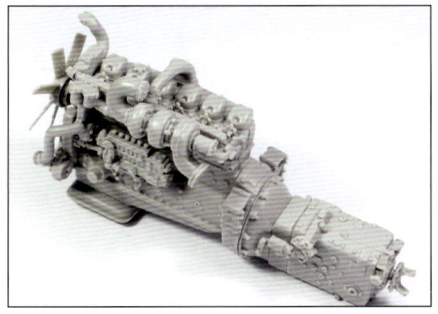

7. While in most engines turbochargers look pretty simple, they are actually quite complex parts. The example in the photo was rebuilt and detailed with bolts on all the flanges.

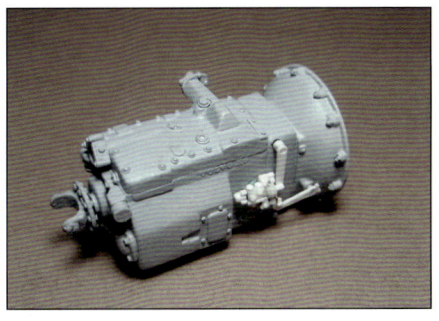

8. The clutch and transmission controls include air and hydraulic valves, which are often missing in the kit. These again provide the chance for detailing and wiring of the whole assembly.

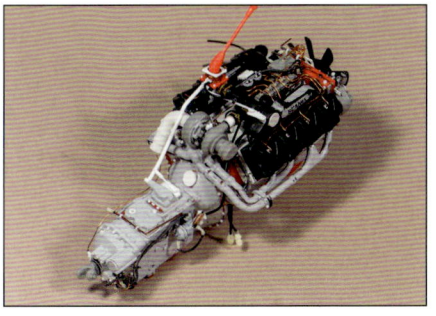

9. On many vehicles the gearstick remains on the engine while the cab is tilted. There is always a linkage between a gearstick and the transmission, but it is missing in many kits.

10. Although the cooler assembly is relatively simple, most can be detailed with photo-etched cooler mesh as it is often seen through the front grille.

11. For piping, fine photo-etched hose clamps are provided by various after-market companies.

12. While some kit parts may look too simple, they can be turned into relatively complex and authentic assemblies such as this air intake pipe, with rubber hose and hose clamps.

TRUCK MODELLING

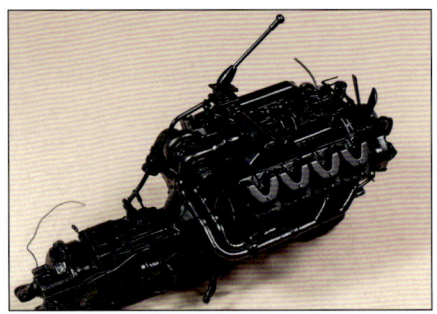

1. When painting an engine I like to start with Mr.Finishing surfacer black as it creates pleasing shadows in every tight corner; these may be difficult to spray or paint.

2. As the hairspray method was planned for painting the aluminium engine parts, all the related components were sprayed with Mr.Color silver.

3. Light green is typical for early Scania engines. The parts were sprayed with my own mix made of Vallejo and Italeri colours.

4. The exhaust manifold was hand-painted with Vallejo acrylics, followed by light dust and old rust pigments.

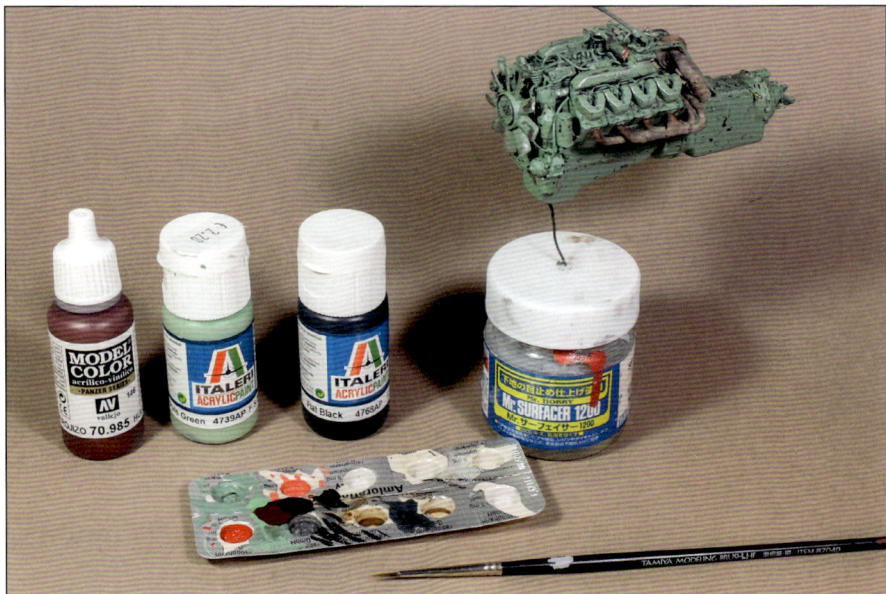

5. In addition to hairspray chipping, more chips on the engine and transmission were hand-painted with Vallejo and Italeri acrylics.

low-temperature section has rubber hose and hose clamps attached to the intake manifold, which again can be done with photo-etched parts. All the turbochargers also have their external lubrication circuit, which means a pair of oil pipes to the narrow central section should be added to provide another worthy detail. Besides the turbocharger, many trucks are also fitted with an exhaust brake. Again there mostly are connecting flanges and an external linkage to control the brake function.

When painting all these parts, make sure that the low-temperature (compressor) side of the turbocharger is not painted in rust tones. The easiest way to ensure a realistic rusted exhaust colour is by using pigments. Those who are more experienced may also make use of various red and brown paint shades. Acrylics have been very popular for this recently, of which Lifecolor varieties are the most frequently mentioned for this task.

Transmission details

Although detailing the transmission may not make sense on conventional US trucks, where it is completely hidden underneath the cab, most cabovers can show the transmission details if not covered with a catwalk. As mentioned previously, detailing any transmission starts with adding all the bosses and bolts to the case flanges and various covers.

Somewhere near the bell housing, most transmissions are fitted with a clutch control mechanism, either just mechanical linkage or a hydraulically assisted power clutch. Both air and hydraulic fluid should be linked to this, providing an opportunity for decent wiring. Furthermore, there is a gear stick linkage that should be connected to the transmission case, which is missing in many kits.

A transmission output is via U-joints, which are again simplified in most kits. Cutting these joints into pieces and detailing them as separate parts with bolts is a pleasing detail clearly visible in the chassis, giving you a chance to score extra points.

6.2.2 ENGINE PAINTING AND WEATHERING

Engines are made for various kinds of painting and weathering techniques. As they are constructed from various metals, corrosion and chipped paint can be represented beautifully. The need for a good reference photo cannot be emphasized enough. These will give you vital views about what an old, worn-

6. PASSION FOR SUPER-DETAILING

" *Detailing the vehicle drivetrain and exposing it by tilting the cab adds another dimension to the model presentation.*

TRUCK MODELLING

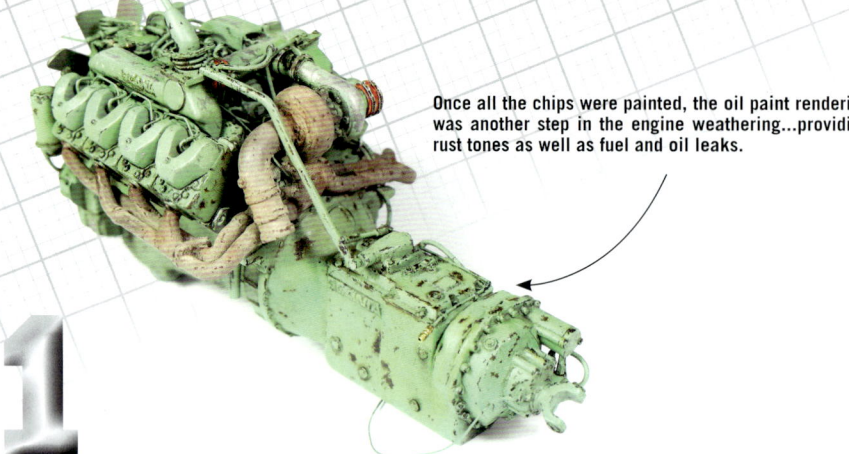

Once all the chips were painted, the oil paint rendering was another step in the engine weathering...providing rust tones as well as fuel and oil leaks.

2. A fine brush and steady hand is required for painting the chips.

3. Speckling was another method for adding another level of fine small chips to the engine and transmission.

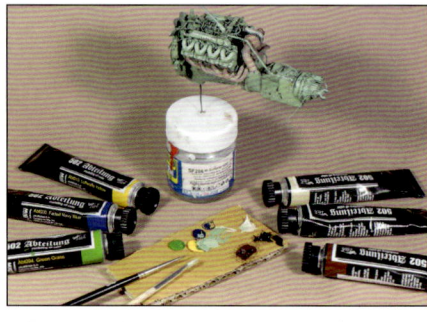

4. The array of colour tones used for engine weathering can be seen on the palette: from black, dark rust to light dust tones and a few more green hues.

5. The visual difference between the rusty steel and bright aluminum part of the turbocharger is obvious. Note also the gear stick with its linkage.

out engine looks like – areas where the paint peels from the aluminium parts, where rust appears, where oil leaks and where dirt collects. Considering every step of the engine painting process is always step zero of my work. In this case, I decided to paint my engine after assembly and detailing was completed. The engine valley details and fuel pipes were especially complex, and painting all the components separately prior to assembly can be challenging.

The Scania 14-litre uses many aluminium parts. The whole intake manifold, as well as all the rocker covers, are aluminium castings, which I wanted to show on my engine and the so-called hairspray technique was a comfortable option. I therefore used Mr.Surfacer Finishing Black primer, followed by Mr.Colour silver on the aluminium parts, and German Grey on the rest of the engine. These were sprayed with AK Interactive Worn Effects fluid, followed by a solid coat of light green mixed from Vallejo and Italeri paints. Just a small amount of water applied with a brush starts dissolving the hairspray under the paint. By using gentle brush strokes over the sharp edges and elevated details, the top coat becomes relatively easy to remove. Any kind of sharp tool such as a toothpick can be used to disturb the paint anywhere, and let the moisture get to the hairspray and this helps with creating the chips if the paint layer is more opaque. This method needs practice, to find the best combination of chipping fluid and paint layer thickness to get some acceptable results, but once mastered is probably the best way to create realistic paint chips.

The next step was painting the exhaust manifolds and turbocharger, and I use mostly acrylic paints and pigment dusts for this. The real working truck engine photos mostly show you that as these engines work really heavily, the rust colour on the exhaust system tends to

The finished engine with all details painted and fully weathered, ready for installation. Note the two pipes with fitting prepared for connecting the diesel fuel lines in the frame.

6. PASSION FOR SUPER-DETAILING

> There are no rules for vehicle livery and accessories, however, often less is more. I did not want the complex livery and many accessories to dominate the model, thus taking away focus from the many little details.

be rather light and often has pink tones too. Bright orange rust can be found on vehicles that are not in regular service. On my engines I therefore use a combination of light dust and old rust tones, which work well together… providing that working engine with exhaust rust tones. Various rust and soot pigments are applied locally to make the part more visually interesting, and small areas of old rust were hand-painted with Vallejo acrylics.

Other details such as the hose clamps and hose were picked out with a brush and Vallejo acrylics. A few drops of white were added to the original light green tone, and fresh paint chips were created over exposed areas.

All the following weathering was done with oil paints. Rather than in separate steps, I was continuously working with oil paints in small areas wherever I felt a need to make it more visually interesting. The paints were either used directly from a palette, or by using AK Interactive Odorless Thinner for wash. I have applied a dark pin wash to highlight all the fine engine details and bolts. Blue and green tones were applied in dots and blended with the surface to add more green tones to the engine colour, and provide shadows and highlights. As there were cast iron areas exposed with chipping, I used rust-brown tones around them too, blending them carefully with a flat brush with a very small amount of thinner.

6.3 CHASSIS

The frame is moulded as one assembly with frame rails and cross members, and split horizontally in halves. During assembly, a seam all around the whole frame is created and it's difficult to sand; the only sensible option is to cover the whole chassis with decking. Frustration set in because I always love to show various plumbing details inside the chassis and, therefore, the original frame was a no-go… but scratch-building my own frame was desirable. Working with 3D CAD software on a daily basis, I got used to using it when scratch-building my own parts. I have never attempted to employ any modern milling or 3D-printing technology in my own work, purely because I have always enjoyed the craftsmanship side of our hobby. But as I am really effective with 3D CAD, I can model both the frame rails and cross members in 3D quite quickly, and create classic paper drawings featuring all the frame holes and details required.

A friend of mine who is an expert on resin casting and scratch-building in general, Ondřej Nadrchal, taught me a great way of transferring the drawings onto plastic sheets. When printing on a laser printer, just lay the drawing over a piece of plastic sheet printed side down. Now apply a small amount of thinner (with a brush for example) and let the drawing get soaked. Acetone works nicely here and finding a good thinner may take you a while, but once done the drawing print transfers to the plastic once you press it down. However, as acetone is rather aggressive I have to remove the drawing from the plastic quickly before it sticks to it. All this needs practice but once managed, it provides a quick way of transferring anything you need from paper to plastic. In the case of scratch-building parts such as these, I cannot imagine a better way as this is far more

1. The front axle comes straight from the box. Again it is of classic design previously seen on the Prostar and Stralis.

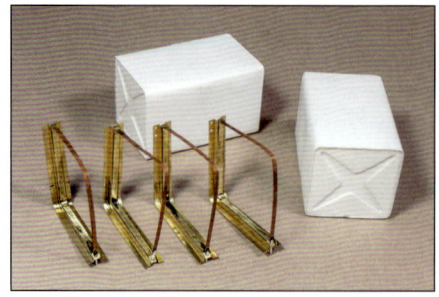
2. The fuel tanks were scratch-built and fitted with photo-etched tank mounts from the CTM detail set.

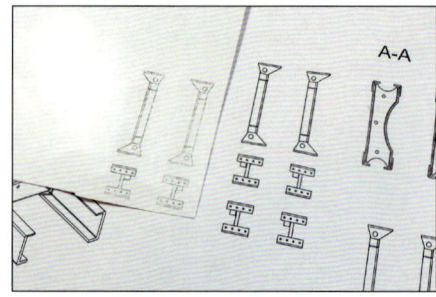
3. The whole frame was modelled in 3D, printed and the drawings were transferred to a plastic sheet.

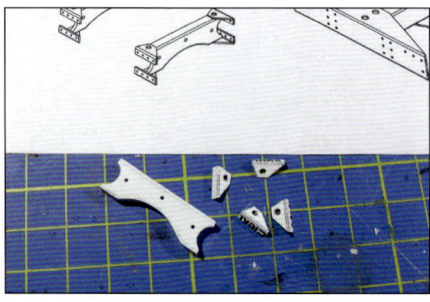
4. This way all the frame components could be made precisely and quickly.

5. Test-fitting can reveal many serious issues that can be corrected when spotted, prior to the parts' painting.

6. Studying the assembled chassis reveals how many parts do not come with the kit. It is actually only the suspension, axles and transmission that are present from Heller's kit.

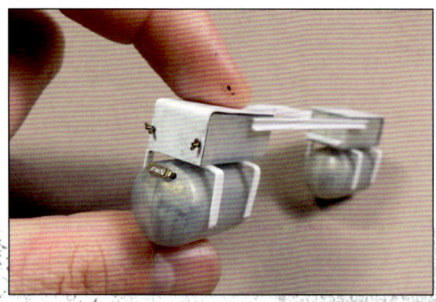
7. The battery box and air tanks assembly were detailed with plastic profiles and photo-etched wingnuts and data sheets.

8. The original chromed bumper (above) compared to the alternative detailed with wiring and photo-etched CTM steps.

9. The complete 5th wheel comes from the Italeri Scania Streamline, and the typical Middle East mudflaps with wire support were scratch-built.

precise than hand-drawn efforts. Therefore, cutting out all the parts and assembling the frame rails and cross members was just an afternoon task. The parts were detailed with bolts and the assembled chassis was left aside to dry overnight.

While the frame design is quite poor, the suspension and axle parts are up to today's standards in 1/24 scale. All I had to do was remove all the mould seams and assemble the parts. Bolts and fittings were added to the assembly, to prepare for the brake air lines, and all the parts were attached to the chassis. Careful measuring was required as there were no holes for locating pins in my frame rails, but the admirably thin frame assembly was worth the extra work.

These old Scania trucks always had a pair of large fuel tanks. Heller's kit has them too, but the parts are rough and require much sanding and filling. For this reason, I made my own fuel tanks - again by using a drawing print-transferred to 1mm plastic sheet. On these tanks, the photo-etched tank mounts from the CTM detail set were used, and the final combination was far above what can be found in the Heller kit.

As the engine was already completed once the frame with suspension was assembled, I test-fitted the engine in the frame rails to revel any clearance issues and prepare the engine mounts. Following the model assembly sequence, I also prepared the battery boxes and large air tanks. Finally, just the basic part shapes were used from Heller's kit and all the mounts and mounting straps were made of styrene sheet and profiles. Here, the CTM sets provide beautiful details: the air tank data sheets and pair of wing nuts for each battery cover. The fifth wheel and its mounting plate come from an Italeri Scania 143 kit, and were detailed with plastic profile and bolts. The front bumper is an out-of-box item but the cab steps come from the CTM detail set… the bumper ends were enclosed with a piece of plastic sheet with a few bolts added.

A noteworthy fact is that on trucks making Middle East runs, large mud flaps were often used and Astran trucks were no exception. I made the front items from a piece of styrene sheet, while those on the rear come from the

10. Once all the components were finished and test-fitted the whole chassis was again split back into pieces and these were painted separately.

CTM White Freightliner detail set, and were detailed with a Scania-Vabis badge from another PE set. The classis 1970s rear lamps are a CTM item too, while the mud flap support frames are made of copper wire bent into shape and glued with cyanoacryate.

I have already mentioned that I am picky about wheels. Those on my Scania are based on KFS rims modified with new bolts. The front axle tyres are standard Italeri items, the drive axle tyres are castings based on wheels taken from a well-detailed diecast model. The front wheel trims come from an Italeri accessory set.

6.4 PLUMBING, WIRING AND DETAILS

Now the fun is about to begin. The model chassis is a large assembly, lacking many details. The very first thing on the list is wiring…or plumbing to be more exact. In case of this vehicle, all air lines are in steel pipes, except a few that run through rubber hoses. That means the wiring process will be slightly different when compared to the two previous models. Both the Prostar and Stralis use flexible vinyl hose, but in the past, steel pipes and fittings were used for distributing the air all around the vehicle.

At first I added straight pipes with fittings (all made from Evergreen profiles) running

11. Note the amount of scratch-built parts. You recognise them easily as they are made of white plastic.

the whole length of the chassis inside both frame rails. These provide the basic background and keep the inside of the frame busy. An electric bundle, made of a few copper wires for the fuel level sensor and rear lights, was attached by the PE cable ties from CTM. The number and position of the air valves in the frame was easily visible on my reference photos. I scratch-built some myself and the rest came from my spares box. Most of the fittings I've used are resin items made for car modellers. A very important step is to drill holes into all the valves and fittings prior to their installation. This will allow clean and simple wire installation in the following steps.

Now the wiring really begins. Fine wire was used to link the rear axle brake chambers to the steel pipes in the chassis, a few more were

added to various valves to make it all a bit more interesting, and a pair in black rubber fibre was used for the front brake chambers. Everything was again fixed properly using the CTM cable ties. The importance of all these fine details, such as various fittings and cable ties, cannot be emphasized enough. This is where the difference between unrealistic wiring and accurate-looking examples is settled.

The next step requires plenty of patience, takes time and demands good reference photos…but is very helpful. While wiring the model with flexible wire, it is quite easy but when reproducing classic steel pipes every single pipe has to be bent into a particular shape, test-fitted and cut to length. Make sure all the bends have sharp corners and all the pipes are perfectly straight, otherwise the result won't be convincing. I use a pair of tweezers and side-cutter pliers for this task. When glued into position, another pipe follows and this way it goes till all the pipes are finished. There are about 20 of them on my model, so you can imagine I spent quite a few hours doing this. However, as most are located around the transmission (which will be easy to view) I believe it was all worth the time. The fuel lines from the fuel tank were made in the same manner.

The battery box assembly was also wired with fine wire and CTM cable ties. A susie bracket was made of plastic strips on top of the assembly and the susie cables were made

1. In the first wiring steps, a few straight pipes made from Evergreen plastic rod were fitted into both frame rails.

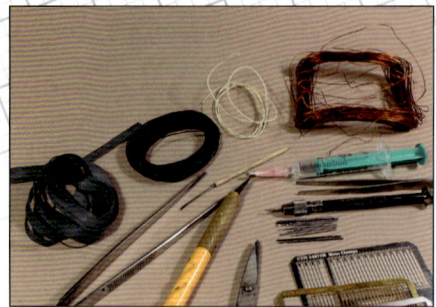
2. All the classic wiring tools and materials were used. For thin steel pipes, copper wire was employed.

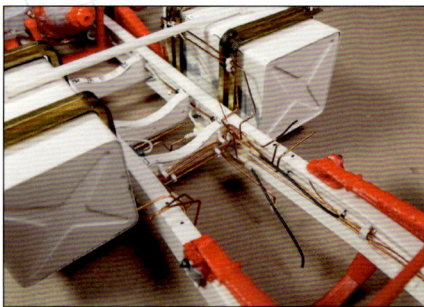
3. A complex pipe structure in the chassis was made by bending and gluing one part after another which required some time and patience.

4. The central chassis section is now busy with all kinds of pipes and fittings.

5. The susie bracket and cables were completely missing in the kit. These were made the same way as on the Prostar and Stralis.

6. A thing missing in virtually any kit is the hydraulic cylinder used for tilting the cab and a small hydraulic pump. All these were added to the RHS frame rail.

from black wire. The air couplings are my own parts I'd cast years ago.

Once the wiring was finished I kept adding more details to the chassis. The rear cab suspension hooks, with levers that prevent the cab from unwanted tilting, were missing entirely, so I made my own from various plastic rod and profiles. A detail missing in all kits is the cab tilting assembly, which comprises a hydraulic pump mostly mounted on the chassis behind the front wheel arch, and a hydraulic cylinder under the cab on the passenger's side. I made my pump of various plastic rods and fitted it on the chassis, just where my reference photos showed. The cylinder is made of two concentric aluminium rods that fitted together perfectly. The barrel is attached to the chassis via a pivot, so it can move while the cab is tilted. The piston is attached to the cab floor in the same way, so the whole assembly acts as a real working cylinder. Once the parts were fitted on the chassis, hydraulic pipes and hoses were added. In this area an air intake filter is fitted as well, and it was somewhat tight in the end. The filter itself comes straight from the box; just the hose clamps on the air intake manifold are photo-etched CTM items.

6.5 THE CAB ASSEMBLY

The cab is one of the kit's strong points. It may seem a bit simple but it actually represents the reality very well. The interior is a little Spartan, but so was the real thing and there is little to complain about. The seats and their suspension look good and will be visible. CTM offers details for inside the cab, such as all the pedals, cab steps and the painted dashboard, which is streets ahead of the Heller's decal.

The front grille details are not too bad, but the painting can be testing as the background usually has a different colour than the grille's horizontal bars. The CTM set provides a worthy solution, with a fine photo-etched background that features the characteristic intake

6. PASSION FOR SUPER-DETAILING

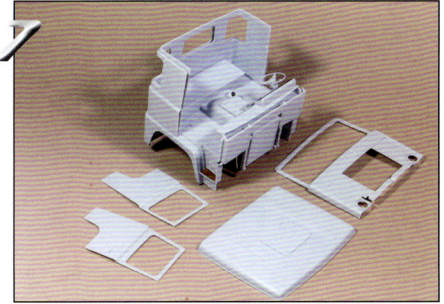

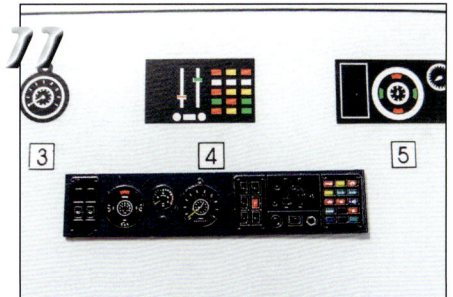

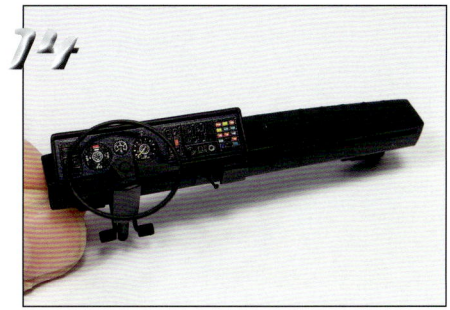

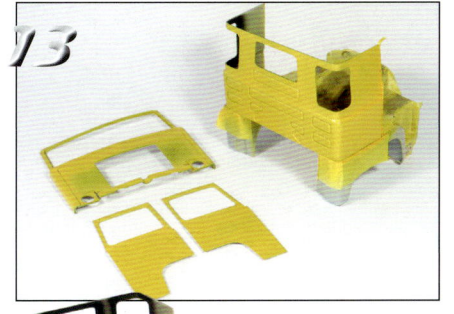

10. As virtually the only one cab on the market the Heller Scania 141 cab is so smartly designed that all the parts can be painted separately prior to the assembly.

7. The cab assembly as per the instruction was straightforward and did not need any modifications.

8. Once again the cab was test fitted to reveal any collisions with the heavily converted chassis and engine.

9. The upholstery texture was made with a Tamiya putty and the seats were painted with Tamiya acrylics and weathered with oils.

11. The difference between the kit decals and the CTM etched and painted dashboard is significant.

12. I started painting the cab from the inside. Once the floor was painted and masked the cream white areas were next to go.

13. The cab outer walls were sprayed with Mr.Color yellow with a few drops of Mr.Retarder Mild.

14. Except for the etched instruments the dashboard comes from the kit.

15. Some fine chips were painted on the exposed edges of the interior parts.

mesh for the cab heaters, and separate grille bars so that all the parts can be painted easily prior to assembly, without any masking. Furthermore, all the badges for the most common versions of these trucks are available from CTM, as well as the fine PE lights. All these little items really bring the cab to life.

Not only does the cab look great, but all the parts including the windows fit perfectly and there is no need for any filling. It all goes together so well that this is one of very few cabs that are worth painting prior to final assembly. In fact, both the painting and assembly of this cab form a continuous process. Although discussed here separately, it is all done at once.

What may seem weird is how the doors are made. Not only are they separate, but the internal structure is moulded together with the glass. It needs masking during painting, but otherwise this is quite a smart concept and once finished it all looks very good. Even the windscreen wipers are so well rendered that there is no need for PE replacements. The only parts I did not use from the kit were the mirror, which did not suit my tastes, so I replaced them with Italeri items and used the original Heller mounts.

As this model represents a long-distance truck, I wanted the interior to be busy with a truck driver's possessions, so I printed some newspapers, road maps and atlas books in 1/24 scale and placed them on the dash. All the cab curtains were printed too. I also made cigarette boxes and placed them around the interior, with one cigarette placed in the ashtray. A couple of Plus Model clear resin bottles were also used, a Coca Cola example on the dash and another for water deeper in the cab. The coffee mug on the dashboard is a scratch-built item. All the accessories were fixed around the interior before the cab shell was closed.

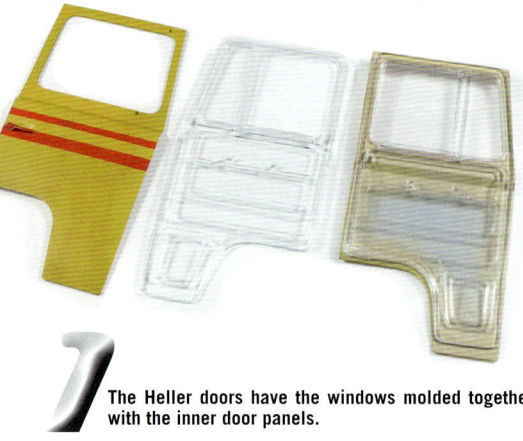

1. The Heller doors have the windows molded together with the inner door panels.

2. The window rubbers were hand painted with Vallejo acrylics.

3. The interior was detailed with a few road maps and magazines.

4. The front grille assembly comes from the CTM detail set.

5. Darker yellow tones were used on the rear cab wall as the basic layer for further weathering.

6. Both the badges and the lights are etched CTM items.

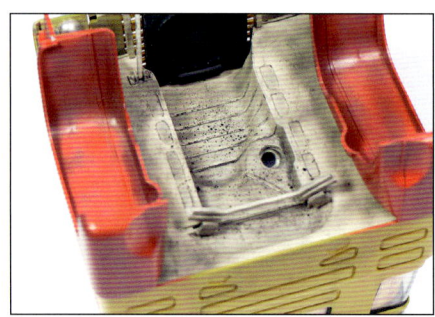

7. The cab was weathered from below as well. These areas get dirty easily but are not washed very often.

8. For painting of the scratchbuilt door locks the Agama spirit based metal paint was used.

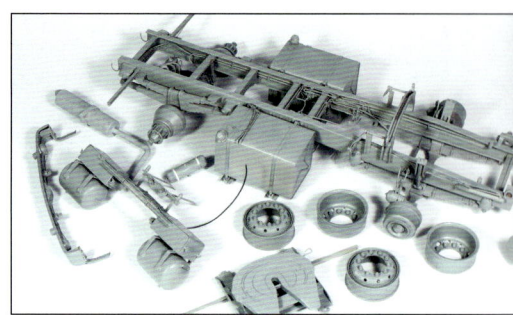

9. All the chassis parts were primed with Mr.Surfacer.

10. For the dark chassis areas a dark brown was used as a first layer.

11. AK Interactive Worn effects chipping fluid was used for creating chips on the chassis parts.

12. The rims and tyres were painted and weathered separately.

TRUCK MODELLING

6. PASSION FOR SUPER-DETAILING

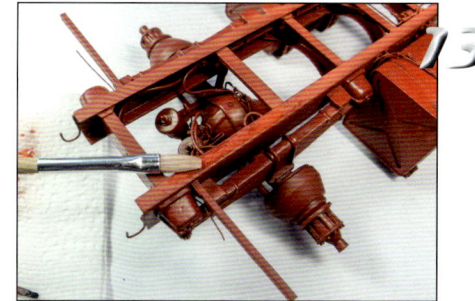

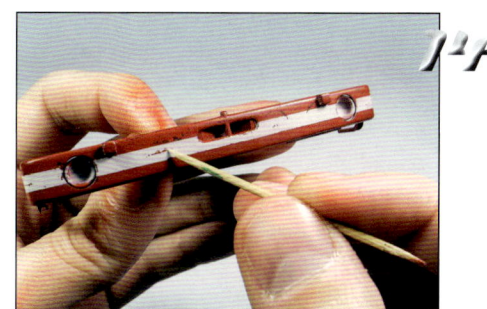

6.6 PAINTING THE MODEL

If the model's assembly is one story, painting it is another. Except for the engine, which was painted separately before construction, I did not start any painting until the whole assembly was finished and the cab and engine test-fitted on the chassis. As there was serious scratch-building involved, I wanted to make sure there would be no issues such as interference between parts and everything would fit perfectly. Test-fitting did reveal some issues, which could be remedied easily with sanding and cutting without destroying the paint finish.

I started with the chassis. As always I primed all parts with a fine coat of Mr.Surfacer. It took a while, as the chassis assembly was quite complex and there were many other parts to consider. I took my time and used all my patience to achieve a fine and smooth surface on all the components.

Since KJN 671P was sprayed in various red and brown colours throughout its life, my plan was to use the hairspray technique to show chipped paint, as it worked well on the engine. I have already pointed out that this technique needs practice; I've used it a few times on my previous models and am getting better, but I definitely do not consider myself an expert.

I sprayed all the parts with dark red-brown to achieve a dark base colour. The rest of the chassis was sprayed with lighter tones, which provided a complete base coat on which the AK Interactive Worn Effects fluid was applied in a fine even coat. Until this point I used Mr. Color and Tamiya paints, diluted with Mr.Color thinner. However, for the paint layers to be chipped I used Tamiya acrylics thinned with tap water alone, as this renders them perfect for the chipping technique.

The first area to be chipped was the top of the frame; both the frame rails and cross members, where I wanted fine chips of the top paint revealing the solid layer below. I added a few drops of XF-55 Buff into Tamiya XF-7 Flat Red and applied a fine coat over the exposed areas. In the next step, a small amount of water was applied over the sprayed surface using a flat brush. As the top coat was very thin, the water started dissolving the hairspray almost immediately, and just gentle work with the brush allowed me to remove the light top coat of paint, creating fine chips. As this was done with two similar tones the contrast was not very strong, but it added another level to the finish. A stronger contrast was obtained on the battery boxes, fuel tanks and the bumper, where the process was repeated with darker undercoat and more opaque red top coat. Here, a toothpick was necessary to disturb the top coat and help with creating chips. Another layer of chips was added to the bumper with the white stripe, under which another coat of the chipping fluid was used.

The next step was hand-painting all the chassis details with Vallejo colours. All the rubber hoses were painted dark grey, most details such as pipes or bolts were highlighted with various red tones, and many fittings and cable ties received light grey. Some chips were hand-painted on all four rims, and for the air filter and inlet manifold, the hairspray chipping method worked a treat.

At this moment the engine was installed into the chassis and a prop shaft was added to connect the gearbox and rear axle. All the

13. Once water is applied over the paint sprayed on the chipping fluid a gentle flat brush motion was used to remove the paint and reveal the dark surface below.

14. Some more solid paint layers may need a sharp tool for creating the chips.

15. One after another all the chassis areas were chipped using the Worn effects fluid.

16. Prior to the weathering the engine was installed and wheels were fitted on the hubs.

wheels were added as well, and from this point the whole chassis was weathered as one complex assembly. All the painting and chipping provided a basic layer on which more effects using oil paints and AK interactive enamel weathering products were applied.

Meanwhile the cab was painted too. Due to simple assembly and precise fitting it was a pleasure, however some patience was still required. Mr.Surfacer primer was applied to all these parts. Painting started in the interior, where the floor was sprayed flat brown together with the bunk, door trims and both seats. In this period both Scania and Volvo cabs were sprayed with a durable cream colour. This was visible in the interior, as well as on the floor when the cab was tilted. I therefore masked the brown floor and sprayed all these areas including all door panels, and hand-painted fine chips on them using my favourite Vallejo acrylics. The dashboard was sprayed with flat black, with a few drops of white added. In the next step, all the yellow areas were sprayed with gloss Mr.Color red after the necessary masking. More masking was done once the yellow coat was dry, and all the red areas of the cab were sprayed again using glossy Mr.Color paints. All the interior parts were sprayed with a mixture of flat brown and cream, while oil paints added more colour tones to the brown areas on the floor, bunk and seats.

Spraying the stripes on the cab was a delicate task as it had to be precise, with sharp edges. I used all my patience during the masking and it was worth it as the result was perfect. The grille assembly was straightforward and all the parts fitted perfectly. The rubber on the windscreen was masked and sprayed while the remaining window rubbers were hand-painted. Surprisingly, all the windows fitted perfectly. The CTM grille badges were sprayed with flat black, which was then sanded away carefully from the letters and numbers.

6.7 FINAL ASSEMBLY, AND WEATHERING

Except for the grille, the cab assembly was completed as per the instruction sheet. Although all the parts were painted prior to

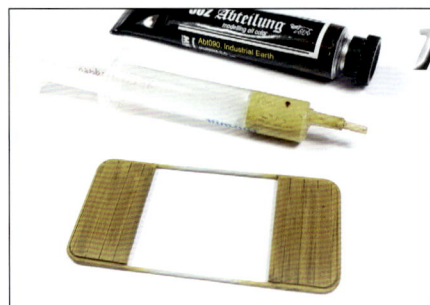

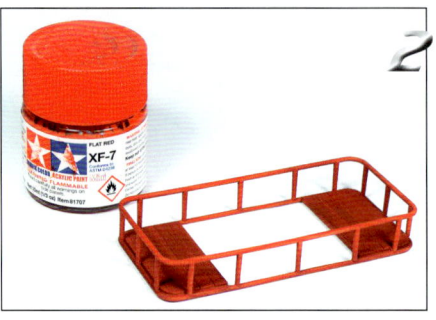

assembly, no issues with fit arose. The only thing I modified was how the doors were attached to the cab. Instead of gluing them to the cab, I made 1mm diameter wire supports and drilled both into the door and the door frame, as I knew the door connection has to be robust on a model being transported to models shows around Europe. Attaching the cab on the chassis was an easy task. The Heller hinge system works pretty well, although it does not require additional pivots as do most Italeri kits.

6. PASSION FOR SUPER-DETAILING

1. The roof racks often had wooden decking. The wood structure on plastic was made with a rough sanding paper and painted with enamels and oils.

2. The wood was then sprayed with the Worn effects fluid followed by Tamiya XF-7 red.

3. Once the paint was dry the wooden floor was chipped with a flat brush and water nicely revealing the wooden structure.

4. The roof AC unit was scratchbuilt. The dimensions were provided by Ashley Coghill.

5. The complete model prior to the final assembly and weathering.

6. On the cab some highly thinned Mr.Color paints were used to create some dust effects and rain marks.

A mixture of AK Interactive enamels and various pigments were applied all over the lower chassis areas and wheels.

7. The upper chassis areas were treated with red and red brown filters, a dark was was applied to highlight the details such as nuts and bolts.

9. Around the fuel tank caps a mixture of black and dark brown oils was applied to create oil stains.

10. On the rear mudflaps some vertical streaks were made with oil paints.

The sand showel was a typical equipment found on the Astran trucks. This white metal casting comes from KFS and was chipped using the hair spray technique.

On the cab there were few more parts to be added. The sun visor is a resin after-market item, the decal was drawn by fellow modeller Petr Hančl and custom printed by a local company. Both the ladder and the roof rack come from Italeri accessories set No.764. While the ladder fits the cab perfectly, the roof rack looked a bit too simple so I decided to make it more interesting. I used my razor saw to create parallel grooves in the rack floor and made it look like it's made of separate planks. Coarse abrasive paper was used to make a rough wood structure. I mixed a brown-yellow shade from a few Mr.Color paints and sprayed the planks. A dark wash comprising 502 Abteilung Industrial Earth oil colour and AK Interactive odorless thinner was applied over the part surface; this highlighted both the grooves between the planks and the wood structure. A few more oils would be beneficial, however for me this was fine and AK Interactive Worn effects was applied. All the parts including the rack floor were sprayed with Tamiya XF-7 flat red. Then, a little water was applied over the wooden planks and the paint was chipped carefully, showing the wood below. The same kind of chipping was done on the shovel that comes from KFS, but the chipping was easier as the shovel itself is a white metal casting, a so just the handle was painted in a wood colour before the hairspray was applied.

The roof air conditioning unit was tackled in two steps. Originally, the item from Italeri's No.764 accessories kit was used. Later, though, I replaced it with a more accurate scratch-built version as Ashley Coghill provided me the dimensions of the real Kysor unit and Ron Johnson supplied the beautiful decals. The inlet hose for the A/C are made of black wire and CTM cable ties.

Once all the details were added, the final weathering stage was started. At first, rain marks and dust were applied on the cab rear and side walls, and on the lower chassis areas. On the cab edges, front grille and rear wall, scratches and chips were painted with bright yellow. In the next step, dark rust was painted inside most of these chips with various rust oil paint tones. In the same manner, rust was added to most of the chips on the bumper, fuel and air tanks and over the chassis. Dust-tone filters made of highly thinned oil paints were applied all over the chassis, bumper and lower cab areas, and a dust wash was used on all the tyres. A highly thinned filter of AK Interactive Rain Marks for Nato tanks enamel was applied to the windscreen, leaving the wipers only partly clean. Once all the filters were dry, more dust and dirt from various AK Interactive enamels was applied over the lower chassis areas, on wheels and the mud flaps where the PE structure was highlighted appropriately. Mud splatters were applied using the 'speckling' method around the wheels and on the front of the vehicle. All these effects were stressed on the rear cab

6. PASSION FOR SUPER-DETAILING

wall, which often belongs to the dirtiest part of the vehicle on which many interesting effects can be shown. Fresh grease on the fifth wheel was made of brown and black oil paints applied directly from the tubes.

6.8 CONCLUSION

Serious detailing and scratch-building was employed on this model. In strong contrast to the Prostar, a large amount of kit parts was replaced, showing that there are many ways to build and detail a truck model. Finally, just the engine actually became an involved project of its own. To make the model as accurate as possible, many reference photos were gathered over several months. All this adds another level to the model's authenticity if an out-of-the-box build no longer satisfies you. However, for such a model one needs many modelling skills. It sometimes does not take much before the model begins to turn into a complex project beyond your abilities. Therefore, when converting a kit, I recommend to start with something simple and move forward in gradual steps. I have seen many who ended up burnt-out with an ambitious, expensive project…only for it to remain an unfinished 'shelf queen'.

I have always loved Astran trucks and wanted to build one for many years. I was pleased with the quality of some of the kit parts, however, for myself a new chassis and new wheels will always be a must. There's no doubt that without modern photo-etched accessories the kit would lack many details, and the CTM set helps considerably in adding more refinement. As the trucks making Middle East runs had a tough life, I applied a few layers of weathering on this model. I started with hairspray and ended with numerous layers of oils and enamels. I must admit that finding good reference images for weathering was not an easy task, as I wanted to show various weathering effects and not just one solid dust layer; but gathering reference material and looking around you in the real world is integral to our hobby. ■

> *The good old times connected with the hard work that both the men and the machines were doing on the Middle east runs are being brought back with this LB 141 in the Astran livery.*

7 LIGHT COMMERC

I can imagine that building trucks may feel a bit tiring from time to time. Suddenly all the work seems too complex and one does not find any motivation. I have experienced this myself in the past and I must admit that building something slightly different helped a great deal.

7. LIGHT COMMERCIAL VEHICLES

7.1 INTRODUCTION

You can find many interesting vehicles in 1/24 and 1/25 scales that are not that far away if your main focus is trucks. There are numerous vans and pick-up kits available from various manufacturers, and many of these are new toolings providing quality that is often above anything you can find among standard truck kits, which also helps us to have fun and relax.

I'd like to point out some of the kits I've had in my hands. Firstly, the nice new Ford F-350 (1/24) from Meng is a must-have for all truck fans. It is so close to big rigs and can play a major role in many dioramas, such as heavy haulage assistance or a service vehicle. A similar machine, but a bit older – the 1971 Ford Ranger (1/25) kit from Moebius Models (also a new-tool kit) can be used the same way with many classic trucks. Far away from US trucks, there is a small, nifty Subaru Sambar (1/24) made by Aoshima…again, a beautifully detailed kit of a vehicle that is small, but still a truck actually, so if there is something unusual you would like to try, maybe this is what you are searching for. If you are bored with poor-quality model truck kits and would like to get your hands on top-quality tooling in 1/24 scale, take a look at what Asuka Models (formerly Tasca) provides. They have a narrow range of superb military vehicles with top tooling. Their latest contribution, an American Bantam (an early Jeep), represents one of the most beautiful injection-moulded plastic kits I have ever seen in 1/24 scale. Recently, both Ebbro and Heller have released classic French light commercial vehicles. While some definitely could have been better with regard to ease of building and fit, they also provide a refreshing change in the automotive scales. Either way there is plenty to choose from.

For an average truck builder these car, van and pick-up kits represent a dramatic change. The kits are more accurate, so there is almost no place for any reworks or conversions. There is almost no necessity for wiring as apart from the engine, everything remains hidden under the body. The kits are smaller and have fewer parts, so it does not take a year to build one model. There is almost no need for any expensive after-market parts, so actually the only thing you pay for is the kit and paints…and that's it. With less drivetrain and chassis detail there is usually a bit more bodywork to deal with, as well as more windows that need patience and care. With an open body or cargo area there is also space for fine cargo – a detail you cannot employ on an average truck. Often there is more opportunity for various weathering effects, as all these cars can be found in poorer condition more often than trucks. Just like I wrote previously: it's vital that everyone should try a change from time to time.

1. When the top quality 1/24 scale tooling is what you want, the beautiful Asuka military kits are a great choice.

2. Subaru Sambar from Aoshima is probably the smallest truck available in 1/24 scale.

3. A range of similar vehicles – just a bit older ones – is available from Moebius models in 1/25 scale. They provide a wide range of various model years of Ford pickup trucks (60's to 70's) with different wheelbases and body versions. All of these kits are from new moulds and are nicely detailed.

Tech Spec — Ford F-350

Kit: Ford F-350 Super duty crew cab, MENG CS-001
Scale: 1:24
Accessories: Custom decals
Notes: An out-of-box built, nice and easy to build kit

7.2 A SAMPLE BUILD: MENG FORD F-350

Meng's kit came as something of an unexpected surprise. Known for super tooling of 1/35 scale kits, I was curious what this civilian product would be like. At the same time, I felt tired of converting and detailing truck models, so building something potentially less stressful was welcome. I wrote a quite positive review on this kit, and after finishing the model I stayed positive and bought another for a future project.

Actually, the whole build could be summarised as: "I used Tamiya Extra Thin Cement, I almost did not need any putty, all the parts fitted perfectly and, due to the smart position of the ejector pins, there was no need to remove any pin marks." That how easy it was. I have never built a car model before and all I know about building kits concerns trucks. On the other hand, while the subject is different, the scale and techniques are the same and I did not find anything that would surprise me in any way. I just followed the instruction sheet and everything went well.

Building the model starts with assembling

Assembling the bodywork was a pure pleasure, Everything fitted perfectly and no filling was necessary.

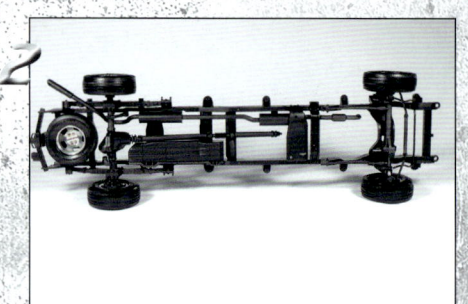

2. The ladder frame and chassis details are nicely molded. However, everything is covered by the bodywork.

3. The suspension on both axles nicely represents the real thing. The front coiled springs can be replaced with wire.

4. The tyres are the weakest part of the kit. Some barely fit the rims.

5. The engine and transmission have very nice details. Unfortunately, just like the chassis, most of the details will be hidden under the cab.

6. The engine front has nice pulleys and belt moulded.

7. The cab is provided as a single piece shell that just needs to have some witness marks removed.

> *I almost did not need any putty, all the parts fitted perfectly.*

7. LIGHT COMMERCIAL VEHICLES

The vehicle concept allows easy dry fitting of all the components - something that is not so easy with truck models in general.

9. The kit contains some beautifully molded parts such as the cooler with a very fine and realistic structure.

10. The dashboard is nicely molded and calls for a careful painting.

11. Except for the decals the kit comes with chromed mirror stickers and a windscreen spray mask.

12. The kit features a working tail gate, a nice detail.

13. All the interior parts were primed with Mr.Surfacer prior to painting.

14. Fitting the engine into the chassis was an easy task. Adding any wiring in this area is questionable as nothing will be visible on the finished model.

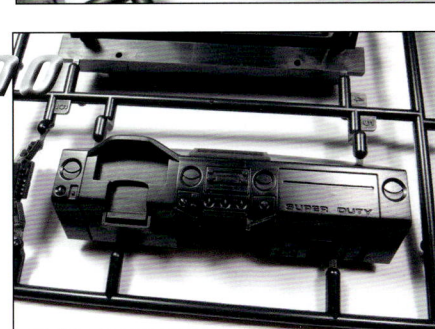

The model was painted in large sub assemblies.

TRUCK **MODELLING**

1. The light grey Mr.Surfacer primer nicely exposes all the chassis details. What a shame this will all soon be hidden under the body.

the chassis and engine. It took just a couple of evenings and was straightforward. The details are perfect and it is a real shame that most will remain hidden underneath. You just need to clean the seams on some of the parts but that is nothing a scalpel wouldn't make short work of in a few seconds. I had doubts about the engine detail, but it looks great after painting. There is some space for adding more embellishments and wiring in the engine bay, but out of box still looks good and I did not add anything. Around 75% of the decal sheet represents various data sheets that belong under the hood and it makes a big difference..

The only thing to criticise are the tyres, but they are the only wrong item in the kit. Not only did they barely fit on the rims, but also tend to slide off them during any manipulation of the model, so that I had to correct their position frequently during the photo shoot. Using Superglue for fixing them on the rims permanently could be a good idea, and in hindsight I should have done just that.

The cab shell is in one piece, which eliminates all the fit issues and it has beautifully moulded detail. The cargo body comprises multiple parts and the alignment could not be better. The interior is quite simple and the seat back rests were the only part in the kit that needed filling. The hood fits the body perfectly and so do the bumpers, so there is no need for any modifications or altering. Heaven on Earth, really.

Even the clear parts were fine to work with and there were just minor errors. The windshield fits perfectly. I even had to use force to press it in and it held in its position without any glue. I had to trim the aperture for the rear window, but it was just a sharp edge preventing the clear part from fitting properly, so no problem at all. The side windows fitted nicely as well as the front lights, and the chromed parts make them realistic. The rear lamps needed trimming to fit the body, but again, this was just a minor improvement. All the bits and pieces around the vehicle are really very good. The wipers have fantastic detail, while the mirrors are provided as self-adhesive stickers, which makes it all easy.

I was afraid of fitting the interior into the cab shell because you need to spread it out significantly when the windows are already positioned. I wasn't sure if all the glazing would stay in, so I used Superglue on all of them. However, there was no problem with the windows at all. I just had to sand a bit of

2. Applying white colours are best done over a black surface, therefore Mr.Color gloss black was sprayed over the entire body.

3. The black was left to dry overnight, then gently polished, followed by Mr.Color white. Note that some vertical streaks and rain marks were applied as a part of the basic paintjob.

7. LIGHT COMMERCIAL VEHICLES

Instead of using chromed parts, all the vehicle accessories were finished in dark grey plastic which is more suitable for a robust, working machine.

4. Vallejo acrylics are the most suitable paints for brush painting.

5. All the vehicle exterior details including the window rubbers were brush painted.

6. The paint chips were painted with Vallejo acrylics as well, using a fine new brush.

7. The windscreen rubber was masked as it is difficult to keep the hands steady enough for long straight brush strokes.

8. The fresh paint chips were done with white, the deeper and older ones with a mixture of dark grey and red brown.

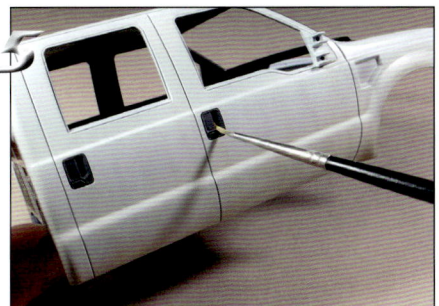

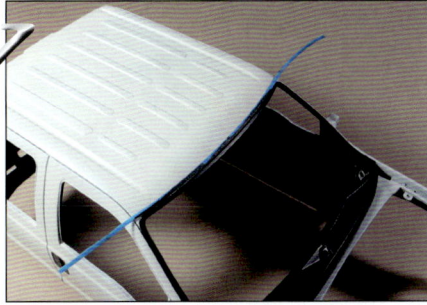

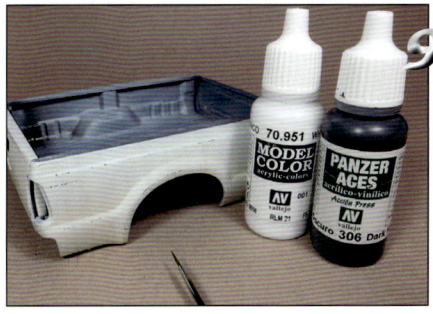

9. One by one, the body panels were chipped. A time consuming process that took several evenings to complete.

10. The simple but very suitable decals were take from the spares box.

TRUCK MODELLING

material in the front door area, where the clearance had been reduced by the clear side window part.

Just like I am used to doing on real trucks with Ford, I also built the whole model and primed all parts to see how it all fitted together before I started painting. What I got was exactly what I expected. A lot of fun during a quick build, which took me just a couple of weeks.

Furthermore, the model looks splendid and I did not compromise in terms of detailing…. something you usually do not see in the world of scale model trucks.

I wanted to build by model as a daily workhorse from the outset. There were many colour combinations in my mind, but I finally decided on plain white and logos from a 1/87 decal sheet from my spares box. To make my model different when compared to other 350 builds, I opted for the chrome-less heavy duty version with black plastic all around the vehicle. The number plates are from Brazil; I found them on the internet and printed them on a laser printer.

The model was painted in sub-assemblies as much as possible (chassis, engine, interior, cab and cargo body). However, the weathering (pigments and oils) was applied to the model after final assembly.

As usual, I primed all the parts with Mr.Surfacer. The bodywork got a coat of Mr.Color gloss black as this is the best way to spray white on vehicles. The Mr.Color gloss white was mixed with a few drops of grey and dust tones during spraying, to create fine vertical dust and rain marks. More dust was added to the lower body surfaces, providing a background for further weathering. Most of the body's fine details were hand painted with my favorite Vallejo Dark Rubber. The only black area that was masked and sprayed was the windscreen frame on both the body and the windscreen. For the clear part, Meng actually provides a spray mask in the kit which is very handy. The lights were painted with Tamiya clear acrylics.

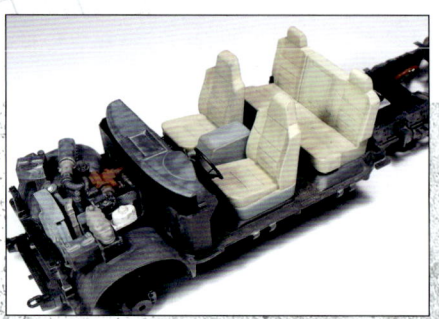

1. The interior was built as per the instructions and weathered with oil paint filters.

2. The dashboard panels were masked and sprayed in different colours. The instrument decals were a bit too large for the aperture in the dashboard.

3. The engine and chassis were weathered heavily. The oil paint, enamel filters and washes were completed with chipping using the sponge method.

7. LIGHT COMMERCIAL VEHICLES

4. The lights in the kit were really beautiful. The favourite Tamiya enamels enhanced them further.

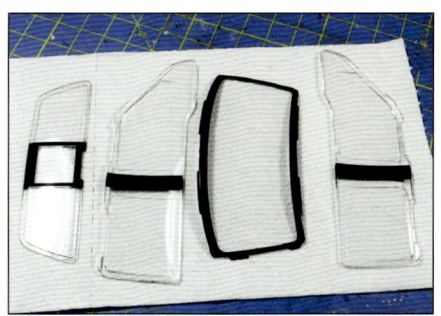
5. The windows' black areas were masked and sprayed flat black.

6. Providing a spray mask for the windscreen is very generous and not common in standard kits.

All the chips around the vehicle were painted with grey and white Vallejo paints. It took me a few evenings but it really brought the model to life. The complete chassis assembly was weathered heavily with oil paint filters. Various tones of AK Interactive enamel weathering products were used here, as well as pigments for rust on the exhaust and dust and mud splatters around the wheels. Finally, most of the effects were covered with the bodywork anyway.

Speaking of what is not considered a standard technique, I would mention the wheels. In the Prostar chapter I mentioned that weathering chromed parts can be difficult. The first step was spraying the rims with a flat clear coat, with the addition of a hint of yellow, which produced a realistic tone. A thin sand dust filter was applied in the next step, fixed by hairspray followed by an acrylic Vallejo dark grey coat, which was removed with moistened brush, and just the small chips of paint were left on the rim (the so-called hairspray method). Black oil paint wash enhanced the colour variation and light grey was used to highlight the details. Two layers of dust and mud filters from AK Interactive's

> *The latest 1/24 release from Meng was turned into a heavy duty working machine with a hard service life.*

125

TRUCK MODELLING

1. No cargo was added, just a few drops of pigments were used to represent dirt and soil in the cargo compartment.

2. The mud splatters were applied using the flicking method, followed by a red-brown filter, applied with an airbrush over the same area.

3

The hood of the model can be posed open, which nicely reveals the cooler structure. Note the dust and dirt on the windshield.

TRUCK **MODELLING**

enamel weathering products were applied to the tyres, which highlighted their structure perfectly.

The windows and lights also received subtle weathering to reduce the shine. A mixture of Rain Marks for Nato Tanks enamel and odorless thinner was applied to the windows by hand (paintbrush) after the windscreen wiper mask was applied over the windscreen. Once dry, it was removed carefully with a cotton swab.

Mud splashes on the body were created in three steps. A thin brown filter of Mr.Color paint was applied as a background with an airbrush. The second layer was done with Dark Mud AK Interactive enamel, and the third with MIG Productions Dark Mud pigment. Both these layers were applied with a brush using the so-called 'speckling' method (without using an airbrush). All the pigments were fixed with MIG Productions Pigment Fixer.

The speckling was also used for creating dirt and insects on the front areas of the hood and the roof, via black and dark grey oil paint. I had many plans for various loads, but in the end, does not carry anything except for a few drops of MIG Productions pigments in the cargo body.

7.3 CONCLUSION

Building this model was a joy. I don't remember the last model I built straight from the box, but this was built in that format and I do not feel any compromise looking at the result. It is a great kit and I wish it would be as easy to build trucks in the same manner. Far away from all the wiring and conversions, I have discovered another world of modelling, to which I'm certain I'll return. ∎

8 ADVANCED RESIN

Injection-moulded kits represent the mainstream of scale truck models, but resin conversions play an important role too. While there is just a limited amount of trucks available in plastic, resin conversions help and broaden the array of subjects.

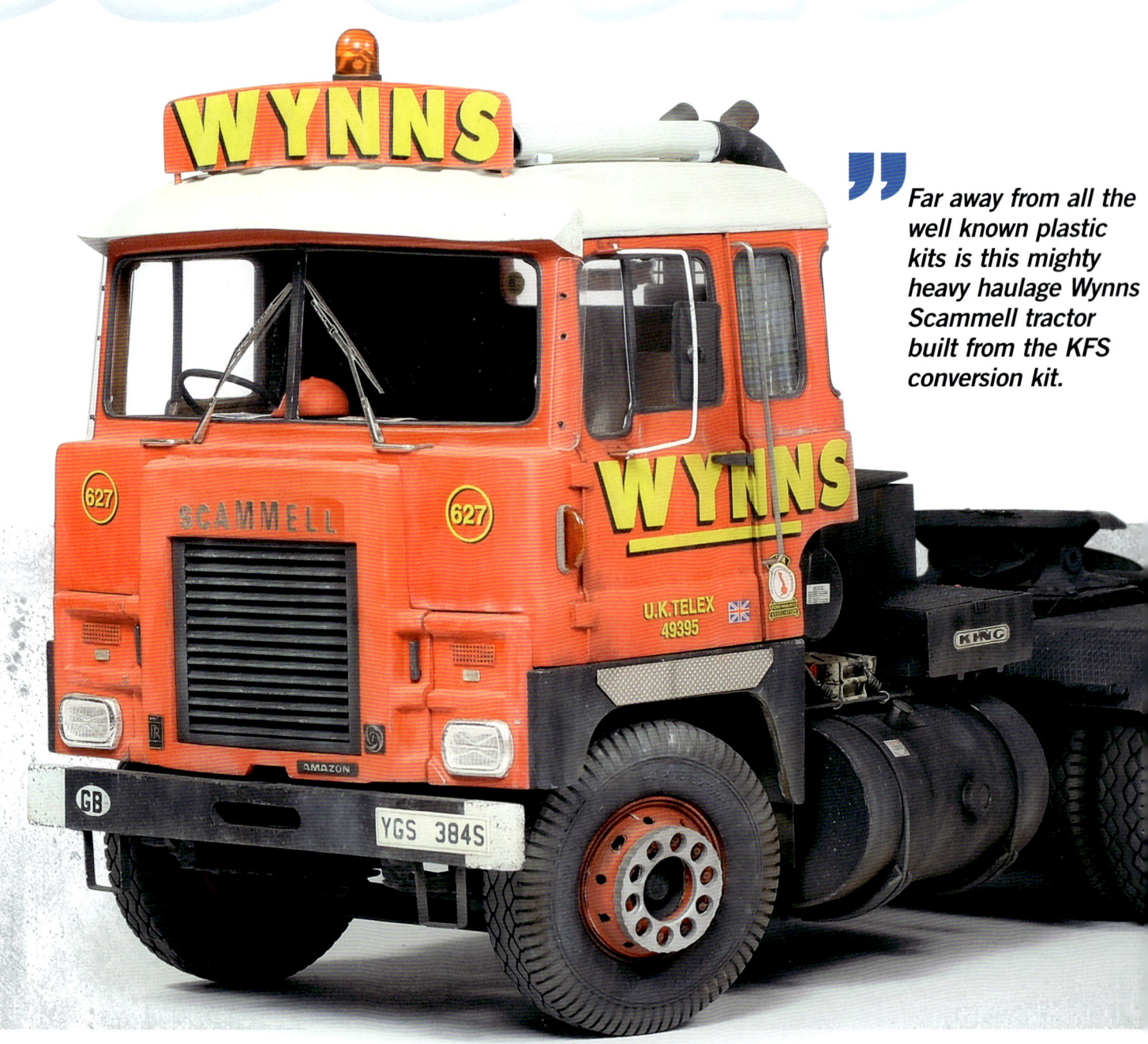

" *Far away from all the well known plastic kits is this mighty heavy haulage Wynns Scammell tractor built from the KFS conversion kit.*

CONVERSIONS

8.1 INTRODUCTION

Available as conversion sets matching some of the donor plastic kits, or full kits that need no donor kit at all, they offer many interesting topics: from classic old-timers and exotic vehicles, to the latest trucks that have not yet been moulded in plastic. Although mostly significantly expensive when compared to injection-molded plastic, and believed to be the realm of experienced modellers only, building a resin kit may actually be easier and faster. Yet quality is what matters here, and it may vary considerably between various producers.

For many years, the phrase "a high-quality resin conversion kit" could be said of all the products offered by British company Kit Form Services (KFS), which has offered a large amount of vehicles as either conversions or full resin kits. High-quality castings and very good fit are common traits with all KFS products, that often need just minor clean-up before painting and assembly. As plastic kit production seems to be at a standstill, other companies are trying to keep up with the times and provide kits of the latest vehicles. Impressive work in this area is being done by A&N Model Trucks, a small Latvian company providing a pleasing, detailed range of resin and photo-etched kits and conversion sets for both European and US trucks. Besides these, there are numerous small companies providing resin cabs and conversion sets for various vehicle types, making the world of scale model trucks diverse and interesting.

1. Except for the classic conversion kits KFS made some full resin kits as well such as this Bedford KM (not all parts shown in the photo).

8.2 A SAMPLE BUILD: SCAMMELL AMAZON

I have always liked vehicles that were a bit different. Scania and Volvo trucks are ever popular in 1/24 scale but I sometimes feel I need to build something different. And that is exactly what many resin kits allow us to do.

Heavy haulage trucks are very popular among truck builders. I wanted to build one myself but I also wanted something unusual when I realised I had the Scammell Crusader kit in my stash. I also had the KFS Wynns decals and other accessories, which could be combined into building one of the well-known heavy haulage Scammell Amazon tractors. I really love classic British trucks and it made perfect sense to build one, as I was about to visit the well-known Gaydon model truck festival. There was one problem, though, as the show was in just eight weeks.

Tech Spec — Scammell Amazon

Kit: KFS TQ Scammell Crusader transkit

Scale: 1:24

Accessories: KFS TQ127x, TQ126x Split rim wheels on tyres from Revells Büssing kit, KFS TQ74 heavy dty fifth wheel, KFS TQ115 Universal Susie bracket, KFS SS47 Orance beacon, KFS Wynns decals, Asuka 24-003 Jerry cans, KFS-50 Generis chassis data plates, KFS-7 UK Number plate set, KFS -84 MOT plates, KFS-3 EC regulation plates

Notes: A resin cab on scratchbuilt chassis, in 2016 the Crusader is to be released by KFS as a full resin kit

> *A great thing with building classic British lorries is that there is a wide range of accessories available for them.*

I was lucky to find a good factory drawing of the Amazon (a heavy duty version of the Crusader) and an internet search provided more than enough photos of the Wynns Amazons, so I had decent reference material and dimensions for building the model. However, with only eight weeks to go I had to keep things simple and focus on finishing the model in time.

SCRATCH-BUILDING

All KFS conversion kits are ready for a plastic donor kit. Most of them are designed to fit the Italeri Volvo F12. However, looking at the sturdy Amazon chassis and suspension, I knew instantly that the Volvo chassis was too far and I needed to scratch-build my own frame. Following the drawings, it took just a couple of evenings and I was more than happy with the result. The front suspension comes from the Heller Scania kit and the rear units are reinforced DAF 3300 items. At the beginning of this project I was struggling with wheels but finally, I combined the KFS split rim wheels and the Revell Büssing tyres I had cast in resin. Fitting the axles with generic resin hubs and wheels gave me a correct chassis riding height, on which the cab was installed. I had to scratch-build the cab suspension but as it

8. ADVANCED RESIN CONVERSIONS

1. The build started with scratchbuilding the frame rather than using a donor kit.

2. The suspension was taken from the Italeri Daf Dutchman kit but a few more leaf springs were added and the wheelbase was extended.

3. A top view of the chassis shows the position of the engine and transmission that came from an old Revell kit.

4. The heavy duty fifth wheel is a KFS item while the support frame and trailer guide up rams were scratchbuilt.

5. The weight of the loaded Amazon tractor was 40 tons, which required a robust suspension.

6. Various accessories such as the jerry cans were stored on the platform behind the cab.

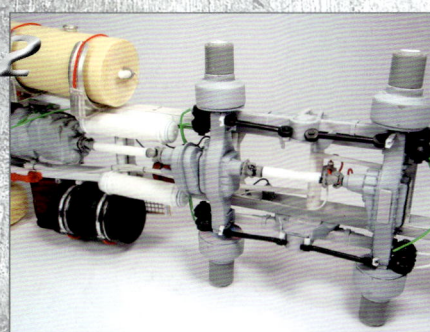

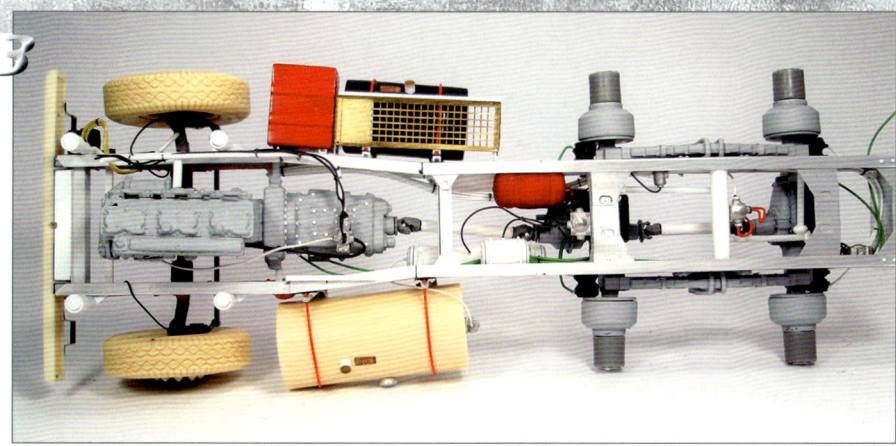
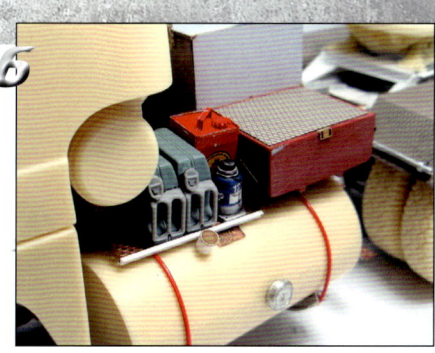

The usually versatile Italeri wheels were too small and modern looking for the Amazon, and were subsequently replaced by cast copies of the Revell Krupp Titan tyres with KFS split type rims.

TRUCK MODELLING

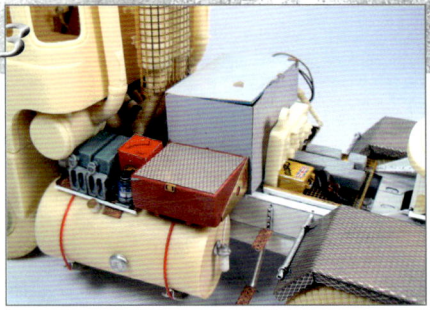

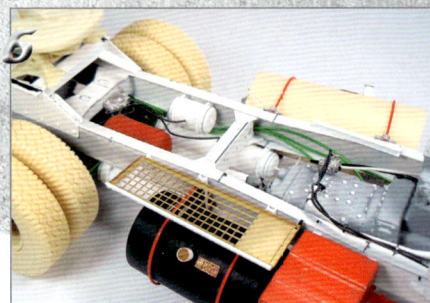

4. The rear mudguards were made from CTM etched treadplate.

5. Extra equipment was stored externally to add further detailed impression.

6. The chassis got some basic wiring. However, much of it, including the transmission details was covered by the accessories and catwalks.

1. The rear cross member was detailed with trailers couplings and bolts made from Plastruct hexagonal rod.

2. All the heavy haulage units are packed with various kinds of accessories, especially large tool boxes where chains, shackles and other pieces of equipment are stored.

3. The area behind the cab is busy with fine little details. Many of them are etched details taken from the spares box.

8. ADVANCED RESIN CONVERSIONS

7. The mirrors are hinged and fully working.

8. The twin exhaust arrangement and the long horizontal air intake pipes are features not commonly seen on other trucks.

is not visible on the finished model, I kept it all simple. The engine is also just a generic item fitted with Eaton transmission, which was detailed with bolts and plumbing that's visible in the chassis behind the cab. The time pressure was relatively high, so I could not afford to spend time on superfluous detail. A pair of extra-long air tanks was scratch built and fitted under the frame rails, and generic plumbing and wiring was added to the chassis. As always, a pair of KFS air valves were used to enhance the chassis detail. All the prop shafts were made from Evergreen profiles and fitted with my own resin U-joints. As the KFS kit contains just one fuel tank, I found a similar item in my spares box and just cut it to length. Most of the remaining details also came from my spares box, which is often a quick and very effective way to find what you need.

THE RESIN CAB
With the basic chassis ready I could turn my attention to what was the centre of this build: the beautifully cast resin cab and its details.

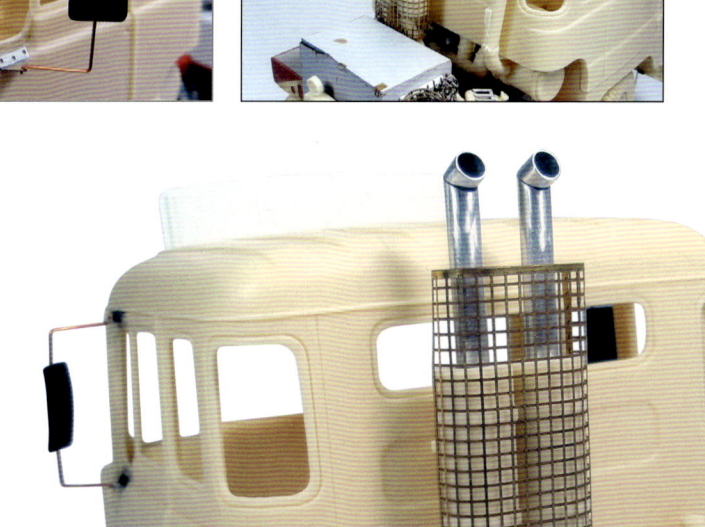

Some improvising was employed during the construction...the exhaust heat shields are actually a part of the CTM etched gitterbox.

1. The complete dry fitting of the un-painted model nicely displays the amount of resin and photo etched parts used in the build.

2. The Amazon cab did not tilt, and the floor plate was therefore fixed on the chassis.

3. The cab interior was spartan on the real machine and the kit included enough detail. The blanket on the bunk was printed on a piece of paper.

4. The cab has nine windows in total, and the rubber around them were brush painted with Vallejo acrylics.

5. Luckily KFS provided a separate decal sheet with the Wynns logos. A pair of these sets were enough to complete all the Amazon signs.

6. To make painting of the chassis easier some components were sprayed separately.

Working with resin conversion sets does not differ from treating any other resin parts, as described in chapter 5.2. As the cab is produced as a one-piece shell, there is no need for any filling and there is almost no need for any cleaning. There was no flash, no air bubbles…so the only thing I had to do was actually paint it, and the same works for the interior. Just the windows needed patience and care, as in the kit there are just stencils and a plain clear sheet available. Every window has to be cut out carefully and there are actually nine necessary here. Otherwise, preparing the cab was much easier than building a plastic version.

Most of the cab details come from the kit. The set provides stainless steel photo-etched parts for all the badges, wipers, dashboard gauges, sun visor and mirror mounts. The cab headboard was made of plastic sheet, while the beacon was an Auslowe after-market item. The complete air intake and exhaust assembly is straight from the kit except for the heatshield, which is actually a part of the CTM gitterbox. The mirror arms are made of fine wire, and the grab handles are made from a hypodermic needle. The tartan on the bunk and curtains was found on the internet, scaled down and printed on paper, and the PE tax disc holder and decals come from a separate detail set.

CHASSIS DETAILING

Detailing the chassis was the last build step prior to painting. I still had a few weeks to go, so I knew I could spend some time creating details that would make the model more accurate. The reference photos showed large stowage boxes behind the cab. The large item is a CTM PE part, while the smaller unit came from my spares box and was just detailed with PE. The various catwalks are a mix of CTM

TRUCK MODELLING

8. ADVANCED RESIN CONVERSIONS

Although the model may look complex, the construction was faster and easier than many plastic kits and finished in approximately seven weeks.

7

8. The rims and tyres were painted separately. Note that the tyres were painted gray rather than black.

135 TRUCK MODELLING

1. The chains were weathered with rust pigments. The data sheets were taken from a KFS set.

2. The vehicle and accessories were weathered with oil paints and enamel weathering products. All the paint chips were made with a fine sponge.

3. The fresh grease on the fifth wheel was simulated with black 502 Abteilung oil paint.

prototype items I had for testing. The drive axle mudguards are made of CTM etched heavy catwalk plate, while the susie bracket and coiled cables are again a KFS item, as were the heavy duty fifth wheel set and details from the Tool and Shackle kit. The hydraulic jack and various oil cans are scratch-built.

Painting the model was simple, as I did not have much time for weathering experiments. All the parts were primed with Mr.Surfacer and sprayed with Tamiya acrylics. I used gloss red on the cab and a mixture of black and grey tones on the chassis, to create color variation. The weathering consists of just black wash around the details and chipping applied with a sponge. All the dust and earth effects were made with AK Interactive enamels applied with a brush, and the grease on the fifth wheel is black oil paint. Chassis data plates and Wynns decals are again a KFS item. I bought a pair (as one wouldn't actually be enough for this vehicle) and combined the logos on the cab, and the headboard and mud flaps. All the small decals come from my spare decal sheets and these provided a pleasing visual enhancement. As the numberplate of the vehicle No.626, I assembled that using KFS British number plate decal set numbering on a piece of plastic sheet (white for the front and yellow for the rear of the vehicle), framed with thin silver pinstripes.

Once the decals were sealed with a clear acrylic coat, I started with the model assembly. The window rubbers were hand painted using my favorite Vallejo acrylics and all the windows were glued in carefully using a very small amount of Superglue. From this point it took just a few hours to assemble the model. Once in one piece, I quickly went over the weathering all around the vehicle and added more dust and dirt tones on the wheels, mud flaps and lower chassis areas.

8.3 CONCLUSION

Luckily, the model was finished just a couple of days before the show. Although, finally, quite a large amount of scratch-building was involved everything went well and quickly. Using the high-quality KFS kit helped greatly, as virtually no cleaning and sanding was required. Therefore, I could focus on detailing and assembly. Compared to a standard 4x2 tractor, this is a little more complex and finishing it within just eight weeks shows that resin kits do not necessarily mean more work, when compared to injection-moulded plastic kits. Furthermore, as this is a rare vehicle it really stands out among standard plastic offerings and brings a fresh breeze to my fleet. I really enjoyed building this British classic and I am sure it will not be the last.

9 MODEL GALLERY

TRUCK MODELLING

9. MODEL GALLERY

Jaroslav Tuláček	Peterbilt 351
Jan Sklenička	Daf NTT
Karel Krejčí	Mack Superliner / Steerable dolly
Ladislav Petřík	DAF CF 6x4 / Iveco Magirus / Mercedes Benz NG
Pavel Behenský	Peterbilt 289 / Kenworth S-900
Petr Rutar	Scania R 500

By: Jaroslav Tuláček

9. MODEL GALLERY

Peterbilt 351

Kit: A heavy conversion based on Strato-models Peterbilt 281 resin kit and AMT Peerless trailer
Scale: 1/25
Notes: Scratchbuilt frame, Hendrickson AMT drive axle suspension

By: Jan Sklenička

9. MODEL GALLERY

Daf NTT

Kit: Italeri 765 DAF NTT
Scale: 1/24
Accessories: CTM DAF N Series detal set
Notes: Cement mixer from AMT

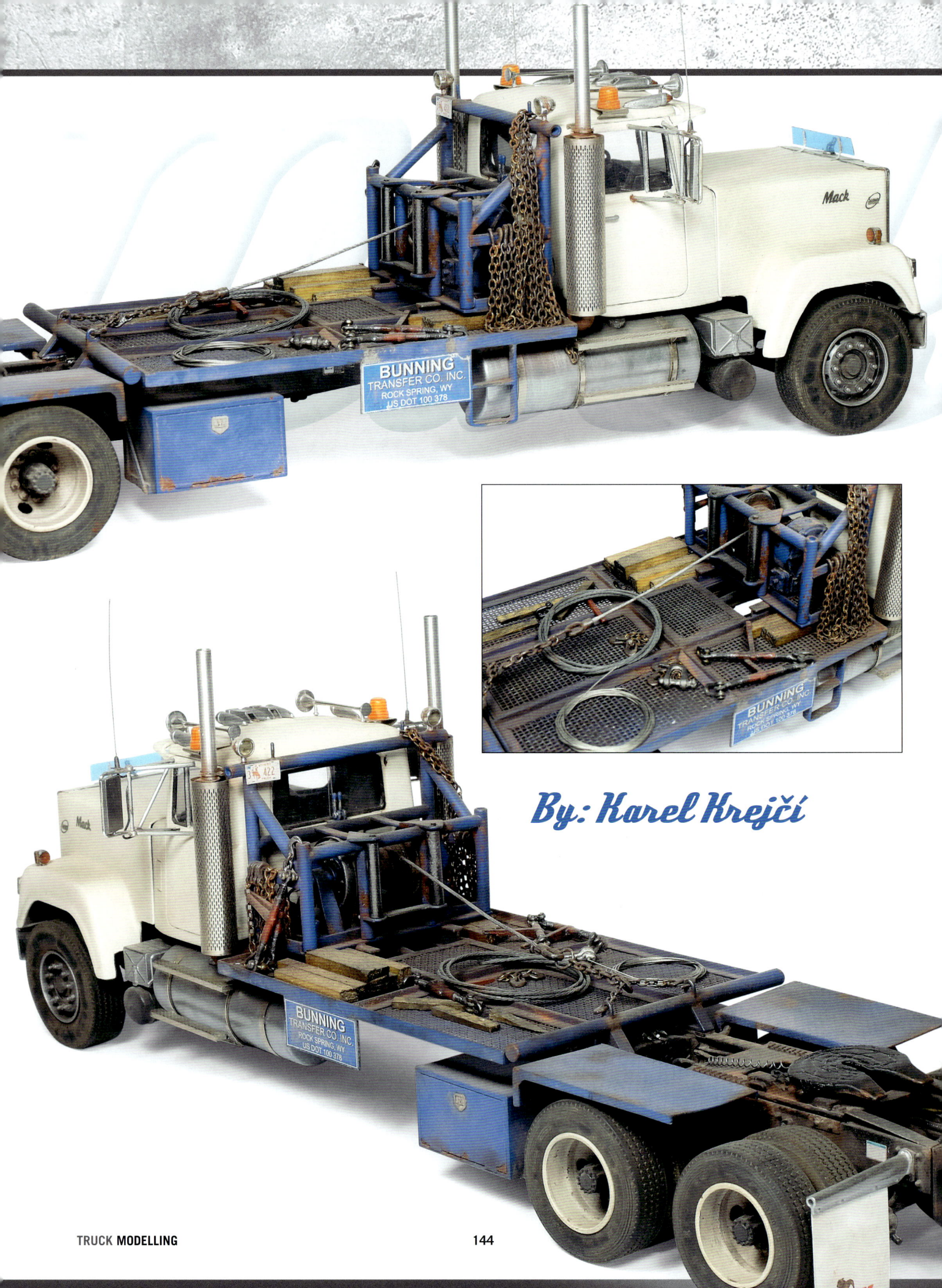

By: Karel Krejčí

TECH SPEC
Mack Superliner

Kit: Italeri Mack Superliner cab (3820). Auslowe Mack V8 and rear Camelback suspension
Scale: 1/24
Notes: Scratchbuilt chassis and bodywork

By: Karel Krejčí

9. MODEL GALLERY

Tech Spec
Steerable dolly

Scale: 1/24
Accessories: KFS resin rims
Notes: Scratchbuilt, cab and frame, Italeri Fruehauf trailer suspension

By: Ladislav Petřík

DAF CF 6x4

Kit: KFS resin cab, Italeri drive axles and suspension
Scale: 1/24
Accessories: KFS DAF Ad Blue kit and white metal steer axle
Notes: Scratchbuilt engine and chassis, custom made decals

By: Ladislav Petřík

9. MODEL GALLERY

Iveco Magirus

Kit: Italeri 3784 Iveco Magirus, box body from Italeri 791 frigo trailer, lifting tail gate from Italeri 776 truck conversion kit
Scale: 1/24
Notes: Revell two axle racing trailer wheels, Revell Schmitz trailer decals

By: Ladislav Petrík

9. MODEL GALLERY

Mercedes Benz NG

Kit: Italeri 757 Mercedes, Italeri 762 canvas body
Scale: 1/24
Notes: Converted chassis and suspension, custom made decals

By: Pavel Behenský

9. MODEL GALLERY

TECH SPEC
Kenworth 8-900

Kit: Strato-models resin kit, master by Pavel Behensky
Scale: 1/24
Accessories: KFS resin spyder wheels

By: Pavel Behenský

9. MODEL GALLERY

Tech Spec
Peterbilt 289

Kit: Revell Peterbilt 359
Scale: 1/25
Notes: Converted to single drive axle

TRUCK **MODELLING**

By: Petr Rutar

9. MODEL GALLERY

Scania R 500
Kit: Italeri 3858 Scania R series conversion, detailed interior and open door conversion
Scale: 1/24
Accessories: CTM etched detail set
Notes: Custom made decals

TRUCK **MODELLING**

Volume 2 offers no less than 8 full building chapters, each focused on different topics and techniques. In addition, a generous reference section is provided, and the book ends with a lavish gallery of models from a selection of first class truck modellers, providing a wealth of inspiration.